Physics for GCSE Combined Science

Project Director
Mary Whitehouse

Project Manager
Alistair Moore

Editor
Mary Whitehouse

Authors
Robin Millar
John Miller
Helen Reynolds
Elizabeth Swinbank
Carol Tear
Mary Whitehouse

OXFORD
UNIVERSITY PRESS

Contents

How to use this book

These pages show you all the different features you will find in your Student Book.
Each feature is designed to support and develop the skills you will need for your
examinations, as well as foster and stimulate your interest in physics.

Chapter openers

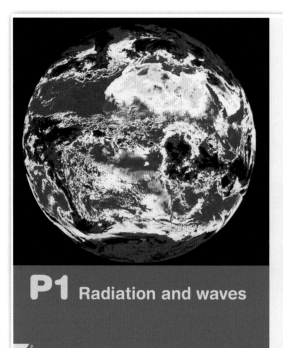

P1 Radiation and waves

Why study radiation and waves?

We use light and sound in many aspects of our everyday lives, and for finding out more about the world around us – including the interior of the Earth itself. Light belongs to a family of radiations that include X-rays and radio waves.

Light and sound behave as waves. By studying waves such as water waves, we can understand more about sound and about radiation, the ways different types of radiation affect us, and how we use radiations in our lives.

What you already know

- Light travels in straight lines.
- Light travels very fast.
- When light meets an object, some may be reflected, some absorbed, and some may pass straight through.
- We see objects when light that is emitted or reflected from them enters our eyes.
- White light is a mixture of colours and can be split up to produce a spectrum.
- Sounds are caused by something vibrating.
- Sound travels fast, though not nearly as fast as light.
- Sound travels in straight lines from its source, getting fainter as it goes.
- Sound travels as longitudinal waves. The frequency of waves is measured in hertz (Hz).

The Science

There are several types of radiation that belong to one 'family', the electromagnetic spectrum. Our communications systems, such as radios and TVs, mobile phones, and computer networks, use electromagnetic radiation to transmit information. Science can explain what happens when radiation is absorbed by our bodies. It can also explain how radiation warms the atmosphere and can predict global warming using computer modelling.

Light, sound, and other types of radiation behave as waves. Studying how waves travel on water helps us predict and explain how light and sound will behave.

Ideas about Science

To make sense of radiation, you need a few things about cause. How sure can thing causes another learn how to evaluate health studies and statements about see some examples were done with had harmful results predicted.

Scientists depend observations. But to interpret the data. Scientists compare the data they collect refine the ideas and understanding of the world.

Why study
This explains why what you are about to learn is useful to scientists as well as to you.

The Science
This summarises the science in the chapter you're about to study.

Ideas about Science
This provides some ideas about how science explanations are developed and the impact of science and technology on society, in the context of the science in the chapter.

What you already know
This is a summary of the things you've already learnt that will come up again in the chapter. Check through them in advance and see if there is anything that you need to recap.

Main spreads

B: How does sound behave?

Find out about

- how sounds are made
- how sound travels
- similarities and differences between sound waves and water waves

regions of compressed air

vibration of loudspeaker cone

direction of travel of sound waves

A loudspeaker has a cone that vibrates. It sends a stream of compression pulses through the air

The distance meter emits a burst of ultrasound. It travels to the end of the room and bounces back to the meter.

Key words

➤ oscillate
➤ echo
➤ ultrasound

Making sounds

Sounds are made by vibrating objects. A source vibrates, causing compressions in the air. Compressed air is 'springy'. As the compression passes, each bit of air springs back, pushing on the next bit of air, which compresses it. A continuous wave of pulses travels through the air. This is a sound wave. A sound wave is a longitudinal wave.

The air itself does not travel when a sound wave travels from a source. If you put a candle flame in the path of a sound, you might see it flicker back and forth if the sound is loud, but it will not blow over.

Sound waves can travel through any gas, and also through solids and liquids (you can hear underwater). You hear sounds because sound waves set up vibrations in your ears. A microphone detects sounds because sound waves make it vibrate. These vibrations produce electrical **oscillations** in the microphone's electric circuit.

Most people can hear sounds that have frequencies in the range 20 Hz to about 20 000 Hz.

Reflected sound

If sound is a wave, then we can predict that, like a water wave, it will be reflected from a barrier.

If you stand some distance away from a wall or a cliff and clap your hands, you hear the **echo** a short time later. An echo is a reflected sound.

You can use echoes to make a rough measurement of the wave speed of sound in air. To work out speed, you use:

$$\text{speed} = \frac{\text{distance}}{\text{time}}$$

You can measure the distance to the wall with a tape measure. Between clapping your hands and hearing the echo, the sound travels twice this distance, there and back.

You need to find a way to measure the time between a clap and hearing its echo.

A distance meter

A distance meter uses the wave speed to measure distances. The wave speed of sound in air is about 340 m/s. The meter sends out a short burst of **ultrasound** towards a wall, and detects its echo coming back. The meter's electronics measure the time between sending the burst of sound and receiving the echo. It uses the time and the wave speed to calculate the distance.

Worked example:
Measuring the speed of sound using an echo

Students bang two blocks of wood together. They are 240 m from a wall. They estimate that it takes 1.5 s for the sound echo to come back from the wall. Use this data to estimate the speed of sound in air.

Step 1: Write down what you know, with the units.

distance travelled = 2 × 240 m
time = 1.5 s

Step 2: Write down the equation that links speed, distance, and time.

$$\text{speed} = \frac{\text{distance}}{\text{time}}$$

Step 3: Substitute the quantities into the equation to work out the speed.

$$\text{speed} = \frac{480 \text{ m}}{1.5 \text{ s}} = 920 \text{ m/s}$$

Answer: estimated speed = 920 m/s

Refracted sound

Because sound is a wave, we predict that sound will be refracted as it travels between regions where the wave speed is different. This does happen, but it can be difficult to observe.

The speed of sound in air depends on the air temperature. At 0 °C the wave speed is about 330 m/s, and at 30 °C it is about 350 m/s.

Different temperatures in the air affect the way we hear sounds. During the day, air near the ground may be warmer than air higher up in the atmosphere. At night, air near the ground is usually cooler. Aircraft noise can be more noticeable at night, because sound from aircraft is refracted upwards during the day and downwards at night.

cool air: sound travels slower here

sound wave

warm air: sound travels faster here

Refraction can make aircraft noise more noticeable at night.

Questions

1 The wave speed of sound in air is 340 m/s. The musical note F below middle C has a frequency of about 170 Hz. What is the wavelength of the note F sound wave in air?

2 **a** List two ways in which sound waves are *similar to* water waves.
  b List two ways in which sound waves are *unlike* water waves.

3 Suggest a reason why it is difficult to observe refraction of sound.

4 The distance meter in the diagram on the previous page is used to measure the size of the sports hall. Sound travels in air at 340 m/s and takes 0.2 s to travel the length of the sports hall and back. How long is the hall?

34

P1.3 How do waves behave? 35

Find out about
Every section in the book has a list of the key points that are explored in the section.

Worked example
Worked examples provide step-by-step instructions for how to carry out calculations and analyse data.

Content that is for Higher Tier only is marked with this tab. If you are studying for the Foundation Tier GCSE then you do not need to know this content.

Questions
Every section has questions that you can use to see if you've understood the content of the section.

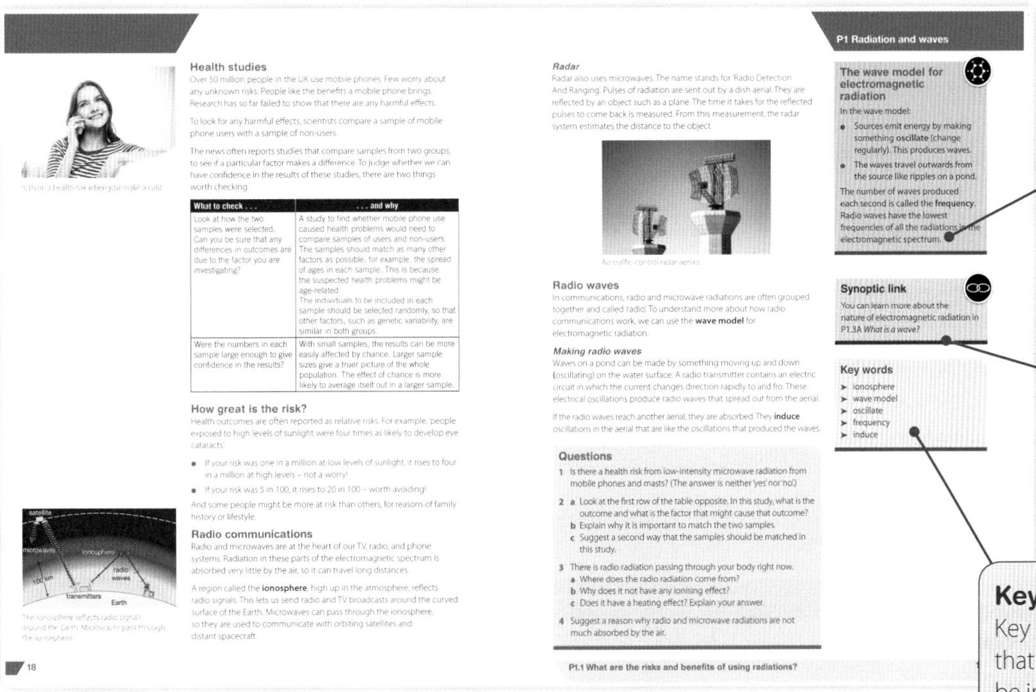

Health studies

Over 50 million people in the UK use mobile phones. Few worry about any unknown risks. People like the benefits a mobile phone brings. Research has so far failed to show that there are any harmful effects.

To look for any harmful effects, scientists compare a sample of mobile phone users with a sample of non-users.

The news often reports studies that compare samples from two groups, to see if a particular factor makes a difference. To judge whether we can have confidence in the results of these studies, there are two things worth checking.

What to check . . .	. . . and why
Look at how the two samples were selected. Can you be sure that any differences in outcomes are due to the factor you are investigating?	A study to find whether mobile phone use caused health problems would need to compare samples of users and non-users. The samples should match as many other factors as possible, for example, the range of ages in each sample. This is because the suspected health problems might be age-related. The individuals to be included in each sample should be selected randomly, so that other factors, such as genetic variability, are similar in both groups.
Were the numbers in each sample large enough to give confidence in the results?	With small samples, the results can be more easily affected by chance. Larger sample sizes give a truer picture of the whole population. The effect of chance is more likely to average itself out in a larger sample.

How great is the risk?

Health outcomes are often reported as relative risks. For example, people exposed to high levels of sunlight were four times as likely to develop eye cataracts.

- If your risk was one in a million at low levels of sunlight, it rises to four in a million at high levels – not a worry!
- If your risk was 5 in 100, it rises to 20 in 100 – worth avoiding!

And some people might be more at risk than others, for reasons of family history or lifestyle.

Radio communications

Radio and microwaves are at the heart of our TV, radio, and phone systems. Radiation in these parts of the electromagnetic spectrum is absorbed very little by the air, so it can travel long distances.

A region called the **ionosphere**, high up in the atmosphere, reflects radio signals. This lets us send radio and TV broadcasts around the curved surface of the Earth. Microwaves can pass through the ionosphere, so they are used to communicate with orbiting satellites and distant spacecraft.

The ionosphere reflects radio signals around the Earth. Microwaves pass through the ionosphere.

Radar

Radar also uses microwaves. The name stands for Radio Detection And Ranging. Pulses of radiation are sent out by a dish aerial. They are reflected by an object such as a plane. The time it takes for the reflected pulses to come back is measured. From this measurement, the radar system estimates the distance to the object.

An air-traffic-control radar aerial.

Radio waves

In communications, radio and microwave radiations are often grouped together and called 'radio'. To understand more about how radio communications work, we can use the **wave model** for electromagnetic radiation.

Making radio waves

Waves on a pond can be made by something moving up and down (oscillating) on the water surface. A radio transmitter contains an electric circuit in which the current changes direction rapidly to and fro. These electrical oscillations produce radio waves that spread out from the aerial.

If the radio waves reach another aerial, they are absorbed. They **induce** oscillations in the aerial that are like the oscillations that produced the waves.

Questions

1 Is there a health risk from low-intensity microwave radiation from mobile phones and masts? (The answer is neither 'yes' nor 'no'.)

2 a Look at the first row of the table opposite. In this study, what is the outcome and what is the factor that might cause that outcome?
   b Explain why it is important to match the two samples.
   c Suggest a second way that the samples should be matched in this study.

3 There is radio radiation passing through your body right now.
   a Where does the radio radiation come from?
   b Why does it not have any ionising effect?
   c Does it have a heating effect? Explain your answer.

4 Suggest a reason why radio and microwave radiations are not much absorbed by the air.

The wave model for electromagnetic radiation

In the wave model:

- Sources emit energy by making something **oscillate** (change regularly). This produces waves.
- The waves travel outwards from the source like ripples on a pond.

The number of waves produced each second is called the **frequency**. Radio waves have the lowest frequencies of all the radiations in the electromagnetic spectrum.

Synoptic link

You can learn more about the nature of electromagnetic radiation in P1.3A *What is a wave?*

Key words

- ionosphere
- wave model
- oscillate
- frequency
- induce

P1.1 What are the risks and benefits of using radiations?

Models

Model boxes describe the main features of a scientific model, how it is used, and its limitations. Read more about models in science in the *Modelling* section at the end of the book.

Synoptic links

Synoptic links highlight where to look if you want to learn more about the ideas discussed in the section.

Key words

Key words boxes highlight words that are useful to know and may be important to understand for your exams. You can look for these words in the text or check the glossary to see what they mean.

Science explanations and Ideas about Science

Science explanations
P1 Radiation and waves

In this chapter you have learnt about the electromagnetic spectrum, different types and sources of radiation, and how they can be both useful and dangerous.

You should know:

- how to think about any form of radiation in terms of its source: its journey path, and what happens when it is absorbed, transmitted, or reflected
- the parts of the electromagnetic spectrum, in order of their frequencies and wavelengths
- that all electromagnetic radiation travels as transverse waves at the same speed through space
- the different properties of the different parts of the electromagnetic spectrum
- what different parts of the electromagnetic spectrum can be used for
- that different types of electromagnetic radiation cause different changes in atoms and molecules, including chemical changes, ionisation, and heating
- why ionising radiation is hazardous to living things and how people can be protected
- how the atmosphere's ozone layer protects living organisms from ultraviolet radiation
- that all bodies emit radiation at different frequencies depending on their temperature, and how this links to global warming and climate change
- that waves are caused by vibrating sources, and the number of waves produced each second is the frequency of the wave
- that waves have amplitude and wavelength, where the amplitude is the distance from the top of a crest or the bottom of a trough to the undisturbed position, and the wavelength is the length of one complete cycle
- the difference between transverse and longitudinal waves
- that wave motion can be described by the equation: wave speed = frequency × wavelength
- how to measure the speed of waves on the surface of water and the speed of sound
- how the effects of refraction can be explained in terms of the changing speed of the waves.

Ideas about Science

To make decisions about both health and climate change, you need to understand not only the electromagnetic spectrum but also some ideas about science. You need to recognise the difference between correlation and cause, and to assess the risks and benefits associated with the electromagnetic spectrum.

Factors and outcomes may be linked in different ways. It is important to distinguish between identifying a correlation, where a change in one factor is linked to a change in the other, and identifying the cause, where there is an explanation of why changing the factor is responsible for the outcome. To show your understanding of these ideas you should be able to:

- suggest and explain everyday examples of correlation
- identify a correlation from data, from a graph, or from a description
- suggest factors that might increase the chance of a particular outcome
- identify that where there is a **mechanism** to explain a correlation, scientists are likely to accept that the factor causes the outcome.

Sometimes scientific advances introduce new risks. It is important to assess the chance of a particular outcome happening and the consequences if it did. People often perceive a risk as being different from the actual risk, sometimes underestimating, and sometimes overestimating. A particular situation that introduces risk will often also introduce benefits, which must be weighed up against that risk.

You should be able to:

- identify risks arising from scientific or technological advances
- discuss both the risks and benefits of a course of action, taking account of who takes the risk and who benefits
- distinguish between real risk and perceived risk
- suggest why people are willing or reluctant to take certain risks.

When reading about the work of scientists you should understand how they develop their ideas and how they agree on the best explanations.

You should be able to:

- describe how scientists use computer modelling to test their ideas
- describe how the process of peer review leads to agreement about the best explanation for scientific phenomena.

Science explanations and Ideas about Science

Every chapter has a summary of the main ideas that you've learnt in the unit. You could use it as a starting point for revision, to check that you know about the big ideas covered.

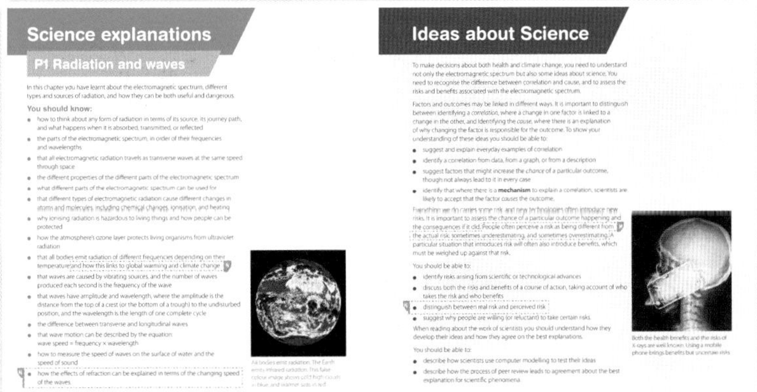

Questions that are for Higher Tier only are marked with this tab. If you are studying for the Foundation Tier GCSE then you do not need to answer these questions.

Review questions

P1 Review questions

1 a List the parts of the electromagnetic spectrum in order of increasing frequency.
   b Which part of the electromagnetic spectrum carries the most energy?
   c Describe some evidence to support your answer.
   d Which part of the electromagnetic spectrum causes the most heating?
   e Describe the changes that take place when a material is heated by electromagnetic radiation.

2 Graph A shows how the percentage of carbon dioxide in the atmosphere has changed over the past 300 years.

   a Describe the trend in graph A and explain the scientific reasons for what the graph shows.
   b Graph B shows how the average temperature of the atmosphere has changed over the past 140 years. Use the two graphs to explain the meaning of correlation.
   c A scientist believes that there is a causal link between carbon dioxide levels and climate change. Write down what else the scientist needs to do so that other scientists will accept this idea.

3 The table lists several different situations in which waves are travelling. In each case something happens to the wave, but which properties of the wave are affected?

Copy this table and complete it by writing either bigger, gets smaller, or stays the same in each cell.

Description of wave	Amplitude	Frequency	Wave speed	Wavelength
waves on the surface of a pond, as they travel away from the disturbance that caused them				
a wave on a long spring, the end is moved up and down more rapidly				
a light ray as it moves from air into a clear glass block				
radio waves as they travel from a satellite to a receiving dish on the ground				
sound waves as they pass from air into a brick wall				

4 All electromagnetic waves travel at a speed of 300 000 km/s in a vacuum (and at a similar speed in air). Sound travels at about 340 m/s in air at room temperature.
   a Calculate the wavelength of sound with frequency 1700 Hz.
   b Calculate the frequency of microwaves with wavelength 3 cm.
   c Explain why we see a flash of lightning in the distance before we hear the thunderclap, but we do not notice a difference between seeing a person's mouth move and hearing them speak when we are in the same room.

5 Describe an observation that shows that when a water wave travels across a ripple tank, the water does not travel with the wave.

6 A student is watching a 100 m sprint and wants to measure the speed of sound. She is standing at the end of the 100 m track. She measures the time between seeing the flash of the starting gun and hearing the bang.
   a Describe how she could use this measurement to find the speed of sound.
   b Explain why this measurement will not give her a very accurate value.
   c Suggest and explain what she could change to improve the accuracy of her experiment.

7 Explain why light changes direction as it passes from air into water.

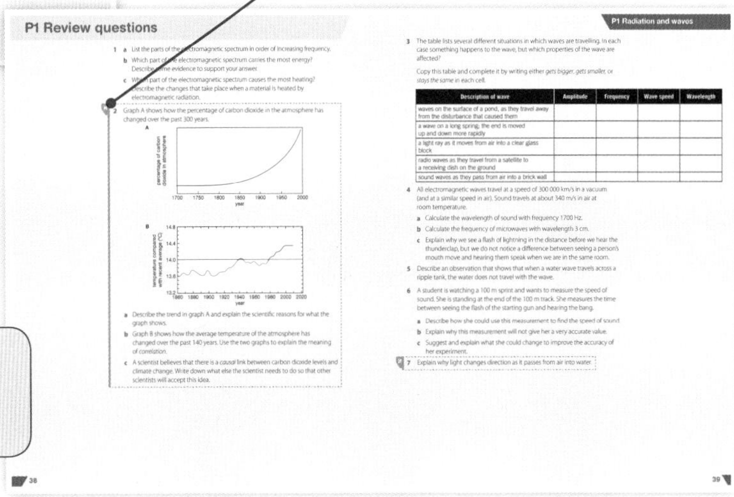

Every chapter has review questions that you can use to test how well you understand the topics in the chapter.

Structure of assessment

There will be four examination papers for GCSE Combined Science.
All of the papers cover all of the chapters. They contain short-answer questions worth up to three marks, structured questions, and questions requiring an extended written response. The papers will assess theory, problem solving, calculations, and questions about practical work.

Paper 1: Biology

Time	Marks available	Percentage of GCSE
1 hour 45 minutes	95	26.4%

Paper 2: Chemistry

Time	Marks available	Percentage of GCSE
1 hour 45 minutes	95	26.4%

Paper 3: Physics

Time	Marks available	Percentage of GCSE
1 hour 45 minutes	95	26.4%

Paper 4: Combined Science

Time	Marks available	Percentage of GCSE
1 hour 45 minutes	75	20.8%

Top tips

In each examination paper, you will have to:

- demonstrate your knowledge and understanding of scientific ideas, techniques, and procedures

- apply your knowledge and understanding to new and familiar contexts

- interpret and evaluate information and data, make judgements and conclusions, and evaluate scientific procedures and suggest how to improve them.

Some questions will use contexts that you are not familiar with, including examples of science from the real world, issues from the news, and reports of scientific investigations. Remember that although the context may be different, the science is the same. The questions are designed so that you can answer them if you combine your own knowledge and understanding with the information given in the question. You should:

- think about how the context is similar to something you have learnt about

- look for information in the question that suggests how you can relate what you know to the new context.

Kerboodle

This book is also supported by Kerboodle, offering unrivalled digital support for building your practical, maths, and literacy skills.

If your school subscribes to Kerboodle, you will find a wealth of additional resources to help you with your studies and with revision:

- Animations, videos, and podcasts
- Webquests
- Activities for every assessable learning outcome
- Maths skills activities and worksheets
- Literacy skills activities and worksheets
- Interactive quizzes that give question-by-question feedback
- Ideas about Science case studies

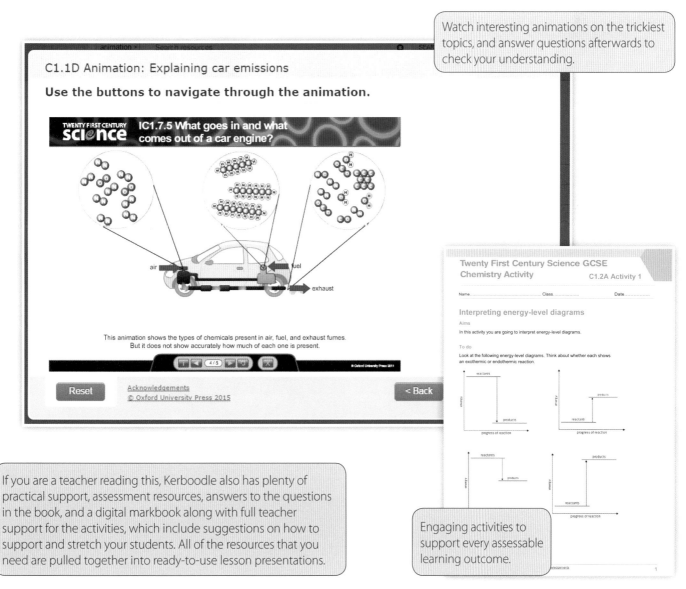

Watch interesting animations on the trickiest topics, and answer questions afterwards to check your understanding.

If you are a teacher reading this, Kerboodle also has plenty of practical support, assessment resources, answers to the questions in the book, and a digital markbook along with full teacher support for the activities, which include suggestions on how to support and stretch your students. All of the resources that you need are pulled together into ready-to-use lesson presentations.

Engaging activities to support every assessable learning outcome.

P1 Radiation and waves

Why study radiation and waves?

We use light and sound in many aspects of our everyday lives, and for finding out more about the world around us – including the interior of the Earth itself. Light belongs to a family of radiations that include X-rays and radio waves.

Light and sound behave as waves. By studying waves such as water waves, we can understand more about sound and about radiation, the ways different types of radiation affect us, and how we use radiations in our lives.

What you already know

- Light travels in straight lines.
- Light travels very fast.
- When light meets an object, some may be reflected, some absorbed, and some may pass straight through.
- We see objects when light that is emitted or reflected from them enters our eyes.
- White light is a mixture of colours and can be split up to produce a spectrum.
- Sounds are caused by something vibrating.
- Sound travels fast, though not nearly as fast as light.
- Sound travels in straight lines from its source, getting fainter as it goes.
- Sound travels as longitudinal waves. The frequency of waves is measured in hertz (Hz).

The Science

There are several types of radiation that belong to one 'family', the electromagnetic spectrum. Our communications systems, such as radios and TVs, mobile phones, and computer networks, use electromagnetic radiation to transmit information. Science can explain what happens when radiation is absorbed by our bodies. It can also explain how radiation warms the atmosphere and can predict global warming using computer modelling.

Light, sound, and other types of radiation behave as waves. Studying how waves travel on water helps us predict and explain how light and sound will behave.

Ideas about Science

To make sense of media stories about radiation, you need to understand a few things about correlation and cause. How sure can we be that one thing causes another? You will also learn how to evaluate reports of health studies and how to interpret statements about risk. You will also see some examples of things that were done with good intentions but had harmful results that were not predicted.

Scientists depend on data and careful observations. But scientists need to interpret the data they collect. Scientists compare their ideas with the data they collect. This helps to refine the ideas and leads to a greater understanding of the world.

P1.1 What are the risks and benefits of using radiations?

A: What is radiation?

Find out about

- different types of radiation
- a scientific model for radiation

Radiation all around

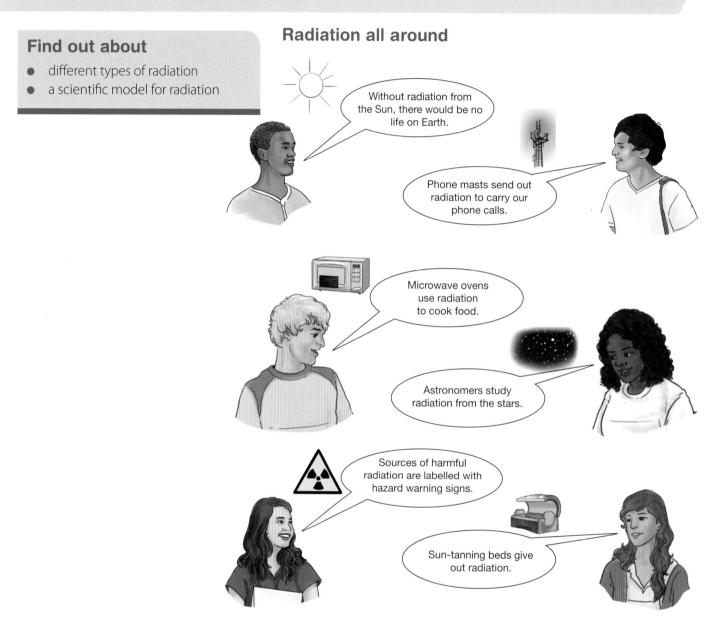

Without radiation from the Sun, there would be no life on Earth.

Phone masts send out radiation to carry our phone calls.

Microwave ovens use radiation to cook food.

Astronomers study radiation from the stars.

Sources of harmful radiation are labelled with hazard warning signs.

Sun-tanning beds give out radiation.

Key words

- ➤ radiation
- ➤ model
- ➤ source
- ➤ emit
- ➤ ray
- ➤ transmit
- ➤ reflect
- ➤ absorb

Light, radio waves, and X-rays are examples of **radiation**. Radiation occurs naturally but we can produce some types as well.

All types of radiation can be useful, though many can also be harmful.

Radiation transfers energy from one place to another.

Modelling radiation

In science, a **model** is a way of describing something that helps us to understand it. Scientific models can be words, pictures, objects, numbers, graphs, or equations.

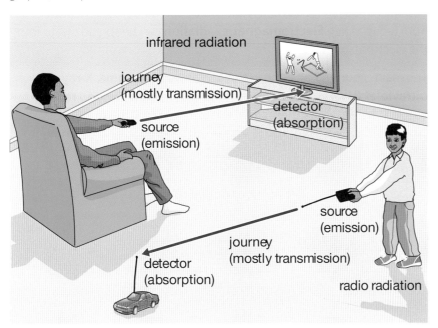

Radiation has a journey from source to detector.

A model for radiation: a journey from source to receiver

Radiation has a **source** that **emits** it. Then it has a journey. It spreads out, or radiates. Lines that show the pathways of radiation are called **rays**. The radiation transfers energy to other objects as it spreads out.

The radiation may be reflected, transmitted, or absorbed.

This model helps describe how energy from the Sun reaches Earth.

Light on a journey

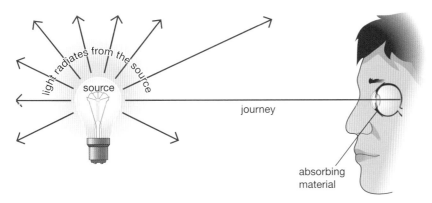

Visible light has a journey from the source to the eye.

Some radiation, at the end of its journey, causes chemical changes at the back of your eye. That radiation is visible light.

Some materials, such as air, let light pass through them. They **transmit** light. They are clear, or transparent. On its way from the source to your eye, light may be **reflected** by other materials. Objects would be invisible if they did not reflect light. Some materials **absorb** light. When light is absorbed it no longer exists as light.

Questions

1 Use the words *source*, *emit*, *transmit*, and *absorb* to describe the radiation's journey when you use a remote control to change channel on a TV.

2 Materials can transmit, reflect, or absorb light. Which one of these does glass do best? Explain your answer.

B: What is the electromagnetic spectrum?

Find out about

- the family of radiation known as the electromagnetic spectrum
- what happens when electromagnetic radiation is absorbed
- why some kinds of electromagnetic radiation are more dangerous than others

A family of radiations

The **electromagnetic spectrum** is a family of types of radiation. They all travel through space at the same speed, which is very fast: 300 000 km/s. You will have seen how visible light can be spread out to form a spectrum from red to violet. **Electromagnetic radiation** can be spread out to form the electromagnetic spectrum.

The main groups of radiation in this spectrum are **gamma**, **X-ray**, **ultraviolet (UV)**, **visible light**, **infrared (IR)**, **microwave**, and **radio**. Visible light is the only member of the electromagnetic radiation family that our eyes can detect. All the others need special equipment to 'see' them.

Type of electromagnetic radiation	Examples, uses, and effects
gamma rays	• emitted by radioactive materials • uses and effects as for X-rays • used for sterilising medical equipment and food
X-rays	• used for X-ray photography • causes fluorescence • causes cancer, but can kill cancer cells
ultraviolet	• causes tanning, skin cancer, and eye damage • causes fluorescence (makes some chemicals glow) • kills bacteria
light	• only type of radiation visible to the human eye
infrared	• radiant heaters and grills • TV and video remote controllers • security alarms and lamps • carries digital signals in fibre optic broadband cables
microwaves	• TV and communications satellites • heating effect used in microwave ovens • mobile phones • telephone links; radar • TV broadcasts
UHF	• FM radio
VHF	
short wave	• amateur radio
medium wave	• local AM radio
long wave	• long-distance AM radio

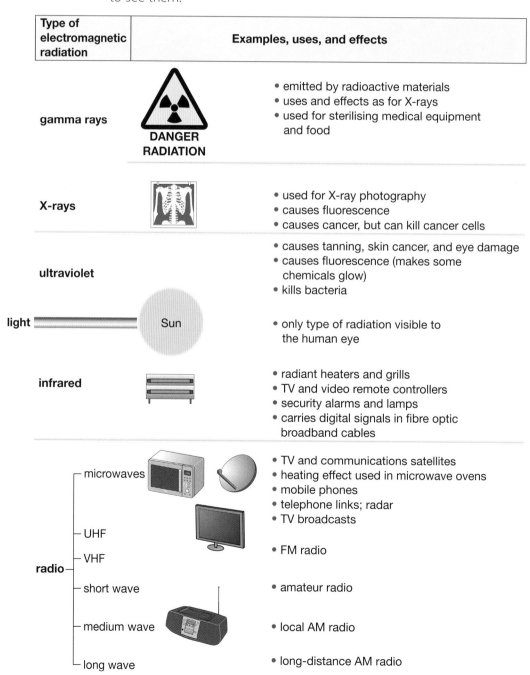

What happens when electromagnetic radiation is absorbed?

When materials absorb electromagnetic radiation they gain energy. Exactly what happens depends on the type of radiation.

A varying electric current in a metal wire

Microwave and radio radiation can carry signals or patterns. These make patterns of electric current in an aerial when it absorbs the radiation. Radios and TVs use these patterns to create sounds and images.

Key words

➤ electromagnetic spectrum
➤ electromagnetic radiation
➤ gamma radiation
➤ X-ray
➤ ultraviolet (UV)
➤ visible light
➤ infrared (IR)
➤ microwave
➤ radio
➤ particle

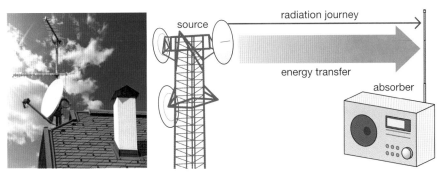

Metal aerials absorb radio and microwave radiation.

A heating effect

If a material absorbs radiation, this may increase the vibration of its **particles** (atoms and molecules). The material gets warmer.

Synoptic link

You can learn more about the nature of electromagnetic radiation in P1.3A *What is a wave?*

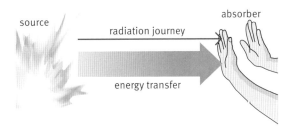

A fire transfers energy to its surroundings. Objects around it, including people, absorb the radiation and gain energy, which warms them.

Chemical changes

If radiation carries enough energy, the molecules in the material that absorbs it become more likely to react chemically. This happens, for example, during photosynthesis and in the retinas of your eyes.

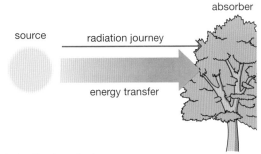

Photosynthesis happens when leaves absorb the Sun's radiation.

Lying in the sunshine, both infrared and visible radiations have a heating effect. Ultraviolet radiation can start off a chemical change that could cause skin cancer.

Damage to living cells

Radiation that carries a large amount of energy may cause chemical reactions in living cells that change the way the cells behave. Healthy cells can become cancer cells. If cells absorb a very large amount of energy, they may die.

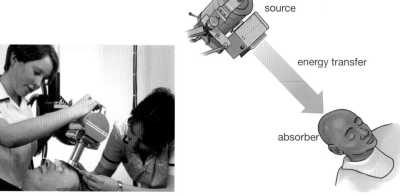

X-rays are being used to kill the skin cancer cells on the patient's head.

Models to explain the effects of electromagnetic radiation

Radiation transfers energy. Two scientific models of electromagnetic radiation can help to explain how it behaves as it travels and when it is absorbed.

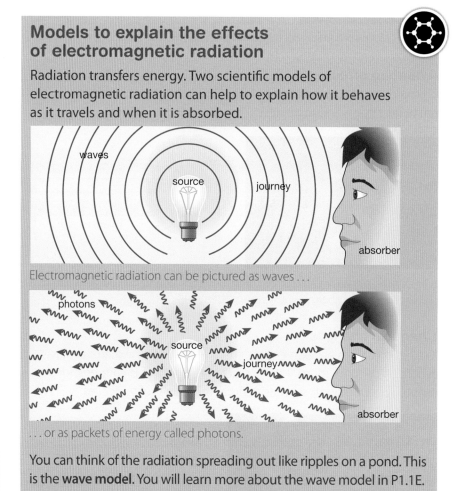

Electromagnetic radiation can be pictured as waves . . .

. . . or as packets of energy called photons.

You can think of the radiation spreading out like ripples on a pond. This is the **wave model**. You will learn more about the wave model in P1.1E.

In the **photon** model, radiation consists of small packets called photons that transfer energy from the source to the absorber. The photon model can help us explain why different types of electromagnetic radiation have different effects.

Key words

➤ wave model
➤ photon
➤ atom
➤ particle model of matter
➤ vibrate

Models of matter

Everything around you, including yourself, is made up of particles called **atoms** and molecules. A molecule is a group of two or more atoms joined together.

We need models for atoms that will help explain some of the effects of electromagnetic radiation on matter.

Synoptic link

You can learn more about the particle model in P6.2 *How does the particle model explain the effects of heating?*

The particle model of matter

The **particle model** gives us a way to visualise how the particles in solids, liquids, and gases are arranged and how they move.

All matter is made of very tiny particles. There are attractive forces between particles. These differ in strength from one substance to another.

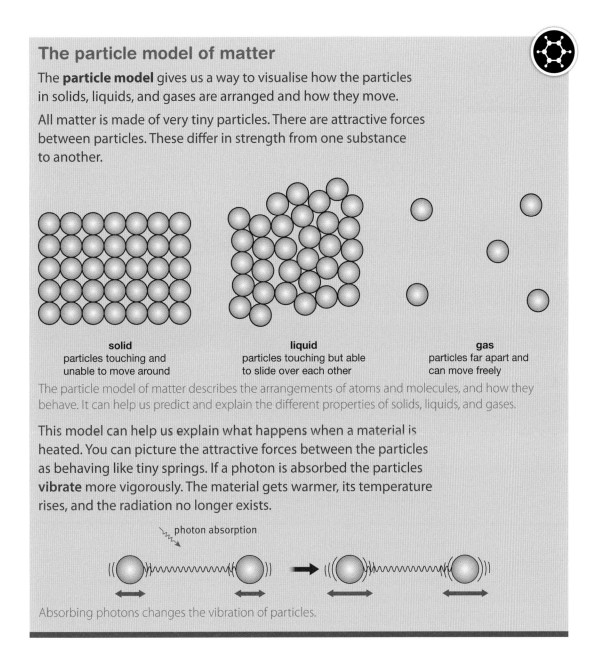

solid
particles touching and unable to move around

liquid
particles touching but able to slide over each other

gas
particles far apart and can move freely

The particle model of matter describes the arrangements of atoms and molecules, and how they behave. It can help us predict and explain the different properties of solids, liquids, and gases.

This model can help us explain what happens when a material is heated. You can picture the attractive forces between the particles as behaving like tiny springs. If a photon is absorbed the particles **vibrate** more vigorously. The material gets warmer, its temperature rises, and the radiation no longer exists.

photon absorption

Absorbing photons changes the vibration of particles.

Key words

➤ intensity
➤ nuclear model of the atom
➤ nucleus
➤ positive
➤ electron
➤ negative
➤ ion
➤ ionisation
➤ ionising radiation
➤ non-ionising radiation

Microwave ovens

A microwave oven uses microwave radiation to transfer energy to absorbing materials. Molecules of water, fat, and sugar are good absorbers of radiation with wavelengths in the microwave part of the spectrum. When they absorb microwave radiation, they vibrate strongly; in other words, their temperature rises. Once the materials have absorbed the energy of the radiation, the radiation ceases to exist.

A potato contains water, so it absorbs microwave radiation. The particles of glass or crockery absorb very little energy from the radiation. It does not increase their vibrations, so bowls and mugs are not heated directly. They are heated by the hot food or drink inside them.

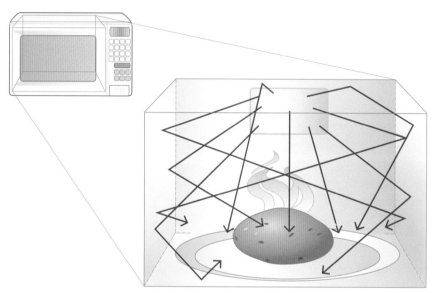

The walls of the microwave oven reflect the microwave radiation. The water in the potato absorbs the radiation.

Safety features

People contain water and fat, two absorbers of microwave radiation. So microwaves could cook you. The oven door has a metal grid to reflect the radiation back inside the oven. A hidden switch prevents the oven from working with its door open.

How well cooked?

Any material that absorbs radiation (such as microwaves) gets hot. The heating effect depends on the type of radiation, the **intensity** of the radiation, and its duration (the exposure time). The intensity of a beam of electromagnetic radiation is the energy that arrives at a square metre of surface each second.

You control the amount of cooking in a microwave oven by adjusting:

● the power setting (to control the intensity)
● the cooking time (to control the exposure time).

Ionisation

The particle model is good at explaining properties of solids, liquids, and gases, but it doesn't help to explain how X-rays can damage living cells. To explain that, we need a more detailed model of the atom – the **nuclear model of the atom**.

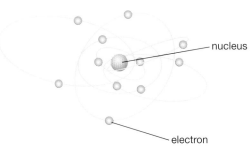

In the nuclear model of the atom, the electrons orbit the central nucleus at different distances.

The nuclear model of the atom

Atoms are very small, but they are made of up of even smaller particles.

At the centre of each atom is a small **nucleus** that has **positive** electric charge.

Orbiting around the nucleus at different distances are one or more **electrons**. These are much smaller than the nucleus and have **negative** electric charge.

When an atom absorbs a photon, it gains extra energy and one of the electrons moves further from the nucleus.

The atom loses its extra energy by emitting a photon of either visible light, ultraviolet, or X-ray.

You will use this nuclear model of the atom often as you learn more science.

If a photon has enough energy, it can move an outer electron right away from the nucleus so that it is no longer part of the atom. The atom, or molecule, left behind has a positive charge and is called an **ion**.

The process of creating ions is called **ionisation**. X-ray, gamma, and some ultraviolet radiations are called **ionising radiations** because a single photon has enough energy to ionise an atom or molecule.

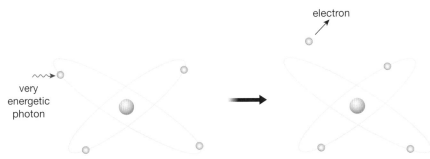

A very energetic photon can ionise an atom by giving an electron enough energy to escape.

If ionisation takes place in a living cell, its chemical reactions might be changed. This can damage the cell by changing the way it behaves, and by heating it. A large amount of ionisation and heating can kill the cell.

Visible, infrared, microwave, and radio are all **non-ionising radiations**. A single photon does not have enough energy to ionise an atom or molecule. The main effect of these radiations is warming.

Questions

1. a Write down four effects that can happen when electromagnetic radiation is absorbed.
   b Which effect do you use if you put a cup of milk in a microwave oven?

2. Suggest how the wave model for electromagnetic radiation could explain why the further you sit from a fire, the less you feel the heat.

3. a Which radiations are on either side of microwave radiation in the electromagnetic spectrum?
   b Which of these carries less energy than microwave radiation?

4. Infrared radiation has a heating effect on most solids. Explain what this tells you about infrared radiation using at least one of these words:
   reflected transmitted absorbed

5. Why is it important that the walls and door of a microwave oven reflect the microwave radiation?

6. a Name three types of electromagnetic radiation that are also ionising radiations.
   b Which of these types has the least energetic radiation?

7. Someone says, 'Radiation is dangerous. Exposure to any sort of radiation can cause cancer.' Explain to them why not all radiation is dangerous.

C: Taking a chance with the Sun

Find out about

- benefits and risks of exposure to sunlight
- how the ozone layer protects life on Earth

Key words

➤ risk
➤ factor
➤ outcome
➤ correlation
➤ cause
➤ ozone layer
➤ atmosphere

Fair skin is good at making vitamin D but it gives less protection against UV radiation than dark skin. Melanoma is the worst kind of skin cancer. One severe sunburn in childhood doubles the risk of melanoma in later life.

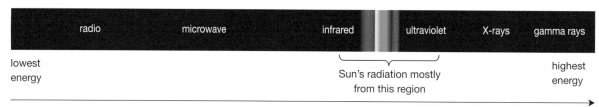

| lowest energy | radio | microwave | infrared | ultraviolet | X-rays | gamma rays | highest energy |

Sun's radiation mostly from this region

increasing energy

The Sun emits visible light and also invisible electromagnetic radiation, mostly infrared and ultraviolet.

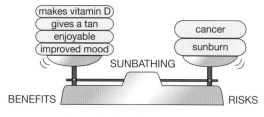

makes vitamin D
gives a tan
enjoyable
improved mood

cancer
sunburn

SUNBATHING

BENEFITS   RISKS

Many people sunbathe. They reckon the benefits outweigh the risks.

People like sunshine. It can alter your mood chemically and reduce the risk of depression. Sunlight includes ultraviolet (UV) radiation. Some UV radiation has enough energy to ionise atoms and molecules, which can change chemical reactions in body cells. This can cause skin cancer. This is why it is advisable to cover up with clothes and sunscreen to reduce the risk on a sunny day.

So is sunlight good for you? There is no simple answer.

Sunlight and skin

Melanin, a brown pigment in skin, provides some protection from UV radiation. People whose ancestors lived in sunnier parts of the world are more likely to have protective brown skin.

We need sunlight on our skin because human skin absorbs sunlight to make vitamin D. This nutrient strengthens bones and muscles. It also boosts the immune system, which protects you from infections. Research suggests that vitamin D can prevent cancers in the breast, colon, ovary, and other organs.

Darker skin makes it harder for the body to make vitamin D. So in regions of the world that are not so sunny there is an advantage in having fair skin. People with dark skin can keep healthy in less sunny countries if they get enough vitamin D from their food.

Balancing risks and benefits

Skin cancer is quickly becoming more common. In the UK, there are now over 13 000 new cases of malignant melanoma, a type of skin cancer, each year. Over a lifetime the **risk** of developing this cancer is now about 1 in 55, compared with less than 1 in 2500 in the 1970s. However, if you try and avoid skin cancer by staying indoors, there are risks too.

Protecting your health involves reducing risks, whenever possible, and balancing risks against benefits.

Correlation or cause?

A study was made of 2600 people. It found that those who were exposed to high levels of sunlight were up to four times more likely to develop a cataract (clouding of the eye lens). Exposure to sunlight is possibly a **factor** in causing cataracts. Eye cataracts are an **outcome**.

There is a **correlation** between exposure to sunlight and eye cataracts. But doctors do not say that exposure to sunlight *will* produce cataracts. It probably increases the risk, but it may not be the only **cause**. There are other risk factors too, such as age and diet.

Protected by the atmosphere

Radiation from the Sun includes infrared radiation, visible light, and UV radiation. Some of this radiation is transmitted through the atmosphere so that it reaches the ground. Fortunately for us, most of the harmful UV radiation is absorbed by the atmosphere as the Sun's radiation passes through it. Life on Earth depends on the **ozone layer** absorbing UV radiation.

The **atmosphere** is a mixture of gases, including oxygen. When these oxygen molecules absorb UV radiation from the Sun, they sometimes split up; some of the oxygen atoms then combine in threes to make ozone. This makes the ozone layer.

The ozone layer is good at absorbing UV radiation. The energy of this absorbed radiation can break up ozone and oxygen molecules, making free atoms of oxygen.

These chemical changes are reversible. Free atoms of oxygen in the ozone layer are constantly combining with oxygen molecules to make new ozone.

"Skin cancer is the last thing I'm thinking about."

Too much exposure to the Sun is dangerous. A Cancer Research UK survey found a worrying gap between how much people know about skin cancer and how little they actually do to protect themselves in sunlight.

Among 16–24-year-olds, 75% believed that exposure to the Sun might cause skin cancer. But only a quarter of this age group apply high-factor sunscreen as protection. And only a third cover up or seek shade from the Sun.

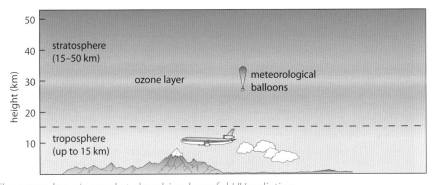

O_2: oxygen O_3: ozone

The ozone layer is good at absorbing harmful UV radiation.

Ozone hole

Humans have created a problem. Some synthetic chemicals, such as chlorofluorocarbons (CFCs) used in old fridges, have been escaping into the atmosphere. They turn ozone back into ordinary oxygen, which means more UV radiation reaches the Earth's surface.

This destruction of the ozone layer happens strongly over the North and South Poles. More UV radiation can reach the Earth's surface through the 'hole in the ozone layer'.

This is an example of an unintended consequence. CFCs were used because they make fridges very efficient. Nobody knew that they would damage the ozone layer.

This image has been made by sensing ozone. Dark colours represent less dense ozone. It shows a 'hole' in the protective layer over Antarctica.

Countries worldwide are now dealing with the problem. Aerosol cans no longer use CFCs. Old fridges have the CFCs carefully removed at the end of their working life. However, the ozone layer may take decades to return to its original thickness.

Old fridges waiting to have CFCs removed.

Questions

1 A person with dark skin moves to live in a region where there are few sunny days. Why should they try to spend a lot of time outdoors?

2 Exposure to sunlight increases your risk of developing skin cancer. List some benefits of staying indoors and avoiding direct sunlight. Suggest some risks of staying indoors.

3 Read the information about the risk of melanoma. Which people are most at risk of developing skin cancer? Suggest a reason why.

4 Suggest why skin cancer is becoming more common in the UK.

5 Why is it important for life on Earth that the atmosphere absorbs most of the UV radiation that comes from the Sun?

6 Describe the multistep process in the atmosphere, involving ozone, that helps protect life on Earth from UV radiation.

D: The risky side of the rainbow

Using X-rays

X-rays were discovered in the 1890s. They soon caught on as a medical tool, and they have saved many lives. How do they work?

An X-ray photon can be emitted when an electron in an atom loses energy. X-rays are produced electrically, in an X-ray tube. A beam of X-rays is shone through the patient and detected on the other side using an X-ray camera.

As the beam passes through the patient, it is partly absorbed. Bone is a stronger absorber than flesh, and so bones show up as 'shadows' on the final image. The intensity of the beam is reduced as more of the X-ray photons are absorbed.

The intensity of any radiation is less if you are further away from the source. This is because the radiation spreads out over a wider and wider **area**.

Find out about
- reducing the risk from ionising radiation
- how ionising radiation can affect body cells

Key words
➤ area
➤ radioactive

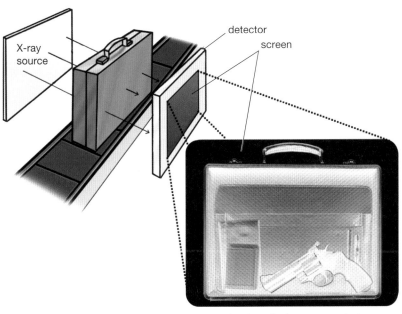

X-ray machines are used in airport security checks. Like bone, metal objects absorb X-rays strongly and reduce the intensity of the beam passing through.

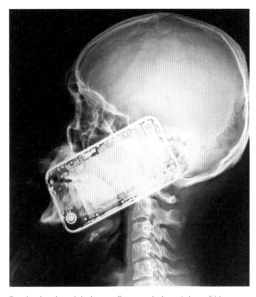

Both the health benefits and the risks of X-rays are well known. Using a mobile phone has benefits but uncertain risks.

Using gamma rays

Gamma radiation is similar to X-rays but it comes from **radioactive** materials. These are substances that emit radiation all the time – you can't switch them off. Gamma radiation is emitted from the nucleus of a radioactive atom. By emitting a gamma ray, the nucleus loses energy.

Gamma radiation is used, like X-rays, for imaging a patient's internal organs. It is also used to destroy cancer cells.

X-rays and gamma rays can be dangerous.

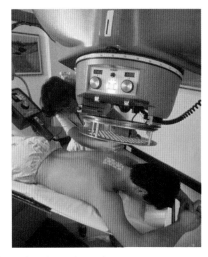

This patient is undergoing gamma radiotherapy. Gamma radiation from the machine above him is directed towards a cancerous tumour in his body.

Discovery of a correlation

Alice Stewart and George Kneale carried out a survey on a large number of women and their children. They discovered a correlation between exposure to X-rays of pregnant women and cancers in their children.

There is a plausible **mechanism** that could explain this correlation. X-ray photons can ionise molecules in your body, which is particularly risky if DNA molecules are affected. This can disrupt the chemistry of body cells, and cause cancer. So the link is more than just a correlation. X-rays can, in a few cases, cause cancer.

This study made doctors more cautious about using X-rays. The radiation is more damaging to cells that are rapidly dividing, such as in a growing fetus or a small child. So the risks associated with X-rays for pregnant women and small children usually outweigh any benefit.

The cancers caused by X-rays are an example of an unintended consequence. X-rays were used because they gave useful information about an unborn baby. Nobody knew that they would cause damage.

Hazards and risks

There is a **hazard** associated with using X-rays and gamma rays. They are ionising. They may cause damage to body cells, which can lead to cancer. This is a risk. Limiting the exposure time and using barriers to reduce exposure can help to minimise the risk.

Reducing the risk

When a patient has an X-ray, the X-ray intensity and exposure are kept to the minimum that will still produce a good image. People who work with ionising radiation must be protected from its effects.

There are several ways to reduce exposure to ionising radiation.

- *Time*: The shorter the time of exposure, the less radiation is absorbed so the smaller the chance of damage to cells.
- *Distance*: Intensity decreases as radiation spreads out from the source.
- *Shielding*: Materials such as lead and concrete, which absorb radiation well, shield people from exposure.
- *Sensitivity*: A sensitive detector means less radiation is needed to produce an image.

Alice Stewart was a British doctor. She collected information from women whose children had died of cancer between 1953 and 1955. Soon the answer was clear. On average, one medical X-ray for a pregnant woman was enough to double the risk of early cancer for her child.

Key words

➤ mechanism
➤ hazard

Synoptic link

You can learn more about ionising radiation in P5.2 *How can radioactive materials be used safely?*

Questions

1 Explain why gamma radiation is sometimes called 'nuclear radiation'.

2 In the article about Alice Stewart, what is the *outcome* she is studying? What is the *factor* that might be causing this outcome?

3 a Why is the link between X-ray exposure during pregnancy and childhood cancer believed to be a cause, and not just a correlation?

   b Why do doctors still use X-rays, despite this link?

E: Communicating with waves

Cooked brain?

Mobile phones use microwave radiation to send signals back and forth to the nearby phone mast. When you make a call, the bones of your skull absorb some of this radiation. But some reaches your brain and warms it, ever so slightly. Vigorous exercise has a greater heating effect than a mobile phone.

Is there a health risk?

The intensity of the radiation from a mobile phone is greatest as it leaves the phone. The radiation spreads out in all directions, so it rapidly gets weaker the further it travels from the phone.

The radiation from the mast is most intense as it leaves the mast. It is more intense than the radiation from a phone. By the time it reaches a distant phone, it is very weak.

People have concerns about radiation from phone masts. If you stood right next to a mast, the heating effect of the radiation absorbed by your body could be quite noticeable.

Fortunately, you cannot get that close. The beam of radiation from a phone transmitter is shaped like the beam of light from a lighthouse. Directly under a mast, its radiation is much weaker than the radiation from your phone.

H
People may not accurately estimate a particular risk. Their **perceived risk** is often different from the **actual risk**. People tend to overestimate the risks of things with invisible effects, such as radiation. Also, they overestimate risks if they feel less in control. For example, people worry more about flying than driving. But when you compare the same number of people travelling the same distance, far more people die on the roads.

Some people think that rail travel is more risky than going by road. But over 20 000 people are killed or seriously injured each year on UK roads. Far fewer people die or are injured on the railways. This is an example of a difference between a perceived risk and an actual risk.

Find out about

- radiation from mobile phones and masts
- how to judge whether a health study is reliable
- the wave model for electromagnetic radiation
- how radio waves are produced and how they carry information

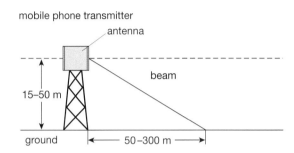

The microwave beam from a mobile phone mast spreads out in all directions.

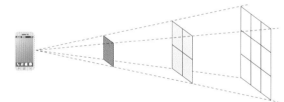

Twice as far away from the phone, the area is four times as great, so only a quarter of the radiation falls on each small square.

Key words
H

➤ perceived risk
➤ actual risk

Is there a health risk when you make a call?

Health studies

Over 50 million people in the UK use mobile phones. Few worry about any unknown risks. People like the benefits a mobile phone brings. Research has so far failed to show that there are any harmful effects.

To look for any harmful effects, scientists compare a sample of mobile phone users with a sample of non-users.

The news often reports studies that compare samples from two groups, to see if a particular factor makes a difference. To judge whether we can have confidence in the results of these studies, there are two things worth checking.

What to check . . .	. . . and why
Look at how the two samples were selected. Can you be sure that any differences in outcomes are due to the factor you are investigating?	A study to find whether mobile phone use caused health problems would need to compare samples of users and non-users. The samples should match as many other factors as possible, for example, the spread of ages in each sample. This is because the suspected health problems might be age-related. The individuals to be included in each sample should be selected randomly, so that other factors, such as genetic variability, are similar in both groups.
Were the numbers in each sample large enough to give confidence in the results?	With small samples, the results can be more easily affected by chance. Larger sample sizes give a truer picture of the whole population. The effect of chance is more likely to average itself out in a larger sample.

How great is the risk?

Health outcomes are often reported as relative risks. For example, 'people exposed to high levels of sunlight were four times as likely to develop eye cataracts'.

● If your risk was one in a million at low levels of sunlight, it rises to four in a million at high levels – not a worry!

● If your risk was 5 in 100, it rises to 20 in 100 – worth avoiding!

And some people might be more at risk than others, for reasons of family history or lifestyle.

Radio communications

Radio and microwaves are at the heart of our TV, radio, and phone systems. Radiation in these parts of the electromagnetic spectrum is absorbed very little by the air, so it can travel long distances.

A region called the **ionosphere**, high up in the atmosphere, reflects radio signals. This lets us send radio and TV broadcasts around the curved surface of the Earth. Microwaves can pass through the ionosphere, so they are used to communicate with orbiting satellites and distant spacecraft.

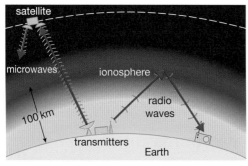

The ionosphere reflects radio signals around the Earth. Microwaves pass through the ionosphere.

Radar

Radar also uses microwaves. The name stands for 'Radio Detection And Ranging'. Pulses of radiation are sent out by a dish aerial. They are reflected by an object such as a plane. The time it takes for the reflected pulses to come back is measured. From this measurement, the radar system estimates the distance to the object.

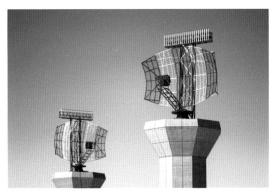

Air-traffic-control radar aerials.

Radio waves

In communications, radio and microwave radiations are often grouped together and called 'radio'. To understand more about how radio communications work, we can use the **wave model** for electromagnetic radiation.

Making radio waves

Waves on a pond can be made by something moving up and down (oscillating) on the water surface. A radio transmitter contains an electric circuit in which the current changes direction rapidly to and fro. These electrical oscillations produce radio waves that spread out from the aerial.

If the radio waves reach another aerial, they are absorbed. They **induce** oscillations in the aerial that are like the oscillations that produced the waves.

Questions

1 Is there a health risk from low-intensity microwave radiation from mobile phones and masts? (The answer is neither 'yes' nor 'no'.)

2 **a** Look at the first row of the table opposite. In this study, what is the outcome and what is the factor that might cause that outcome?
   b Explain why it is important to match the two samples.
   c Suggest a second way that the samples should be matched in this study.

3 There is radio radiation passing through your body right now.
   a Where does the radio radiation come from?
   b Why does it not have any ionising effect?
   c Does it have a heating effect? Explain your answer.

4 Suggest a reason why radio and microwave radiations are not much absorbed by the air.

The wave model for electromagnetic radiation

In the wave model:

● Sources emit energy by making something **oscillate** (change regularly). This produces waves.

● The waves travel outwards from the source like ripples on a pond.

The number of waves produced each second is called the **frequency**. Radio waves have the lowest frequencies of all the radiations in the electromagnetic spectrum.

Synoptic link

You can learn more about the nature of electromagnetic radiation in P1.3A *What is a wave?*

Key words

➤ ionosphere
➤ wave model
➤ oscillate
➤ frequency
➤ induce

A: What is global warming?

Find out about

- links between temperature, energy, frequency, and wavelength of radiation
- H how the Earth is warmed by the Sun
- how the atmosphere keeps the Earth warm

Key words

- ➤ principal frequency
- ➤ principal wavelength

We're all radiators

Hot objects glow brightly. They emit visible light. Hot objects emit high-energy photons. Very hot objects, such as the hottest stars, emit radiation whose photons are mainly in the UV part of the electromagnetic spectrum.

All objects emit some electromagnetic radiation, even cool ones. Animals (including people) are not hot enough to emit visible light, but they give out invisible infrared radiation. Special cameras can detect this infrared radiation. Security lamps have sensors that detect infrared radiation from a person's body, and switch on the lamp.

The camera detects infrared radiation from the house. It shows where it is losing energy because of poor insulation.

Objects with temperatures far below 0 °C emit infrared or microwave radiation. This radiation has photons with very low energy. Astronomers use telescopes that can detect infrared and microwave radiation. This comes from cool clouds of gas between the stars and from stars that are not hot enough to emit visible light.

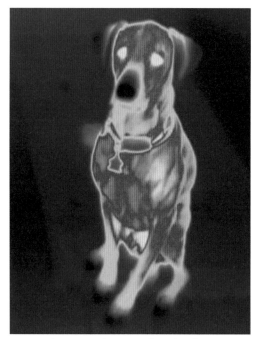

A special camera detects infrared radiation from people and animals. It creates a 'false colour' image called a thermogram. The colours change from hot (white) to cold (blue).

Radiation and temperature: two models

According to the photon model, the hotter the object, the higher the *energy* of the photons it emits.

The wave model describes the *frequency* of the radiation emitted. The hotter the object, the higher the **principal frequency**, or main frequency. So, the hotter the object, the shorter the **principal wavelength** of the radiation it emits.

Vibrating molecules

Infrared radiation is emitted and absorbed by vibrating molecules. When a molecule absorbs an infrared photon it gains energy, the substance gets warmer, and the radiation no longer exists.

Vibrating molecules can also *lose* energy by *emitting* infrared photons. The molecules then vibrate less strongly; in other words, the temperature falls.

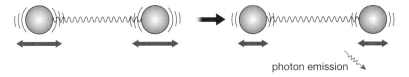

photon emission

Emitting infrared photons changes the vibration of a molecule.

False-colour image of part of the Orion Nebula. This picture was created using an infrared telescope on an Earth-orbiting observatory.

Climate change threatens coastal towns

Climate change means a change in average weather patterns over many years.

Key words

➤ climate
➤ climate change
➤ global warming
➤ greenhouse effect
➤ greenhouse gas

Synoptic link

You can learn more about climate change in C1.3 *What is the evidence for climate change and why is it occurring?*

Climate change

You have probably seen stories in the media about **climate change**. It means a change in the average weather in a region over many years. For example, the average temperature could change, and changes in wind patterns and rainfall could lead to drought or flooding.

To understand climate change and to decide what actions to take, you need to know about the possible causes of climate change. You need to find evidence for what is really happening.

Global warming is linked to climate change. Global warming means an increase in the average temperature of the whole Earth. Global warming of even a few degrees could be enough to cause climate change.

The Earth's average temperature depends on the electromagnetic radiation from the Sun. That radiation is transmitted, absorbed, and reflected by the Earth's atmosphere and surface, which affects the temperature.

Radiation from the Sun and Earth

The Sun's surface temperature is about 5800 °C. The principal wavelength of the radiation it emits corresponds to visible light. It emits a lot of UV and infrared radiation as well. The Sun also emits some gamma, X-ray, microwave, and radio radiation, but these are of lower intensity than the visible and UV.

The Earth also emits electromagnetic radiation. It is much cooler than the Sun, so the principal frequency of its radiation is much lower. It emits infrared and microwave radiation.

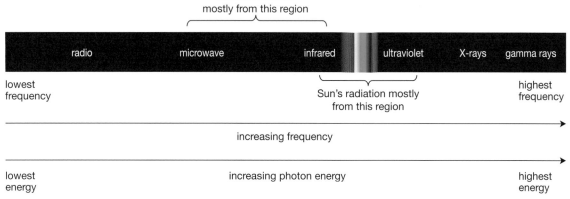

The principal frequencies of the Earth and the Sun. They both emit electromagnetic radiation. The intensity and principal frequency of the radiation depend on temperature.

A comfortable temperature for life

The Earth's average temperature is about 15 °C, which is very comfortable for life. Why does it have this temperature?

- The Earth's surface absorbs radiation from the Sun, and this warms the Earth. At the same time, the Earth emits radiation back into space.

- During the day, our part of the Earth is facing the Sun. The Earth absorbs the Sun's radiation. It warms us up and the temperature rises.

- At night, we are facing away from the Sun. Energy radiates away into space and our part of the Earth gets colder.
- The Earth is cooler than the Sun, so the radiation it emits has a lower principal frequency. This radiation can be absorbed by the atmosphere.

Without the Sun to keep topping up our energy, the Earth's temperature would soon fall to the temperature of deep space, about −270 °C.

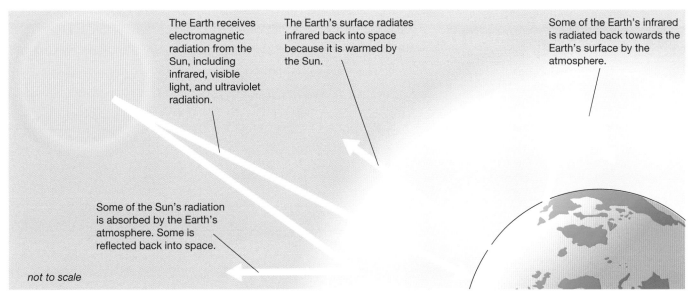

The Earth receives electromagnetic radiation from the Sun, including infrared, visible light, and ultraviolet radiation.

The Earth's surface radiates infrared back into space because it is warmed by the Sun.

Some of the Earth's infrared is radiated back towards the Earth's surface by the atmosphere.

Some of the Sun's radiation is absorbed by the Earth's atmosphere. Some is reflected back into space.

not to scale

The atmosphere lets through infrared radiation from the Sun. But not all the infrared emitted by the Earth escapes into space. This is because the Earth's radiation has lower frequencies than the Sun's. The Earth's radiation is more easily absorbed by the atmosphere.

The greenhouse effect

Without its atmosphere, the Earth's average surface temperature would be −18 °C. That's how cold it is on the Moon. This warming of the Earth by its atmosphere is called the **greenhouse effect**. (By the way, this is *not* how greenhouses keep warm!)

Life on Earth depends on the greenhouse effect. Without it, our water would be frozen. Water in its liquid form is essential to life.

The atmosphere is mainly nitrogen and oxygen, but these gases do not bring about the greenhouse effect. Tiny amounts of a few other gases make all the difference. Carbon dioxide, methane, and water vapour absorb some of the Earth's infrared radiation. They are called **greenhouse gases**.

If we added more greenhouse gases, more of Earth's infrared radiation would be absorbed by the atmosphere and reflected back towards the surface. This radiation would heat the atmosphere and the Earth's surface, leading to global warming.

Questions

1 When a metal bar is heated up, it glows red then yellow. Explain why the colour changes from red to yellow.

2 Which of the following gases found in the Earth's atmosphere are *not* greenhouse gases?
nitrogen   methane
oxygen   carbon dioxide
water vapour

3 Draw a diagram to show the steps by which an increase in greenhouse gases would cause an increase in the temperature of the Earth.

B: What is the evidence for climate change?

Find out about

- evidence for global warming
- why the amount of carbon dioxide in the atmosphere is changing
- ways of reducing the amount of carbon dioxide released into the atmosphere

Key word

➤ computer model

Getting warmer?

Are summers now hotter and winters milder than they once were? You cannot answer this question from personal experience, because you can only be in one place at a time and memory can be unreliable. Instead, you need to collect and analyse lots of data.

Weather stations have kept temperature records for over a century. There is a clear pattern. The Earth's average temperature has been rising since 1800. This conclusion is supported by evidence from nature such as growth rings in trees, ocean sediments, and air trapped in ancient ice.

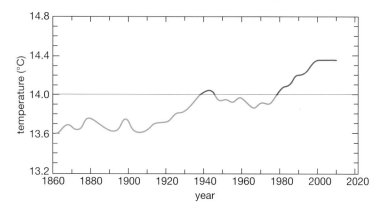

This graph of data from weather stations shows that the Earth's surface temperature has risen over the past 150 years.

Nature's records

The polar ice caps are frozen records of the past. In parts of the Antarctic, ice made from layers of snow each year is 4 km thick. That ice contains tiny bubbles of air. These give a record of the atmosphere over 800 000 years. It shows that the climate has always changed. There have been ice ages and warm periods.

But temperatures have never increased so fast as during the past 50 years.

Data collected by the Met Office shows that Bognor Regis gets more hours of sunshine than any other town in England. This data is more reliable than personal experience.

This ancient ice drilled from Antarctica contains tiny bubbles of air, trapped hundreds of thousands of years ago.

Climate change and carbon dioxide

Over the past 200 years, people have produced more carbon dioxide (CO_2) by burning fuels to release energy. They have also cut down lots of forests, which absorb CO_2 from the atmosphere.

Most climate scientists think that the rising level of CO_2 in the atmosphere is causing the rise in temperatures. Why?

● Temperatures and CO_2 levels have risen at the same time.

● Evidence from the distant past suggests that temperature and CO_2 levels go up and down together.

● Scientists can explain how CO_2 in the atmosphere absorbs radiation and raises the temperature.

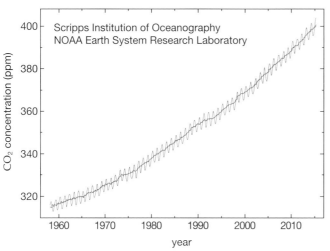

Carbon dioxide concentrations have been recorded at Mauna Loa in Hawaii since 1958. They rise and fall each year, but the overall trend is upwards.

Climate-change sceptics

Thousands of climate scientists have studied how human activities are affecting the climate. They publish their results in scientific journals and test each other's ideas.

A few scientists and many other people have challenged aspects of this work. These people are sometimes called climate 'sceptics' or 'deniers'. Despite these challenges new evidence usually supports climate scientists' ideas.

Human activities affect the atmosphere

People want to live comfortably. For most people this means clean water, electricity, manufactured goods, and bigger houses and cars. All of these things require energy.

But whenever fossil fuels (coal, oil, and gas) are burned, they increase the amount of CO_2 in the atmosphere. Cutting down or burning forests (deforestation) also releases CO_2 and reduces the amount removed by photosynthesis. Methane is another greenhouse gas. It is produced by grazing animals and from rice paddies.

Climate modelling

The atmosphere and oceans control climate. Climate scientists use **computer models** to predict the effects of rising CO_2 levels.

Climate models are similar to the models used for day-to-day weather forecasting. They use what climate scientists know about how the atmosphere and oceans behave.

Computer models are tested using data about the Earth's climate in the past. If they can predict accurately from past data, it is more likely that their predictions for the future will be accurate. If a model cannot account for past data, then the model might not be quite correct.

By working on their models to get a better match with the data, climate scientists improve their understanding of climate change. However, the further the model looks into the future, the greater the uncertainty in the predictions.

This power station supplies enough electricity for a major city. Every day it uses several trainloads of coal and sends thousands of tonnes of carbon dioxide into the atmosphere.

Science has the solution

Several solutions have been proposed to help reduce carbon (CO_2) emissions.

- Spread iron granules on the southern oceans. This would help the growth of plankton, which use CO_2 dissolved in the ocean. More CO_2 from the atmosphere could then dissolve into the oceans.

- Capture the CO_2 produced at power stations. Then compress it into a liquid and pump it beneath the seabed.

- Cement production produces 5% of the greenhouse gases generated worldwide. A new type of 'eco-cement' absorbs CO_2 while setting, and goes on absorbing for up to a year afterwards.

These suggestions are being evaluated. Scientists and engineers are well aware of the risks of rushing into a solution without considering possible side effects.

Questions

1 All of the statements about climate change and carbon dioxide in this section describe correlations. Which statement is also about cause and effect?

2 Make a list of the scientific uncertainties mentioned in this section.

3 Do you think people should rely on technical solutions to global warming like those suggested in the 'Science has the solution' article? Justify your answer.

Computer models show that:

- Human activities contribute more to global warming than natural factors.

- If CO_2 concentrations rise much further, climate change may become irreversible.

- To stabilise climates, carbon dioxide emissions should be reduced by at least 70% worldwide.

Effects of climate change

The risks associated with global warming are enormous.

- Extreme weather events, such as violent storms and heat-waves, will be more likely. Higher temperatures will cause greater convection in the atmosphere, and there will be more evaporation of water from both oceans and the land.

- Water in the oceans will expand as it gets hotter, so sea levels will rise. In addition, continental ice sheets – such as in Antarctica and Greenland – may melt, adding to the volume of the oceans. Low-lying land will be flooded, particularly affecting people living in river deltas such as the Ganges delta in Bangladesh, or on low-lying islands.

- Reduced rainfall may make it impossible to grow staple crops in some areas. Tropical areas may become drier, leading to the expansion of deserts such as the Sahara.

- Malaria will spread if mosquitoes can breed in more places.

What can we do?

Climate change is a global problem. International organisations, such as the European Union and the United Nations, work to bring countries together to tackle the problem.

The UK Government aims to reduce greenhouse gas emissions:

- 20% by 2020
- 80% by 2050.

The baseline is 592 million tonnes emitted in 1990.

In March 2015, the UK Government announced that, over the previous year, UK emissions had fallen by 8.4% to just over 400 million tonnes of CO_2. This was the biggest fall since 1990.

But it can be difficult to get agreement between countries, and it is hard for governments to change people's behaviour. People may protest and businesses may fight to protect their profits.

Technological solutions

There are many proposals for using technology to reduce the amount of CO_2 entering the atmosphere. However, these projects may take a long time to develop and build, and their outcomes may be uncertain.

A: What is a wave?

A wave is a repetitive vibration. It transfers energy from place to place without transferring matter. Ripples on water are one example of waves. There is evidence that light and sound travel as waves, along with all other electromagnetic radiations. To understand this evidence, we need to know more about waves.

You can use a slinky spring to make two different types of wave:

- To make a **transverse wave**, move the end from side to side or up and down, at right-angles to the length of the spring.

- To make a **longitudinal wave**, move the end of the spring in and out. This makes a series of compressions travel along the spring.

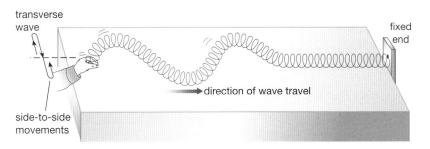

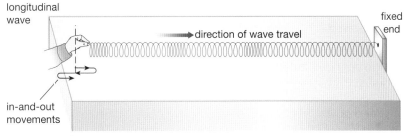

Two types of wave on a slinky spring.

Find out about

- how waves travel
- how we measure waves
- how waves behave at barriers and boundaries
- how electromagnetic waves get their name
- the nature of electromagnetic waves

Key words

- ➤ transverse wave
- ➤ longitudinal wave
- ➤ amplitude
- ➤ wavelength

Measuring waves

If we draw a simple diagram of a wave, we can define two important quantities:

- The **amplitude** is the height of a wave crest above the undisturbed level.

- The **wavelength** of the wave is the distance from one crest to the next (or from one trough to the next).

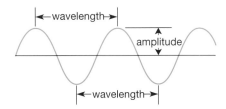

These properties are important when describing a wave.

Key words

- ➤ frequency
- ➤ period
- ➤ wave speed
- ➤ medium
- ➤ wave equation

Frequency and period of a wave

Imagine that you are making transverse waves travel along a spring. Your hand is the vibrating source of the waves. You can do two things to change the wave:

- Move your hand from side to side by a greater amount. This will give waves with a bigger amplitude.

- Move your hand faster, so that it produces more waves per second. This increases the **frequency** of the waves.

The frequency is the number of waves that pass a point each second. It is the same as the number of times the source vibrates each second. Frequency is measured in hertz (Hz). '1 Hz' means '1 wave per second'.

The **period** is the time taken to make a complete vibration to and fro (or up and down), ending back at the starting point. It is the same as the time for one complete wave to pass any point. Period is a time, so it is measured in seconds.

The connection between frequency and period

If the frequency is 5 Hz, this means five waves are made per second. So the period of one wave is one-fifth of a second:

$$\frac{1\text{ s}}{5} = 0.2\text{ s}$$

If the period is 2 s, it takes 2 s to make a wave. Only half a wave is made per second, so the frequency is $\frac{1}{2}$ Hz, which is usually written 0.5 Hz.

$$\text{frequency (Hz)} = \frac{1}{\text{period (s)}} \quad \text{and} \quad \text{period (s)} = \frac{1}{\text{frequency (Hz)}}$$

Wave speed

No matter how you move your hand when you make waves on a slinky spring, you cannot increase the wave speed. To change the speed of the waves, you would need to use a different spring.

Wave speed is the speed at which each wave crest moves. It is measured in metres per second (m/s).

The speed of a wave can be calculated using the equation:

$$\text{speed} = \frac{\text{distance travelled}}{\text{time taken}}$$

Frequency and wave speed are completely different things. The frequency depends on the source – how many times it vibrates every second. The wave speed depends only on the **medium** or material the wave is travelling through.

The wave equation

Imagine that you are making transverse waves travel along a spring. Moving your hand to and fro faster will increase their frequency. The diagram of the waves looks different, because their wavelength decreases.

The waves travel out from your hand at a fixed speed. They travel a certain distance in one second. If you make more waves in one second, they will have to be shorter to fit into the same distance.

Synoptic link

You can learn more about measuring the speed of waves on water in P8H *Observing waves on water*.

Suppose a source vibrates five times per second. It produces waves with a frequency of 5 Hz. If these have a wavelength of 2 m in the medium they are travelling through, then every wave moves forward by 10 m (5 × 2 m) in one second. The wave speed is 10 m/s. In general:

$$\text{wave speed (m/s)} = \text{frequency (Hz)} \times \text{wavelength (m)}$$
$$v = f\lambda$$

This **wave equation** links the three wave quantities: speed v, frequency f, and wavelength λ (lambda). It applies to every kind of wave.

wave begins

wave one second later

◄2 m►◄2 m►◄2 m►◄2 m►◄2 m►

The link between wave speed, frequency, and wavelength.

Worked example: Calculating wave speed

A source makes 20 waves per second. The distance between the peaks is 30 cm. What is the speed of the wave?

Step 1: Write down what you know, with the units.

frequency f = 20 Hz
wavelength λ = 30 cm = 0.30 m

Step 2: Write down the equation you will use to calculate the wave speed.

wave speed = frequency × wavelength
$v = f\lambda$

Step 3: Substitute the quantities into the equation and calculate the wave speed. Include the units in your answer.

v = 20 Hz × 0.3 m
v = 6 m/s

Answer:

wave speed = 6 m/s

Worked example: Calculating wavelength

An earthquake wave has a speed of 6 km/s. The frequency of the wave is 0.5 Hz. What is its wavelength in km?

Step 1: Write down what you know, with the units.

wave speed v = 6 km/s = 6000 m/s
frequency f = 0.5 Hz

Step 2: Write down the equation that links wave speed, frequency, and wavelength.

wave speed = frequency × wavelength
$v = f\lambda$

Step 3: You are trying to find the wavelength, so you need to rearrange the equation to get wavelength on its own.

$\dfrac{v}{f} = \dfrac{f\lambda}{\cancel{f}}$

Divide both sides of the equation by f.

$\lambda = \dfrac{v}{f}$

Step 4: Substitute the quantities into the equation and work out the wavelength. Include the units in your answer.

$\lambda = \dfrac{6000 \text{ m/s}}{0.5 \text{ Hz}}$

λ = 12 000 m

Answer:

wavelength = 12 km

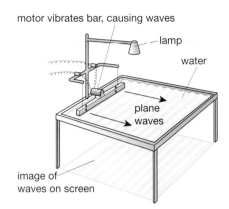

motor vibrates bar, causing waves

lamp

water

plane waves

image of waves on screen

A ripple tank producing a steady stream of plane waves (straight waves).

Waves in a ripple tank

We can learn more about waves by studying water waves in a ripple tank. Waves are created on the surface of the water. A lamp projects an image of the waves onto a screen.

If the water is all one depth, waves on it are equally spaced. This shows that the waves do not slow down as they travel. As the wave travels, it loses energy (because of friction). Its amplitude gets less, but its speed stays the same.

Reflection

Water waves are **reflected** by a straight barrier placed in their path. If you draw a line at right-angles to the barrier, the reflected wave makes the same angle with this line as the incoming wave.

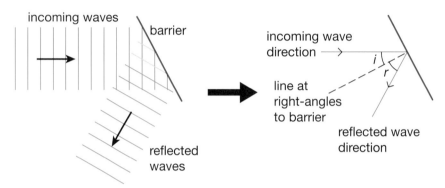

incoming waves

barrier

reflected waves

incoming wave direction →

line at right-angles to barrier

reflected wave direction

Reflection of water waves at a plane barrier.

Refraction

If waves cross a boundary from a deeper to a shallower region, they are closer together in the shallower region. Their wavelength is smaller. This effect is called **refraction**. It happens because water waves travel more slowly in shallower water.

The frequency is the same in both regions, so the slower wave speed means that the wavelength must be shorter.

If the waves are travelling at an angle to the boundary between the two regions, their direction also changes. You can work out which way they will bend by thinking about which side of the wave gets slowed down first.

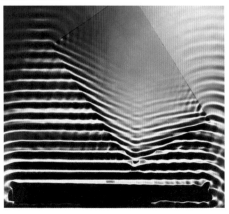

At a boundary between deep and shallow water, the waves are refracted. They change direction.

What are electromagnetic waves?

Making radio waves

If you look at water waves, you can see the water moving up and down. With sound waves, you cannot see the compression pulses, but you can detect them fairly easily. A candle flame in front of a loudspeaker flickers, showing the movement of the air. But with light, it is much harder to detect anything vibrating.

To get some more clues about the nature of light waves, we can think about another member of the electromagnetic spectrum 'family'. Radio waves are produced by electrical vibrations or oscillations in an aerial. The waves travel outwards at right-angles to the aerial. We can picture these oscillations as rather like your hand making a transverse wave on a slinky spring.

The electrical oscillations in a radio aerial produce both electrical and magnetic oscillations. These travel outwards from the aerial. The oscillations are at right-angles to the direction of wave travel, so the radio waves are transverse.

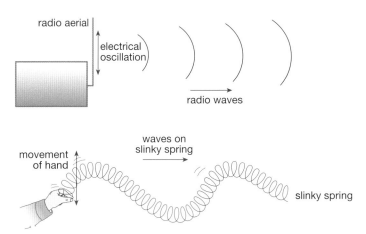

Electrical oscillations produce radio waves. Radio waves are transverse, like the transverse wave on a slinky spring.

The nature of electromagnetic waves

Radio waves have the lowest frequencies and longest wavelengths of all the electromagnetic radiations. We can picture all other electromagnetic waves as being like radio waves, but with much higher frequencies and shorter wavelengths. For example, rapid electrical oscillations in a vibrating molecule produce infrared radiation.

All electromagnetic waves are transverse. All electromagnetic waves involve *electrical* and *magnetic* oscillations. This is what gives them their name.

Unlike any other waves, electromagnetic waves can travel in a **vacuum**. It seems odd to have a wave where there is nothing at all, not even air. But it is possible to have electrical and magnetic effects in a vacuum. In fact, electromagnetic waves travel fastest in a vacuum, where their wave speed is 300 000 km/s. Anything else slows them down, though air slows them down only very slightly.

Key word

➤ reflect
➤ refraction
➤ vacuum

Light waves

In the wave model for light, the colour of light is related to its frequency. Red light has the lowest frequency of all visible light, and violet light has the highest frequency. The frequency of violet light is almost twice the frequency of red light. In any given medium, violet light has about half the wavelength of red light.

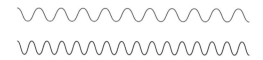

The blue waves have a higher frequency than the red waves, so their wavelength is shorter.

The frequencies of visible light are *much* higher than the frequencies of sound, and the wavelengths of light are *much* shorter. In air, the longest wavelength of visible light is about 750 nanometres and the shortest is about 380 nanometres. One nanometre (nm) is 1/1 000 000 000th of a metre (1×10^{-9} m).

The lowest frequency of visible light is about 400 terahertz and the highest frequency is about 790 terahertz. One terahertz (THz) is 1 000 000 000 000 Hz (1×10^{12} Hz).

The wave equation links the wavelength to the frequency and wave speed.

Worked example: Calculating frequency

A certain colour of green light has a wavelength of 500 nm in air. What is its frequency?

Step 1: Write down what you know, with the units.

To calculate frequency in Hz we need the wavelength in m and the wave speed in m/s.

wavelength λ = 500 nm = $\dfrac{500 \text{ m}}{1\,000\,000\,000}$ = 0.000 000 5 m = 5×10^{-7} m

In air, the speed of light is 300 000 km/s

1 km/s = 1000 m/s so

wave speed = 300 000 km/s = 300 000 000 m/s = 3×10^{8} m/s

Step 2: Write down the equation that links wave speed, frequency, and wavelength

wave speed = frequency × wavelength

$v = f\lambda$

Step 3: You are trying to find the frequency, so you need to rearrange the equation to get frequency on its own.

Divide both sides of the equation by wavelength.

$\dfrac{v}{\lambda} = \dfrac{f \times \lambda}{\lambda}$

$f = \dfrac{v}{\lambda}$

Step 4: Substitute the quantities into the equation and work out the frequency. Include the units in your answer.

$f = \dfrac{3 \times 10^{8} \text{ m/s}}{5 \times 10^{-7} \text{ m}}$

$f = 600\,000\,000\,000\,000$ Hz

Answer:

frequency = 600 THz

Questions

1 Using a ruler, measure the drawings of the slinky springs (at the start of this section) as follows:

   a Find the wavelength of the transverse wave: measure the distance from the crest of one wave to the next.

   b Find the wavelength of the longitudinal wave: measure the distance from the centre of one compression to the next.

2 Suppose you shake the end of a rope with a frequency of 2 Hz, making waves whose wavelength is 1.5 m.

   a What is the period of the vibrations?

   b What is the wave speed along the rope?

3 **a** Some water waves meet a straight boundary between a region of deep water and a region of shallower water. Draw a diagram to show how the wave direction changes.

   b How would the waves' direction change if they travelled from shallow to deep water?

4 **a** List two ways in which electromagnetic waves are *similar to* waves on a rope.

   b List two ways in which electromagnetic waves are *unlike* waves on a rope.

5 Describe a behaviour of light that you have observed and that provides evidence that it has wave properties.

6 The BBC broadcasts World Service radio programmes to Europe on a frequency of 648 kHz. Calculate the wavelength of the signal.

Find out about

- how sounds are made
- how sound travels
- similarities and differences between sound waves and water waves

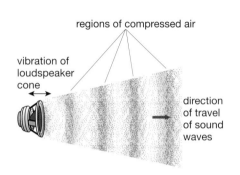

A loudspeaker has a cone that vibrates. It sends a stream of compression pulses through the air.

The distance meter emits a burst of ultrasound. It travels to the end of the room and bounces back to the meter.

Key words

➤ oscillate
➤ echo
➤ ultrasound

Making sounds

Sounds are made by vibrating objects. A source vibrates, causing compressions in the air. Compressed air is 'springy'. As the compression passes, each bit of air springs back, pushing on the next bit of air, which compresses it. A continuous wave of pulses travels through the air. This is a sound wave. A sound wave is a longitudinal wave.

The air itself does not travel when a sound wave travels from a source. If you put a candle flame in the path of a sound, you might see it flicker back and forth if the sound is loud, but it will not blow over.

Sound waves can travel through any gas, and also through solids and liquids (you can hear underwater). You hear sounds because sound waves set up vibrations in your ears. A microphone detects sounds because sound waves make it vibrate. These vibrations produce electrical **oscillations** in the microphone's electric circuit.

Most people can hear sounds that have frequencies in the range 20 Hz to about 20 000 Hz.

Reflected sound

If sound is a wave, then we can predict that, like a water wave, it will be reflected from a barrier.

If you stand some distance away from a wall or a cliff and clap your hands, you hear the **echo** a short time later. An echo is a reflected sound.

You can use echoes to make a rough measurement of the wave speed of sound in air. To work out speed, you use:

$$\text{speed} = \frac{\text{distance}}{\text{time}}$$

You can measure the distance to the wall with a tape measure. Between clapping your hands and hearing the echo, the sound travels twice this distance, there and back.

You need to find a way to measure the time between a clap and hearing its echo.

A distance meter

A distance meter uses the wave speed to measure distances. The wave speed of sound in air is about 340 m/s. The meter sends out a short burst of **ultrasound** towards a wall, and detects its echo coming back. The meter's electronics measure the time between sending the burst of sound and receiving the echo. It uses the time and the wave speed to calculate the distance.

Worked example:
Measuring the speed of sound using an echo

Students bang two blocks of wood together. They are 240 m from a wall. They estimate that it takes 1.5 s for the sound echo to come back from the wall. Use this data to estimate the speed of sound in air.

Step 1: Write down what you know, with the units.

distance travelled = 2 × 240 m

time = 1.5 s

Step 2: Write down the equation that links speed, distance, and time.

$$speed = \frac{distance}{time}$$

Step 3: Substitute the quantities into the equation to work out the speed.

$$speed = \frac{480 \text{ m}}{1.5 \text{ s}}$$
$$= 320 \text{ m/s}$$

Answer: estimated speed = 320 m/s

H Refracted sound

Because sound travels as a wave, we predict that sound will be refracted as it travels between regions where the wave speed is different. This does happen, but it can be difficult to observe.

The speed of sound in air depends on the air temperature. At 0 °C the wave speed is about 330 m/s, and at 30 °C it is about 350 m/s.

Different temperatures in the air affect the way we hear sounds. During the day, air near the ground may be warmer than air higher up in the atmosphere. At night, air near the ground is usually cooler. Aircraft noise can be more noticeable near the ground at night, because sound from aircraft is refracted upwards during the day and downwards at night.

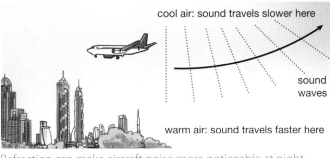

Refraction can make aircraft noise more noticeable at night.

Questions

1   The wave speed of sound in air is 340 m/s. The musical note F below middle C has a frequency of about 170 Hz. What is the wavelength of the note F sound wave in air?

2   **a** List two ways in which sound waves are *similar to* water waves.

    b List two ways in which sound waves are *unlike* water waves.

3   Suggest a reason why it is difficult to observe refraction of sound.

4   The distance meter in the diagram on the previous page is used to measure the size of the sports hall. Sound travels in air at 340 m/s and takes 0.2 s to travel the length of the sports hall and back. How long is the hall?

Science explanations

P1 Radiation and waves

In this chapter you have learnt about the electromagnetic spectrum, different types and sources of radiation, and how they can be both useful and dangerous.

You should know:

- how to think about any form of radiation in terms of its source, its journey path, and what happens when it is absorbed, transmitted, or reflected
- the parts of the electromagnetic spectrum, in order of their frequencies and wavelengths
- that all electromagnetic radiation travels as transverse waves at the same speed through space
- the different properties of the different parts of the electromagnetic spectrum
- what different parts of the electromagnetic spectrum can be used for
- that different types of electromagnetic radiation cause different changes in atoms and molecules, including chemical changes, ionisation, and heating
- why ionising radiation is hazardous to living things and how people can be protected
- how the atmosphere's ozone layer protects living organisms from ultraviolet radiation
- that all bodies emit radiation of different frequencies depending on their temperature and how this links to global warming and climate change H
- that waves are caused by vibrating sources, and the number of waves produced each second is the frequency of the wave
- that waves have amplitude and wavelength, where the amplitude is the distance from the top of a crest (or the bottom of a trough) to the undisturbed position, and the wavelength is the length of one complete cycle
- the difference between transverse and longitudinal waves
- that wave motion can be described by the equation:
  wave speed = frequency × wavelength
- how to measure the speed of waves on the surface of water and the speed of sound
- H how the effects of refraction can be explained in terms of the changing speed of the waves.

All bodies emit radiation. The Earth emits infrared radiation. This false-colour image shows cold high clouds in blue, and warmer seas in red.

Ideas about Science

To make decisions about both health and climate change, you need to understand not only the electromagnetic spectrum but also some ideas about science. You need to recognise the difference between correlation and cause, and to assess the risks and benefits associated with the electromagnetic spectrum.

Factors and outcomes may be linked in different ways. It is important to distinguish between identifying a *correlation*, where a change in one factor is linked to a change in the other, and identifying the *cause*, where there is an explanation of why changing the factor is responsible for the outcome. To show your understanding of these ideas you should be able to:

● suggest and explain everyday examples of correlation

● identify a correlation from data, from a graph, or from a description

● suggest factors that might increase the *chance* of a particular outcome, though not always lead to it in every case

● identify that where there is a **mechanism** to explain a correlation, scientists are likely to accept that the factor *causes* the outcome.

Everything we do carries some risk, and new technologies often introduce new risks. It is important to assess the chance of a particular outcome happening and the consequences if it did. People often perceive a risk as being different from [H] the actual risk: sometimes underestimating, and sometimes overestimating. A particular situation that introduces risk will often also introduce benefits, which must be weighed up against that risk.

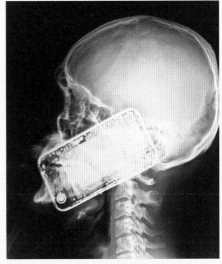

Both the health benefits and the risks of X-rays are well known. Using a mobile phone brings benefits but uncertain risks.

You should be able to:

● identify risks arising from scientific or technological advances

● discuss both the risks and benefits of a course of action, taking account of who takes the risk and who benefits

[H] ● distinguish between real risk and perceived risk

● suggest why people are willing (or reluctant) to take certain risks.

When reading about the work of scientists you should understand how they develop their ideas and how they agree on the best explanations.

You should be able to:

● describe how scientists use computer modelling to test their ideas

● describe how the process of peer review leads to agreement about the best explanation for scientific phenomena.

P1 Review questions

1 **a** List the parts of the electromagnetic spectrum in order of increasing frequency.

   b Which part of the electromagnetic spectrum carries the most energy? Describe some evidence to support your answer.

   c Which part of the electromagnetic spectrum causes the most heating? Describe the changes that take place when a material is heated by electromagnetic radiation.

H 2 Graph A shows how the percentage of carbon dioxide in the atmosphere has changed over the past 300 years.

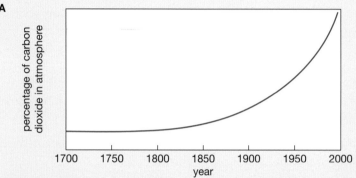

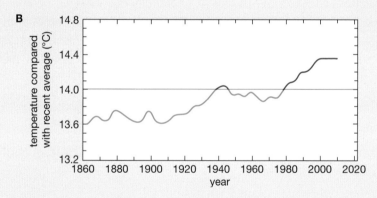

   a Describe the trend in graph A and explain the scientific reasons for what the graph shows.

   b Graph B shows how the average temperature of the atmosphere has changed over the past 140 years. Use the two graphs to explain the meaning of *correlation*.

   c A scientist believes that there is a *causal* link between carbon dioxide levels and climate change. Write down what else the scientist needs to do so that other scientists will accept this idea.

3 The table lists several different situations in which waves are travelling. In each case something happens to the wave, but which properties of the wave are affected?

Copy this table and complete it by writing either *gets bigger*, *gets smaller,* or *stays the same* in each cell.

Description of wave	Amplitude	Frequency	Wave speed	Wavelength
waves on the surface of a pond, as they travel away from the disturbance that caused them				
a wave on a long spring; the end is moved up and down more rapidly				
a light ray as it moves from air into a clear glass block				
radio waves as they travel from a satellite to a receiving dish on the ground				
sound waves as they pass from air into a brick wall				

4 All electromagnetic waves travel at a speed of 300 000 km/s in a vacuum (and at a similar speed in air). Sound travels at about 340 m/s in air at room temperature.

a Calculate the wavelength of sound with frequency 1700 Hz.

b Calculate the frequency of microwaves with wavelength 3 cm.

c Explain why we see a flash of lightning in the distance before we hear the thunderclap, but we do not notice a difference between seeing a person's mouth move and hearing them speak when we are in the same room.

5 Describe an observation that shows that when a water wave travels across a ripple tank, the water does not travel with the wave.

6 A student is watching a 100 m sprint and wants to measure the speed of sound. She is standing at the end of the 100 m track. She measures the time between seeing the flash of the starting gun and hearing the bang.

a Describe how she could use this measurement to find the speed of sound.

b Explain why this measurement will not give her a very accurate value.

c Suggest and explain what she could change to improve the accuracy of her experiment.

H **7** Explain why light changes direction as it passes from air into water.

P2 Sustainable energy

Why study energy?

How to maintain our energy supply is one of the major issues facing society in the immediate future.

To have an informed opinion about our supply and use of energy, you need to understand the figures and calculations behind the headlines.

Electricity supplies many of our energy needs. Most of us take electricity for granted. But our power stations are becoming old and will need replacing. How should we generate electricity in the future? Can we reduce our impact on the environment without reducing our quality of life?

What you already know

- Energy stores include food and fuels, moving objects, stretched springs, and objects that are raised up.
- Energy can be transferred by using a force, by an electric current, or by heating.
- The energy transferred by a device depends on the power rating of the device and the length of time it is used.
- Energy is measured in joules or kilowatt-hours.
- When energy is transferred in a system, the total energy after the transfer is equal to the energy available at the start.

The Science

Energy cannot be made or destroyed. Whenever we use energy, some is lost to the surroundings. We need ways of using energy more efficiently.

Mains electricity is distributed to our homes using the National Grid.

Most UK electricity is generated by burning gas or coal to drive generators. All the methods of generating electricity have advantages and drawbacks.

Ideas about Science

Generating electricity and maintaining our energy supply brings problems no matter which types of energy resource we use. There are different risks with using each energy resource. But who should be making the decisions?

P2.1 How much energy do we use?

A: What's the big energy picture?

Find out about

- how to identify different energy stores
- how energy is transferred between stores by different devices

Key words

➤ energy store
➤ work
➤ electric current
➤ heating
➤ electromagnetic radiation
➤ radiation

Is there enough energy to last us for hundreds of years? Is there enough energy for the lifestyle that we want? These are very important questions. To answer them we need to know how to keep track of the energy we use.

A comfortable lifestyle uses a lot of energy. Is there enough for the future?

Energy stores and energy transfers

One way of keeping track of energy is to think of **energy stores**. Here are examples of stores that we use.

Type of energy store	Example of this store
chemical	a large pile of coal together with lots of oxygen
thermal	a hot bath
kinetic	a fast-moving car
gravitational	a skier at the top of a hill
elastic	a stretched elastic band
nuclear	the Sun, or a large amount of a radioactive material such as uranium
electrostatic	two opposite charges held apart
electromagnetic	the opposite poles of two magnets held apart

These stores are not like food stored in a cupboard, because energy is not an object that you put somewhere to be used later. Energy in a store is a quantity in joules that you can calculate.

Transferring energy – mechanically

You can transfer energy by **working**. Working is energy transfer using a force. When the skiers ski down the slope, a force due to gravity does work on them. Energy is transferred from a gravitational store to a kinetic store while they are speeding up. Forces acting over a distance do work.

As the skiers move away from the centre of the Earth, the energy in the gravitational store of their bodies and of the Earth increases.

Transferring energy – electrically

Energy can be transferred using an **electric current**. When you connect up a circuit, forces act on electrical charges in the circuit. These forces transfer energy to the components in the circuit, such as lamps or motors. This is electrical working.

Transferring energy – by heating

Energy is transferred by **heating** when there is a temperature difference. Energy is transferred through solids, liquids, and gases by conduction. Liquids and gases also transfer energy by movement (convection).

Transferring energy – by radiation

Energy is transferred by sound waves or by **electromagnetic radiation**, such as light, microwaves or infrared spreading out from a source (radiating). There is much more about **radiation** in P1.

A microwave oven transfers energy by electromagnetic radiation. Energy in the chemical store of fuel and oxygen at the power station is transferred to energy in the thermal store as the popcorn is heated up.

The big energy picture

You can describe many energy transfers in everyday life this way:

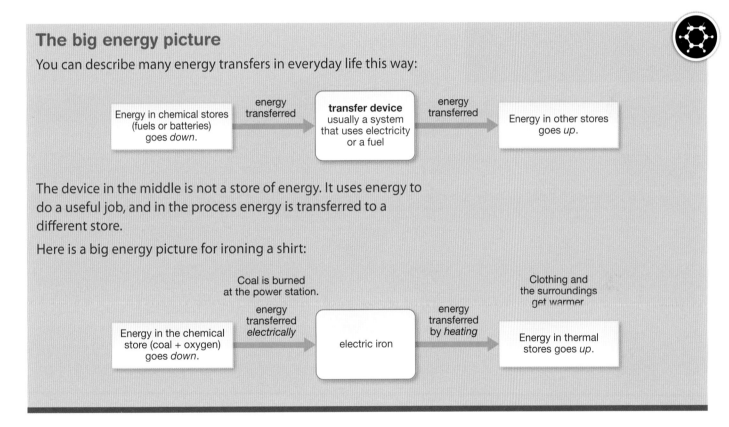

The device in the middle is not a store of energy. It uses energy to do a useful job, and in the process energy is transferred to a different store.

Here is a big energy picture for ironing a shirt:

It is the device in the middle of a big energy picture that is useful. Some devices use fuels directly; others use fuels via electricity.

● Energy transfers get you to school. A bus is a device that uses fuel directly.

● Energy transfers allow you listen to music or style your hair. DVD players and hair straighteners use fuels via an electric current.

Energy in the chemical store of a battery is transferred to a kinetic store as the drill speeds up.

Most UK electricity is generated by burning fossil fuels.

Why use electricity?

We use many electrical devices, either with a battery or connected to the mains supply.

- An electric current is a clean and convenient way of transferring energy from one store to another over a large distance.
- Many electrical devices do jobs that could not be done by burning fuels directly.

People rely on the energy store in their phone battery to keep them connected.

Charging a mobile phone transfers energy from the chemical store at the power station to the chemical store in the battery of the phone.

As you send a text, the store of usable chemicals in your phone battery gets smaller. The phone emits light which is absorbed by your eye (so you are a tiny bit hotter) and by the surroundings. Using your phone heats things up.

It is important to realise that energy transfers happen at the *same time*. The surroundings heat up at the same time as the chemicals in the battery get used up.

The battery is recharged by connecting it to the mains supply. **Mains electricity** is produced at a power station. The fuel and oxygen at the power station are used up to recharge the battery. Each time the battery charges and discharges, chemical reactions take place inside it.

Questions

1 In these situations, an energy store is decreasing. Name each type of store.
   a a cup of tea cooling down
   b a woman rebounding on a bungee jump so the elastic is getting shorter
   c rubbing your hands to keep warm
   d wood burning on a fire

2 For each device, name the useful method of energy transfer.
   a a kettle of water
   b a battery-operated radio
   c a lift

3 Draw the big energy picture for an electric oven as it cooks a meal. Show the energy stores and transfers.

Key word

➤ mains electricity

B: How much energy do appliances transfer?

Calculating the energy transferred

An electrical appliance has a label showing the **power** of the appliance. If the **power rating** is higher, the appliance will transfer more energy per second. The chemicals in the battery are used up faster, or the fuel at a power station is burned more quickly.

The energy transferred by an electrical appliance is measured with a meter. The amount of energy transferred W depends on:

- the power P of the appliance
- the length of time t it is used.

The power is the amount of energy transferred each second. An appliance with a power of 1 watt (1 W) transfers 1 joule of energy (1 J) every second. The amount of energy transferred is given by:

energy transferred = power × time
(joule, J)   (watt, W)   (second, s)

$$W = Pt$$

Find out about

- how to calculate the energy transferred by an electrical appliance
- how to calculate the cost of electrical energy
- changes in the amount of energy in different stores as you use appliances

Key words

➤ power
➤ power rating

Speakers with a power rating of 10 W transfer 10 J of energy every second.

Powerful appliances such as power showers and ovens have power ratings of several thousand watts.

Worked example: Calculating energy transfers

Calculate the energy transferred by two speakers in 1 hour. The power of each speaker is 10 W.

Step 1: Write down what you know, with the units. Convert to standard units.

power P = 2 × 10 W = 20 W = 20 J/s
time t = 1 hour = 60 min
t = 60 s/min × 60 min = 3600 s

Step 2: Write down the equation you will use to calculate energy transfer

energy transferred = power × time
$W = Pt$

Step 3: Substitute the quantities into the equation and calculate the energy transferred. Include the units in your answer.

W = 20 J/s × 3600 s
W = 72 000 J

Answer:

energy transferred = 72 000 J

An electricity meter measures the number of kilowatt-hours transferred by all the appliances in the house.

Key words

➤ kilowatt
➤ kilowatt-hour

One joule is a tiny amount of energy. Many domestic appliances have a power rating of a few **kilowatts (kW)**. 1 kW = 1000 W.

To describe the energy transferred in a domestic appliance, we use the **kilowatt-hour (kWh)**. 1 kWh is the energy transferred by a 1 kW appliance switched on for 1 hour.

$$\begin{array}{ccc} \text{energy transferred} & = & \text{power} \quad \times \quad \text{time} \\ \text{(kilowatt-hour, kWh)} & & \text{(kilowatt, kW)} \quad \text{(hour, h)} \end{array}$$

Worked example: Energy in kilowatt-hours

Calculate the energy transferred by a 10 kW shower that you use for 15 minutes.

Step 1: Write down what you know, with the units. Convert to standard units.

power P = 10 kW
time t = 15 min = 0.25 h

Step 2: Write down the equation you will use to calculate the energy transferred.

energy transferred = power × time
$W = Pt$

Step 3: Substitute the quantities into the equation and calculate the energy transferred. Include the units in your answer.

W = 10 kW × 0.25 h
W = 2.5 kWh

Answer:

energy transferred = 2.5 kWh

Paying for energy transferred

On an electricity bill, 1 unit means 1 kWh. To find the cost of the energy transferred, multiply the number of units by the price of 1 unit.

$$\begin{array}{ccccc} \text{cost of energy transferred} & = & \text{number of units used} & \times & \text{price of 1 unit} \\ \text{(pence, p)} & & \text{(kWh)} & & \text{(p/kWh)} \end{array}$$

We pay for a fuel to be burned at a power station, to generate a voltage to transfer the energy to run our appliances.

Meter: **326565**		Tariff: **Domestic**	
cost of energy	**number of units used**	**unit charges**	**cost**
13.25p/unit for first 227 units	883	227 at 13.25p	£30.08
7.88p/unit for remaining units		656 at 7.88p	£51.69
			£81.77

The electricity bill shows the number of units (kWh) to be paid for.

Worked example: The cost of a shower

Calculate the cost of using the 10 kW shower for 15 minutes (see the previous example). The price is 10p/unit, or 10p/kWh.

Step 1: Write down what you know, with the units. Convert to standard units.

power P = 10 kW
time t = 15 min = 0.25 h
cost of energy = 10p/kWh

Step 2: Calculate the energy transferred.

$W = Pt$
W = 10 kW × 0.25 h
W = 2.5 kWh

Step 3: Calculate the cost of energy. Include the units in your answer.

cost of energy = 2.5 kWh × 10p/kWh

Answer:

cost of energy = 25p

Changes to energy in stores

Many appliances such as cookers, irons, and kettles transfer energy from chemical to thermal stores. Others, such as DVD players, have a motor. Some energy is transferred to a kinetic store as the motor turns.

Questions

1 Calculate the energy transferred (in joules) when an 800 W microwave oven is used for 2 minutes.
2 Look at the tasks in the table.
   a Calculate the energy in kilowatt-hours that each task uses.
   b A unit costs 10p. Calculate the cost of each task.

Task	Appliance used	Power rating (W)	Length of time used
make tea	electric kettle	2000	4 min
write homework	computer	250	2 h
listen to music	mp3 player	0.2	2 h
wash dirty clothes	washing machine	1850	2 h
play a game	games console	190	1 h

3 Think about how you use electricity at home. Suggest two ways you could reduce your electricity use without making a big difference to your life.

C: How can we use less energy?

Find out about

- how energy is dissipated
- how to reduce unwanted energy transfer
- the law of conservation of energy
- efficiency and how to increase it
- using a Sankey diagram to show energy transfers

Key words

➤ dissipated
➤ lubrication
➤ insulation
➤ closed system
➤ law of conservation of energy

Energy is dissipated

When you use an appliance to do a job, some energy ends up in a store that is not useful. Eventually the energy transferred ends up in the thermal store of the surroundings. The air and the ground become a little bit (or a lot) hotter. You cannot use this energy to do another job. The energy is **dissipated**.

Here are some examples of energy ending up in a less useful store.

Transfer	Effect	So energy ends up in...
friction between parts of a car engine	the parts of the engine heat up	the thermal store of the engine parts
conduction between water in a kettle and the plastic of the kettle	the plastic gets hot	the thermal store of the kettle
radiation from the front of a hot oven	the room warms up	the thermal store of the surroundings

A store has useful energy if it can be used to do a job. This includes:

- heating things
- doing work (with forces or electricity).

When you heat a pan of water, you transfer energy to both the thermal store of the water and the thermal store of the surroundings. The hot water in the pan is useful. You can't do anything with the energy in the thermal store of the surroundings – it is dissipated.

The job of the stove is to transfer energy from the chemical store of the fuel and oxygen to energy in the thermal store of the water. But energy is also transferred to the thermal stores of the pan, the air, and the stove.

Reducing unwanted transfer

If a device is increasing the thermal store of the surroundings, this wastes energy. We can reduce the transfer of energy into stores that are not useful in two main ways.

When surfaces are touching, such as the parts of an engine, work is done to move the surfaces over each other. This work transfers energy to the thermal store of the parts, so they heat up. **Lubrication** reduces the work done when surfaces rub over each other, so less energy is dissipated.

Oil lubricates an engine.

Insulation slows down the transfer of energy between two objects at different temperatures. This is done by putting a layer of material that does not conduct well between the two objects.

The conservation of energy

The total amount of energy in a **closed system** does not change. A closed system has clearly defined stores at the start and end of a process. If you analyse a process in a closed system, then you need to account for all the energy. There must be the same amount of energy at the end as there was at the start.

This is the **law of conservation of energy**. It says that energy cannot be created or destroyed, only transferred. So when analysing the process of heating water on a stove you would need to include:

- the energy from the chemical store of the gas and oxygen
- the energy used to heat the water
- the energy that heats the pan, the stove, and the air around the stove.

Loft insulation slows the transfer of energy through the roof.

A model for energy

Energy is a bit like money. If you leave home with £10 and spend £4 then you know, without looking in your wallet, that there is £6 left. How much money you have left tells you what you can buy.

Energy is like that. Energy is conserved. The amount of energy available tells you what is *possible*, not what *will* happen.

Energy always adds up, just like money.

Why do buildings cool down?

In winter we need to keep the heating on to keep the temperature of our homes comfortable. What is happening in terms of energy transfer?

A thermal imaging camera shows the temperature of the outside of the house.

A boiler burns a fuel, such as gas, to heat water, which travels around the radiators. This process:
- heats the rooms (the job that you want)
- heats the environment outside (the job that you don't want).

Energy is transferred through the walls, floor, windows, and roof because there is a temperature difference between the inside and the outside of the house.

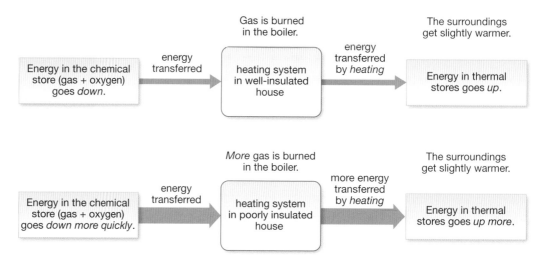

A poorly insulated house needs more energy to keep it warm than a well-insulated house. Energy is transferred from the house to the thermal stores of the surroundings more quickly. The width of the arrow indicates the amount of energy transferred.

Older buildings often have thick walls, which provide some insulation as well as strength.

How thick are the walls?

In modern buildings the walls have several layers of different materials, including insulation.

In some old buildings there is an inner and an outer wall, but the middle is filled with twigs and other natural materials. The walls can be nearly 1 m thick.

Two similar houses have walls of different thicknesses.

Imagine two similar houses, but the walls have different thicknesses. There is the same temperature difference across them. Eventually both rooms will both cool down to the same temperature. However, the room with thicker walls will take a longer time to cool down.

The temperature falls more quickly if the walls are thinner.

What are the walls made of?

There are lots of different types of building materials, and new ones are being designed all the time.

When choosing materials for walls, builders need to consider several factors, such as:

- strength (holding up floors and ceilings)
- appearance
- cost
- durability (how long it will last).

Key word

➤ thermal conductivity

They also need to think about the **thermal conductivity** of the material. The thermal conductivity tells you how fast energy is transferred by conduction through a material that has an area of 1 m², a thickness of 1 m, and a temperature difference across it of 1 °C.

Suppose the two similar houses have walls of different thermal conductivity.

A

outside: 2 °C | inside: 22 °C

material of lower
thermal conductivity

B

outside: 2 °C | inside: 22 °C

material of higher
thermal conductivity

Two similar houses have walls of different thermal conductivities.

Builders reduce energy transfer by putting thick insulation in the walls. It is made of a material with a low thermal conductivity.

House B will cool down faster than house A. The temperature falls more quickly if the thermal conductivity is higher.

Modern insulation materials have a very low thermal conductivity.

What is efficiency?

We can save fuel at the power station if we switch off appliances such as lights when we are not using them. We should also choose appliances that are *efficient*. This means they are better at making the energy transfers that we want, rather than the ones we do not want.

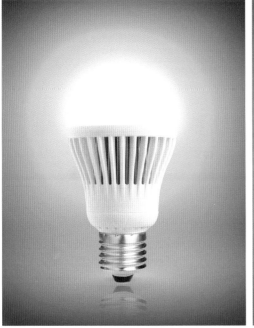

All three light bulbs emit the same amount of light per second. The LED lamp on the left does less heating than the CFL in the middle, or the filament lamp on the right.

Synoptic link

You can learn more about LED lights in P7.1 *How can solar energy make a difference?*

Calculating efficiency

In electrical appliances, only some of the energy being transferred ends up doing the job that we want. The rest usually heats up the surroundings – it is dissipated.

The **efficiency** of an appliance is:

$$\text{efficiency} = \frac{\text{useful energy transferred}}{\text{total energy transferred}} \times 100\,\%$$

The efficiency tells us how good the appliance is at doing its job.

Filament lamps are very inefficient. They get very hot. Most of the energy from the electricity supply is transferred to the surrounding air and heats it up. Only a small amount of energy is transferred as light. The lamp heats the room much better than it lights the room. This is why the EU has banned sales of new filament lamps.

Compact fluorescent lamps (CFLs), halogen lamps, and **light-emitting diodes (LEDs)** are more efficient than filament lamps. An LED lamp is about 15 times more efficient than a filament lamp of the same brightness. The LED lamp also lasts much longer.

Worked example: Calculating efficiency

In 1 second, 75 J of energy are supplied to a 75 W filament lamp. Only about 10 J of energy are usefully transferred as light. Calculate the efficiency.

Step 1: Write down what you know, with the units.

energy supplied = 75 J
useful energy transferred = 10 J

Step 2: Write down the equation to calculate efficiency.

$$\text{efficiency} = \frac{\text{useful energy transferred}}{\text{total energy transferred}} \times 100\,\%$$

Step 3: Calculate the efficiency.

$$\text{efficiency} = \frac{10\ \text{J}}{75\ \text{J}} \times 100\,\%$$

Answer:

efficiency = 13%

Sankey diagrams

Sankey diagrams are a way of showing the efficiency of energy transfers. These diagrams use branching arrows to show how energy is transferred. The width of each arrow shows the amount of energy. The total width of all the arrows stays the same, because energy cannot be lost or gained overall.

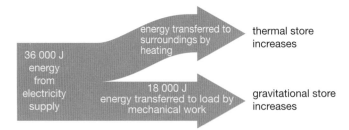

Sankey diagram for an electric motor lifting a load with an efficiency of 50%.

Making more efficient devices

In 2014 three physicists won the Nobel prize in physics for inventing an LED that emits blue light. This invention has changed the nature of lighting all around us. It is now possible to make LEDs that give out white light. Before this they were only red or green.

Because LEDs do not waste much energy heating the surroundings, they have a much lower power rating than other bulbs.

New technology can produce more efficient devices, such as blue LEDs. Scientists also use technology to make existing appliances more efficient, such as by using materials that reduce unwanted energy transfer.

Key words

➤ efficiency
➤ CFL (compact fluorescent lamp)
➤ LED (light-emitting diode)
➤ Sankey diagram

Questions

1 You are riding your bike to school.

   a State the type of energy store that fills up because of the friction between the axles and the wheels.
   b State one way that you could reduce this dissipated energy.

2 Use ideas about energy stores and transfers to explain why some cups are insulated.

3 Suggest why it is difficult to do an experiment to prove the conservation of energy.

4 List A, B, and C in order showing how fast the rooms will cool down, starting with the quickest.
   A thick walls made of a material with a high thermal conductivity
   B thick walls made of a material with a low thermal conductivity
   C thin walls made of a material with a low thermal conductivity

5 Using the big energy picture for a poorly insulated house given at the start of this section, explain how increasing the thickness of insulation in the wall of a house would affect the energy bill.

6 The inside of a house is at a constant temperature, even though the heating is on. Describe and explain what is happening in terms of energy stores and transfers.

7 Calculate the efficiency of an electric motor that transfers 170 J to a kinetic store for each 200 J supplied.

8 Draw a Sankey diagram for the electric motor in question **7**.

9 A fundamental law of physics is that energy is always conserved. Energy cannot be created or destroyed. Explain how a Sankey diagram shows this.

10 Describe a situation where LED lighting is used, and explain why it is better than using filament lamps.

11 More efficient light bulbs do not do as much heating as less efficient light bulbs. Explain why using more efficient light bulbs might not reduce your energy bill. (Hint: think what a room lit with LEDs would feel like, compared with a room with normal light bulbs.)

A: Which energy resources do we use?

Find out about

- the main energy resources on Earth
- the difference between renewable and non-renewable resources

Key words

➤ energy resources
➤ fossil fuel
➤ biofuel
➤ nuclear fuel

Modern living demands large-scale use of energy resources.

We use more **energy resources** now than people did in the past. There are several reasons for this.

- The world population is increasing.
- Modern transport, buildings, possessions, and communications need energy.
- People travel further and faster than before.

The demand for energy resources is likely to continue to increase in the future.

We need to understand the energy resources that are available to make choices about energy use.

Energy resources

We have only the Sun and resources on Earth to meet our energy needs.

We can use energy transferred by radiation from the Sun. There are also many energy resources on Earth. For example, we can release energy from chemical stores by burning fuels. The table shows how the main energy resources are used in the UK.

Burned for heating	Transport	Generating electricity
fossil fuels, biofuel	fossil fuels	fossil fuels, nuclear fuel, biofuel, wind, hydroelectricity, the Sun

Fuels

Crude oil is a valuable energy resource, but drilling for oil has an impact on the environment.

- **Fossil fuels** have been formed over millions of years by the decay of plant and animal remains. Coal, crude oil, and natural gas are all fossil fuels. When they burn, fossil fuels produce carbon dioxide (CO_2) and other pollutants such as carbon particles. Crude oil is used to produce petrol, oil (for boilers), diesel, and other fuels. Crude oil is also an important feedstock for making useful chemicals, including polymers.

- A **biofuel** is a fuel that has come from recently living material. Wood, straw, sewage, and sugar are all used as biofuels. Like fossil fuels, biofuels produce CO_2 when they burn.

- **Nuclear fuel** releases energy without burning, so it does not make CO_2. Nuclear fuels are used to generate electricity in nuclear power stations.

Stores and resources

Energy resources are not the same as energy stores.

- An energy store is a way of keeping track of energy. The type of energy store tells you how to calculate an amount of energy.

- An energy resource is a physical thing, such as a lump of coal or wood, or moving water or air. The energy in the chemical store of the coal (and oxygen) can be used for heating or generating electricity.

Synoptic link

You can learn more about CO_2 and climate change in P1.2B *What is the evidence for climate change?*

Key words

- non-renewable
- renewable
- solar power
- hydroelectric power
- wind power
- tidal power
- wave power

Renewable and non-renewable resources

Straw pellets can be used to generate electricity.

Some resources are running out. Fossil fuels take a very long time to form. We are using them faster than they are forming, so eventually they will all be used up. They are **non-renewable** resources. Nuclear fuels are minerals taken from the ground, and are another non-renewable resource.

Other energy resources are not used up because they are replaced all the time. They are **renewable**.

Renewable resources

There are many types of renewable resource.

- Electromagnetic radiation from the Sun provides **solar power**. The Sun will shine for about another 5 billion years.

- Water heated by the Sun evaporates, and then falls as rain. Rain falling on high ground can be stored behind a dam. Then it can be used in a **hydroelectric power** station as it flows downhill.

- The Sun affects the weather and causes winds. **Wind power** can be used to generate electricity.

- The pull of gravity between the Earth and Moon causes the tides. The wind produces waves. Water movement due to tides and waves can generate electricity, using **tidal power** and **wave power**.

- Biofuels are materials such as wood, grass, biogas from sewage, or bioethanol from sugar cane. They can be replaced quickly. Some biofuels, such as bioethanol, could replace oil as fuel for transport.

To help meet the increasing demand for energy resources in the future, we need to make the best use of both renewable and non-renewable resources for heating, transport, and generating electricity.

Questions

1 Explain why coal is not a renewable resource.

2 Explain why hydroelectric power and wind power depend on energy from the Sun.

3 Here is a quote about energy use: "In the UK we rely too much on fossil fuels." Suggest why the speaker might have this opinion.

B: What happens at a power station?

Energy companies generate electricity and distribute it to your home.

Generating electricity

You can generate an electric current by moving a magnet into, or out of, a coil of wire. The movement of the magnet **induces** a **voltage** across the ends of the coil. 'Induced' means that it is caused by something else – in this case, the movement of the magnet.

You need three things to generate electricity:

- a magnet to induce a voltage
- a coil of wire in which to induce the voltage
- a change in the magnetism in and around the coil – usually achieved by moving the magnet or the coil.

If the coil is part of a complete circuit, the induced voltage makes a current flow.

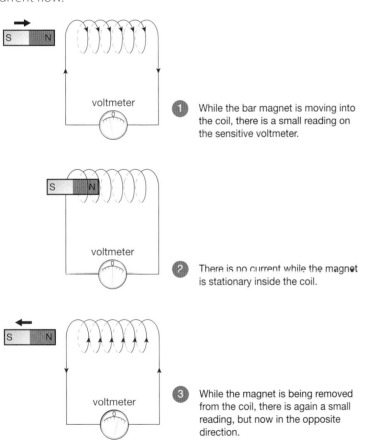

voltmeter

1 While the bar magnet is moving into the coil, there is a small reading on the sensitive voltmeter.

voltmeter

2 There is no current while the magnet is stationary inside the coil.

voltmeter

3 While the magnet is being removed from the coil, there is again a small reading, but now in the opposite direction.

Moving the magnet induces a voltage in the coil.

Simple generators

Before LEDs were used for bicycle lights, some bicycles had a simple **generator** called a dynamo attached to the wheel. Inside the generator were a magnet and a coil. As the wheel turned, the movement made the magnet spin inside the generator. This generated the voltage for the bicycle lights.

Find out about

- how we generate electricity
- how fossil fuels and biofuels are used
- the sequence of events inside a thermal power station
- what happens in a nuclear power station
- some benefits and risks of nuclear power
- how renewable sources can be used to generate electricity

Key word

➤ induce
➤ voltage
➤ generator

In a dynamo, the turning wheel makes the magnet spin, generating an electric current while the bicycle is moving.

Generators for power stations generate electricity on a large scale.

Bigger generators

The technician in the photograph is constructing this generator. Wires are wound around the outside. A turbine will make electromagnets rotate in the centre.

You can only induce a very small voltage using a magnet and a coil. To generate mains electricity at a much higher voltage, you need:

- much bigger generators (many metres across)
- a very strong magnet (a large electromagnet)
- a way of spinning the magnet inside the coil very quickly.

The electromagnet spins inside the coil. The way of making it spin depends on the type of energy resource being used to generate electricity.

What happens at a thermal power station?

In a fossil-fuel power station, the fuel is burned to boil water and make steam at high **pressure**. Biofuels such as wood can be used in the same way. Any power station that works like this is known as a **thermal power station**.

At a thermal power station, steam passes through a **turbine**. This is a bit like a windmill, which turns as the steam passes over the vanes. As the turbine turns, it makes a generator rotate. This induces a voltage, which drives a current through the coils. After passing through the turbines, the steam condenses to water. It can be fed back into the boiler and used again.

Steam collects in cooling towers, where it condenses back to water.

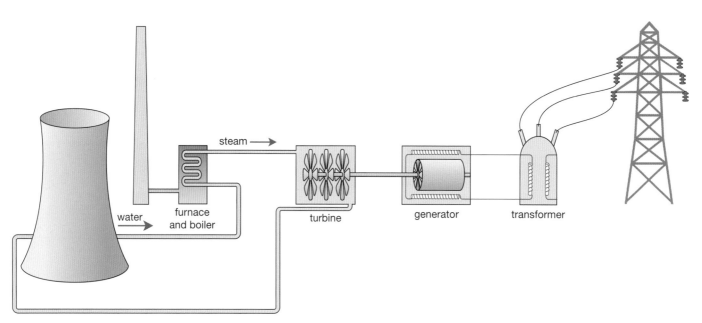

The same processes take place in all thermal power stations.

Reducing waste

At a thermal power station, only some of the energy from the burning fuel is transferred electrically. A lot of energy is wasted because steam and exhaust gases heat up parts of the power station and the surroundings.

Burning fuels produce CO_2 and other waste products. Some of these are removed from the exhaust gases before they can escape into the atmosphere.

Key words

➤ pressure
➤ thermal power station
➤ turbine

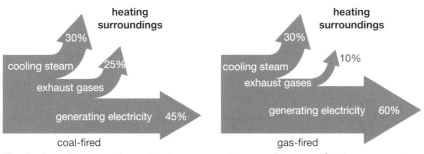

Many processes inside a power station heat the surroundings, wasting energy.

The Sankey diagrams show that less energy is wasted in a gas-fired power station than in a coal-fired power station.

More efficient power stations could reduce the cost of electricity, and produce less CO_2. To make it more efficient, a gas-fired power station can have an extra turbine that is driven by the exhaust gases. But there are arguments both for and against building more gas-fired power stations.

Weighing up the arguments – should we build more gas-fired power stations?

That electricity bill again

The cost of electricity comes from a variety of sources:

● the cost of the fuel

● the cost of maintaining power stations and building new power stations as the old ones are shut down

● the cost of getting the electricity to people's homes.

These costs can change, for many reasons. To keep the cost of electricity as low as possible, all the processes involved in shifting energy between stores need to be as efficient as possible.

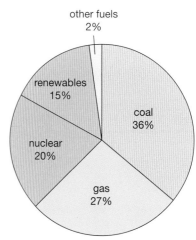

In the UK, most electricity is generated by burning fossil fuels. (Data from 2013)

What about nuclear power?

There are nine **nuclear power stations** in the UK. Seven of these power stations will come to the end of their life by 2024. There are plans to build new nuclear power stations on the sites of existing ones.

Nuclear power stations use solid fuel that contains uranium. In a nuclear reactor, uranium atoms split. This releases energy, so the nuclear fuel becomes very hot. The hot fuel boils water to make steam that drives turbines. The turbines turn generators to produce electricity. The nuclear fuel gradually becomes solid nuclear waste that cannot be used as fuel.

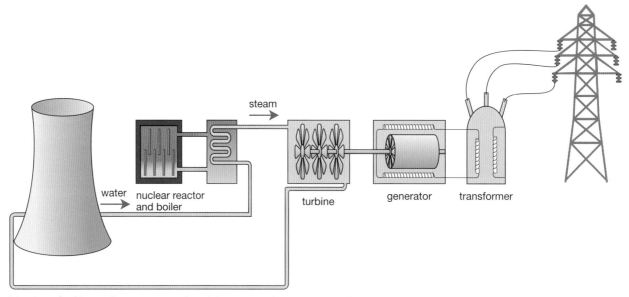

Uranium fuel is used to generate electricity at a nuclear power station.

Nuclear fuel and waste

Nuclear fuel and nuclear waste are **radioactive**. They give out **ionising radiation**. Ionising radiation can change cells in your body and increase your risk of cancer.

Some **nuclear waste** will be radioactive for thousands of years. Nuclear waste must be safely stored to make sure it does not contaminate the atmosphere, water supply, or soil. There are strict regulations controlling the way radioactive materials are used and stored. At the moment, most of the waste produced by the nuclear power stations in the UK is stored at the Sellafield nuclear reprocessing site in Cumbria. There are laws about how the waste must be stored to reduce the risk of contamination.

Old power stations are closed down as they reach the end of their useful life. The buildings must be taken apart and made safe. This is called **decommissioning**.

Contamination and irradiation

Radioactive **contamination** occurs when radioactive material lands on or gets inside something. Exposure to ionising radiation is called **irradiation**. Limits for irradiation are set by law.

Key words

➤ nuclear power station
➤ radioactive
➤ ionising radiation
➤ nuclear waste
➤ decommissioning
➤ contamination
➤ irradiation

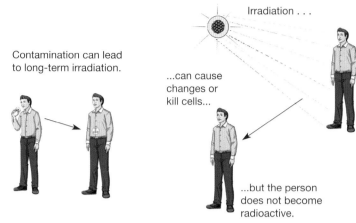

Contamination can lead to long-term irradiation.

Irradiation . . .

...can cause changes or kill cells...

...but the person does not become radioactive.

Contamination and irradiation.

Benefits and risks of nuclear power

Nuclear fuel releases far more energy than the same amount of fossil fuel. 1 g of uranium fuel can provide as much energy as 8 kg of fossil fuel.

A nuclear power station produces much less waste than a fossil fuel power station.

A nuclear reactor does not burn fuel, so no CO_2 is produced.

Suppose there is an accident and fuel leaks out?

We can't see radiation, how can we judge the risk?

There are no uranium mines in Britain. I am worried about relying on imports.

Why should we be exposed to risks so that everyone can have cheap electricity?

What if nuclear waste falls into the hands of terrorists?

They can't store waste at Sellafield, with sea levels rising. It's on the coast!

Many people are concerned about nuclear power stations.

How are renewables used to generate electricity?

Many renewable resources are used to generate electricity. How the electricity is generated depends on the type of resource being used.

Using a generator

Water released from behind a dam can be used to turn turbines to generate electricity, just as steam turns the turbines at a thermal power station. In the UK there are hydroelectric power stations in hilly places where there is fast-flowing water.

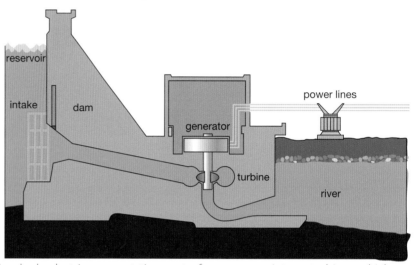

In a hydroelectric power station, water from a reservoir turns turbines, which turn a generator.

Wind turbines use the wind to drive a generator to produce electricity. However, the wind does not blow all the time. A wind farm is a group of wind turbines. We could build wind farms all around the coast of the UK. This would be more difficult and more expensive than building them on land.

The pull of gravity between the Earth and Moon causes two tides every day. The motion of water in tides, and from waves hitting the shore, can be used to drive a generator to produce electricity. We could build lots of tidal generators and wave generators because the UK is surrounded by sea. They have to be designed so that they are not damaged in storms.

An offshore wind farm saves space on land that could be used for other things, such as growing food.

Energy from the Sun

In the UK, electromagnetic radiation from the Sun provides an average of about 100 W of solar power per square metre of ground. **Solar thermal panels** use the Sun's radiation to heat water or buildings directly. A different kind of solar panel uses the Sun's radiation to generate a voltage and produce electricity. These are called photovoltaic (PV) panels, or **solar cells**.

Generators in a tidal stream can generate electricity, but are difficult to build and maintain.

Synoptic link

You can learn more about solar energy in P7.1 *How can solar energy make a difference?*

Questions

1 State two things that you need in order to induce a voltage across the ends of a coil of wire.

2 Suggest one problem with using a simple generator to produce electricity for bicycle lights.

3 Suggest and explain why you cannot use a small hand-held generator to operate a kettle.

4 Look at the pie chart on page 59. What percentage of UK electricity is generated using:
   a nuclear fuels?
   b fossil fuels?

5 At a thermal power station, suggest two places where energy from the fuel is transferred to the thermal store of the surroundings.

6 Look at the Sankey diagrams on page 59. What is the typical efficiency of:
   a a coal-fired power station?
   b a gas-fired power station?

7 Compare the diagrams of a thermal power station and a nuclear power station on pages 58 and 60.
   List the parts that are:
   a the same
   b different.

8 Describe one advantage of a nuclear power station over a thermal power station.

9 a Suggest one reason why people who live near a nuclear power station might be concerned about their drinking water.
   b Suggest one reason why they should *not* be concerned about their drinking water.

10 Use the information about generating electricity from renewable resources to explain why solar cells are the odd one out.

11 Suggest why tidal power might be more reliable for electricity generation than wave power.

12 Building offshore wind farms frees up land for other uses. Suggest two disadvantages of building offshore wind farms.

Key words

➤ solar thermal panels
➤ solar cells

C: What is the mains supply?

Find out about

- the domestic supply in the UK
- the National Grid
- why transformers alter the voltage
- the different wires inside a plug

When you plug in a device, you connect it to an alternating mains supply.

When you plug a device into a socket, you are using 'the mains' to transfer energy. The mains is another name for the **domestic electricity supply**. It is an **alternating current (a.c.)** at a frequency of 50 Hz.

Generating the voltage

Alternating voltage

An **electric current** flows in a device because there is a voltage across it. An alternating **voltage** produces an alternating current in a mains device such as a kettle.

You can generate an alternating voltage with a simple generator. You rotate a magnet near one end of a coil. As the magnet rotates, the magnetic field around the coil is constantly changing. This induces a changing voltage across the ends of the coil, which causes an alternating electric current in the circuit.

Synoptic link

You can learn more about voltage in P3.2B *Potential difference.*

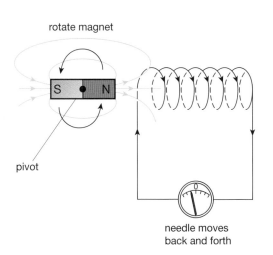

As the magnet rotates, it induces an alternating voltage across the coil.

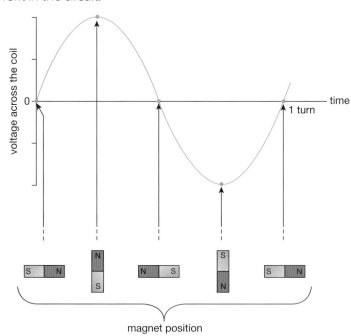

In a typical power station generator, an electromagnet is rotated inside a fixed coil. As it spins, an a.c. is generated in the coil. In power stations in the UK, the rate of turning is set at 50 cycles per second, or 50 Hz. The domestic supply has a voltage of about 230 V.

Direct voltage

A direct voltage produces a **direct current** in a battery-powered device, such as a phone. The voltage produced by a battery does not change direction. If a voltmeter was connected across the terminals of the battery, its reading would not change.

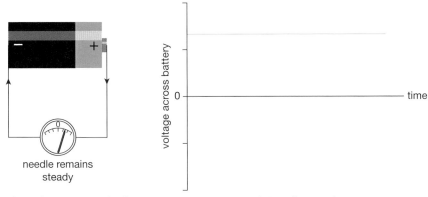

The voltage across the battery remains constant. It is a direct voltage.

Generating voltage on a large scale

To produce a big enough voltage to operate domestic appliances, we need a larger generator than the simple generator in the diagram on the opposite page. This could be a stand-alone generator that runs on diesel. Until 2003 there were places in the UK that were not connected to the mains, and used these generators. Now most people have mains electricity, which uses the generators in power stations. However, diesel generators are still maintained as a back-up in situations where a power cut could be catastrophic.

This maintenance technician maintains the hospital diesel generator to ensure it is always ready to keep the hospital going in the event of a power cut.

Key words

➤ domestic electricity supply
➤ alternating current
➤ electric current
➤ voltage
➤ direct current

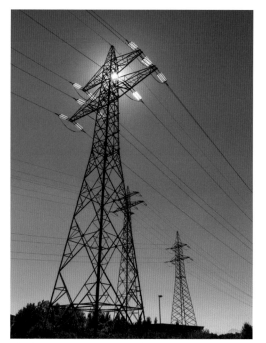
The high-voltage wires of the National Grid are supported by tall pylons.

How is mains electricity distributed?

Power stations are built where there is a nearby supply of their energy resource, such as fossil fuel, or where there is plenty of cooling water. This may be far away from the homes and businesses where the electricity is needed. The electricity is distributed around the country by a network of cables called the **National Grid**.

All the power stations in the UK are connected to the National Grid, and so are all the electricity users. This means that individual power stations can be switched on and off without cutting off the electricity supply.

High voltage

The National Grid covers large distances, so there is a lot of wire.

When an electric current flows in a wire, the wire gets hot. Some energy is transferred to the thermal store of the surroundings. This energy is not getting to electrical devices in the homes and businesses that need it. It is possible to reduce the wasted energy by using a very high voltage.

It is more efficient to use a high voltage than a low voltage to distribute electricity. A higher voltage can deliver the same power but using a smaller current in the wires. With a smaller current, less energy is lost heating the wires.

In the UK the mains voltage is 230 V. You can see in the diagram that parts of the Grid transmit at 275 000 V.

Transformers at local substations step down the voltage so that you can use mains devices in your home.

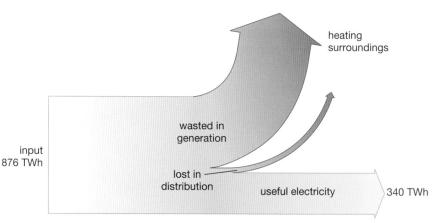
In 2013 the UK used about 876 TWh of energy to supply 340 TWh of electricity. 26 TWh were lost in the distribution process. 1 TWh is one thousand million kWh.

Transformers

The voltage of the electricity supply is altered using **transformers**.

The National Grid uses *step-up transformers* to increase the voltage for electricity to be transmitted. *Step-down transformers* at the local substations reduce the voltage down to 230 V.

Transformers are not only used at substations. Every time you plug in a laptop or tablet you are using a transformer to step down the voltage.

What is inside a plug?

A plug connects a device to the mains. Two wires make the device work. There are other components that are designed to protect you, or the device, or both.

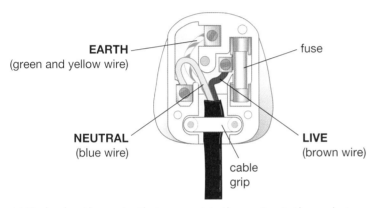

EARTH
(green and yellow wire)

fuse

NEUTRAL
(blue wire)

LIVE
(brown wire)

cable grip

A UK plug has three pins that connect to three wires in the socket.

You know that you need a complete circuit to make a device work. The two wires that do this are:

● the **live wire** (the brown wire)

● the **neutral wire** (the blue wire).

These two wires connect the device to the National Grid. The voltage between the live wire and the neutral wire is 230 V. This voltage drives the current in your device to make it work. If the device is working properly then only these wires are used. A switch is always connected in the live wire. When the switch is off, the device is isolated from the mains circuit.

The **earth wire** (the green and yellow wire) is there for your safety and to protect the device.

The green and yellow earth wire prevents a device from becoming live.

Synoptic link

You can learn more about transformers in P3.3A *Electrical power*.

A laptop mains adapter contains a step-down transformer. It also converts the alternating mains voltage to a direct voltage.

Key words

➤ National Grid
➤ transformer
➤ live wire
➤ neutral wire
➤ earth wire

There are laws that make sure that plugs are as safe as possible.

It is possible that a fault might develop inside a device. The live wire may end up touching the case of the device. If this happens, we say that the device is 'live'. If you touched the device, there would be a voltage across you. The ground would become the 0 V terminal of a circuit. You would be like a circuit component – a current would flow through you. You could be severely injured.

The earth wire prevents this happening. It does not connect the device to the National Grid. It connects the case of the device, or anything on the outside of the device that you might touch, to an earth wire in your home. The end of that wire is connected to a large metal spike buried in the ground.

If the live wire touches the case, then the current flows through the live wire and earth wire to earth, and not through anyone touching the case. The current in the live wire would be very large. It would quickly melt a thin piece of wire inside the fuse, which is connected to the live wire. This breaks the circuit, so the large current will not damage the appliance either.

When you plug in a device, the earth pin connects to the earth wire first. With modern sockets you cannot connect the other two pins to the National Grid until the earth wire has been connected.

Some appliances, such as hairdryers, have a casing made of plastic. Plastic is an insulator so the casing cannot become 'live' and they don't need an earth wire. They still have an earth pin on the plug, but it does not connect the appliance to the earth wire in the building.

Questions

1 State the frequency and voltage of the mains supply in the UK.

2 Describe the difference between the alternating current produced by a power station and the direct current from a battery.

3 The output of the generators in villages that were not connected to the mains needed to be the same voltage as the mains supply. Explain why.

4 What does a step-up transformer do to the voltage?

5 Use the Sankey diagram on page 66 to calculate the overall efficiency of electricity generation and distribution in the UK.

6 a Where would you find a step-down transformer in the National Grid?

  b Explain why it is used.

7 Explain the function of each wire in a three-pin plug.

8 Explain why a radio with a plastic case does not need to be connected to the earth wire in your home.

9 State and explain how much current the earth wire carries when the appliance is working normally.

10 In some countries plugs have only two pins. Suggest one way that this system can be safe for users.

D: What's the solution to the energy problem?

Sustainable energy

Sustainable energy means using energy resources in a way that will allow people in the future to have sufficient energy for their needs. Some of the energy resources we use are running out, and some of our use of energy resources is damaging the environment. This is not sustainable.

How are energy resources used in the UK?

Each year the UK Government publishes information about how the country uses energy resources, including:

- natural gas
- oil, including petrol, diesel, and other fuels made from oil
- other fuels, including coal and wood
- fuels and renewable resources that are used to generate electricity.

In the UK most energy resources are used by industry, transport, and homes.

We also use energy resources for growing food; in schools, hospitals, and other public buildings; and for shops and businesses.

Building homes and maintaining roads use a range of resources. The black tar (bitumen) that is used to make roads comes from crude oil.

Computer servers are at the core of many businesses and at the heart of the internet. They need resources to produce electricity to drive the computers and also to cool them down.

In our homes, we might use gas, oil, or other fuels for heating and cooking. For almost everything else we use electricity. Electricity can be used for many different tasks and it is easy to distribute using cables and wires.

Resources for generating electricity

One of the most important choices for the future is the type of resource that we use to generate electricity. The pie chart shows how much electricity is needed by each sector.

The graph shows which resources have been used to generate electricity since 1970. You can see that our use of renewable and non-renewable resources has changed since 1970. There are many reasons for this change.

Resources can be used for different things. For example, we can use oil not only to generate electricity and as a fuel, but also to make useful products such as petrol or plastics.

Find out about

- sustainable energy
- how energy resources are used at home, in industry, and for transport
- arguments for and against using various energy resources

Key word

➤ sustainability

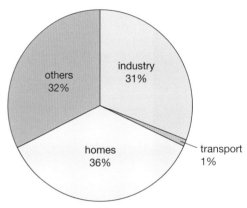

UK electricity demand in each sector in 2012.

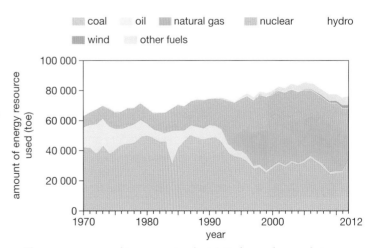

The resources used to generate electricity have changed since 1970. The unit is the 'toe', tonnes of oil equivalent.

What are the alternatives to fossil fuels?

Fossil fuels are not a sustainable resource for generating electricity. There is a limited supply and they produce carbon dioxide, which is a greenhouse gas. The table shows some of the arguments for and against the alternative options.

	For	Against
Nuclear	Nuclear fuel is the only energy resource that can meet a large electricity demand. It releases almost no CO_2. The best way to use uranium is as fuel in nuclear power stations to generate electricity. It can also be used for making nuclear weapons. UK nuclear power stations use tried-and-tested technology. Safety systems meet high standards. Waste disposal is a problem that we can solve.	Nuclear power stations may release little CO_2 while operating, but large amounts of CO_2 are released when they are built and decommissioned. Most importantly, they produce radioactive waste that lasts for years. New reactors take about 10 years to build and cost roughly £2 billion each. Insurance companies will not cover their risks. If anything goes wrong the public will have to pay.
Renewables	The UK should use its own energy resources and not rely on imports. Recent studies suggest that renewable energy sources could provide the UK with a reliable supply of electricity. We need a full range of generators, both big and small, at sites all around the country. Building wind generators and solar cells on the rooftops of offices and homes is relatively cheap and easy. Using power from the Sun and winds releases little CO_2.	Renewable energy is unreliable. The wind doesn't always blow. The Sun doesn't always shine. Renewable sources would not provide enough energy for this country. Wind farms should not be built where people live and work. Wind turbines are huge noisy machines. Wave and tidal generators harm wildlife. Large hydroelectric schemes damage the countryside. The main renewable energy resources are not in the same places as power stations. We would have to connect them to the National Grid using more power lines across the countryside.
Use less energy	The amount of energy resources used by the UK rises year by year. In your lifetime, you are likely to use as much energy as all four of your grandparents put together. This is not sustainable. It is using up energy resources and damaging the environment. We must make better use of resources or they will run out. There are ways of saving energy without changing our lifestyle. We can: ● switch off appliances ● use appliances that are more efficient. The Government can help by making sure that: ● new buildings are energy efficient ● grants help householders improve heating and power systems such as solar cells ● new appliances are energy efficient ● fossil fuels are highly taxed.	Energy resources, and electricity, improve our standard of living and our health. We can't give up improvements and return to the way our grandparents lived. In the UK we need energy for technology to feed, clothe, and house our large population. Everyone has a right to a good standard of living at home.

Predicting the future

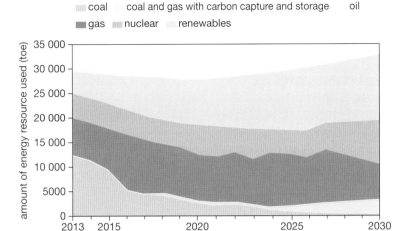

The way that we use resources to generate electricity will change in the future, but how? This is one prediction.

The chart shows how the balance of energy resources we use to generate electricity might change in the future. Some coal- and gas-fired power stations will capture the carbon dioxide produced and store it (carbon capture and storage [CCS]). There will be pros and cons to any plan, and it may not be possible to get everyone to agree on the best solution.

Battersea power station in London stopped generating electricity in 1983, and the building was decommissioned. Past plans to convert it to shops and offices have hit problems. There is an 'energy cost' to decommissioning.

The energy debate

There isn't a simple answer to the energy question. There will have to be a mix of energy sources, as there is now. No single source can meet all our needs. This leaves us with more questions:

● Who should make the decisions about which energy sources are in the mix – the energy companies, the government, or scientists?

● Who should have the last word when a few local people object to a new power station that will meet the needs of many more people?

● How do you weigh the benefits of 'clean' energy from wind turbines against the change in view across the hills?

Different people have different views on ways to use energy in a more sustainable way. What is certain is that we need to find a way that relies less on fossil fuels.

Questions

1 Compare the use of fossil fuels and wind energy to generate electricity since 1970.

2 What does 'a sustainable supply of energy' mean?

3 Look at the arguments for and against nuclear and renewable energy resources.

a Draw balance diagrams for each option, listing statements on each side.

b Distinguish statements of fact from opinion, by putting a tick next to the facts.

4 The cost of decommissioning power stations adds to the price of electricity. It is much higher for nuclear power stations than for stations burning fossil fuels. Explain why.

5 Look at the graph showing a possible future energy mix.

a Describe the differences in how electricity is predicted to be generated in 2030 compared with now.

b Is that the mix you would propose? Explain your answer.

Science explanations

P2 Sustainable energy

In this chapter you have learnt that a sustainable energy supply is essential for the future of both humans and the Earth. An understanding of energy and energy resources will allow us to make sensible choices in the future.

You should know:

- that energy cannot be created or destroyed, but that when it is used to do work, some energy is usually dissipated in the surroundings
- that power is the rate at which energy is transferred
- that energy transferred = power × time
- that the efficiency of any energy transfer can be calculated using the equation:

$$\text{efficiency} = \frac{\text{useful energy transferred}}{\text{total energy transferred}}$$

- how to interpret and construct Sankey diagrams
- some examples of how unwanted energy transfers can be reduced, for example, using lubrication or insulation
- the main energy sources available for use on Earth
- the difference between renewable and non-renewable energy resources
- the ways in which the main energy resources are used for generating electricity and the risks and benefits of each
- that the domestic supply in the UK is an a.c. at 50 Hz and about 230 V, and how to explain the difference between direct and alternating voltage
- why electricity is distributed through the National Grid at high voltage, although the mains supply voltage to our homes is 230 V
- the differences in function between the live, neutral, and earth mains wires, and the implications for using electricity safely
- that the demand for energy is continually increasing, so we need to consider carefully the availability of resources and the environmental effect of using them
- how to evaluate energy resources, using data where appropriate, in terms of:

  - in which sector they are used (for industry, transport, or domestic use in homes)
  - factors that affect the choice of resource (such as the environment, economics, and waste products produced)
  - the advantages and disadvantages of power stations using non-renewable resources (fossil fuel and nuclear) and renewable resources (biomass, solar, wind, and water).

Finding ways to generate sufficient electricity in a sustainable way is a key issue for scientists and engineers.

Ideas about Science

In this chapter you have developed an understanding of the use and generation of electricity. This involves assessing the risks and benefits associated with different ways of generating electricity and using energy. We need to consider many different issues when making decisions about the use of science and technology.

Everything we do carries some risk, and new technologies often introduce new risks. It is important to assess the chance of a particular outcome happening, and the consequences if it did, because people often perceive a risk as being different **H** from the actual risk: sometimes less, and sometimes more. A particular situation that introduces risk will often also introduce benefits, which must be weighed up against that risk.

You should be able to:

- identify risks arising from scientific or technological advances
- interpret and assess risk presented in different ways
- **H** distinguish between perceived and calculated risk
- suggest reasons for people's willingness to accept a risk
- discuss how risk should be regulated by governments and explain why it may be controversial.

Science-based technology provides people with many things they value. However, some applications of science can have undesirable effects on quality of life and on the environment. Benefits need to be weighed against costs. You should be able to:

- identify the groups affected by the introduction of a new technology, and the main benefits and costs to each group
- suggest reasons why different decisions on the same issue might be taken in different social and economic contexts
- identify examples of unintended impacts of human activity on the environment
- explain the idea of sustainability, and use data to compare the sustainability of different processes
- in cases where an ethical issue is involved, say clearly what the issue is and summarise different views that may be held
- explain why scientists should communicate their work to a range of audiences.

Deciding how much renewable energy to include in the energy mix is a decision for citizens, not for scientists.

P2 Review questions

1   Describe the energy transfers that take place when a mains electric drill is used to drill a hole in wood.

2   An electric heater is rated as 1500 W.

   a   What is this rating in kilowatts?

   b   Calculate the energy transferred by the heater in 5 hours.
      Give your answer in kWh.

   c   Calculate the cost of using the heater for 5 hours, if 1 kWh of electrical energy costs 8p.

3   The hot water storage tank for a house is in the roof space of the house. Explain why insulating the storage tank will reduce the energy bills for the house.

4   The manufacturer of an LED lamp with a rating 13.5 W claims that it emits the same light as a 75 W filament lamp. Use this example to explain why an LED lamp is more efficient than a filament lamp.

5   The Sankey diagram shows the energy transfers of a modern power station.

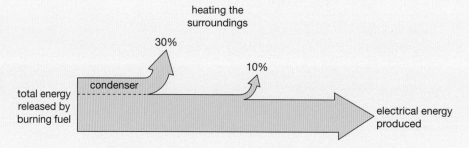

   a   Use the diagram to calculate the efficiency of the power station in producing electrical energy.

   b   One way to waste less energy is to use the heat energy from the condenser to heat homes and businesses near the power station. Assuming half of the heat from the condenser can be used in this way, what is the efficiency of the power station in providing useful energy output?

6   **a**   Copy and label the diagram of a coal-fired power station.

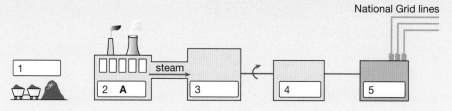

      Put the letters **A**, **B**, **C**, **D**, and **E** in the correct boxes on the diagram. One has been done for you.

      A   furnace

      B   transformer

      C   fuel

      D   turbine

      E   generator

b Many power stations use a carbon-based fuel. Which greenhouse gas is produced when the fuel is burnt?

c Coal is a non-renewable energy source. Which two of the following are renewable energy sources that are used to generate electricity?

natural gas   nuclear fuel   wind power
oil   wave power

7 Many wind farms are being constructed to generate electricity for Britain. The pie chart below shows the various costs of setting up and operating a wind farm.

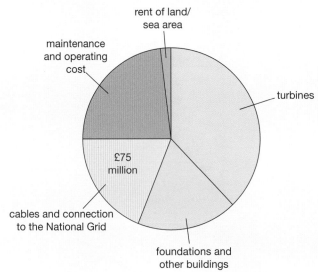

a Which one of the following is the best estimate of the cost of the turbines?

£40 million   £75 million   £150 million   £200 million

b Which one of the factors costs £90 million?

8 On a typical June day in the UK, electricity was reported to be generated from the following sources. (1 GW = 1 000 000 kW.)

Resource	Power (GW)	Percentage of total power (%)
coal	6.75	20
nuclear	7.27	21
gas	11.88	34
wind	3.75	11
imports	2.63	8
other	2.18	6

a Suggest what the resource classed as 'other' might be.

b 'Imports' describes electricity transferred through cable connections with France, the Netherlands, and Ireland. Suggest and explain why there might be concerns if the amount in this category increased significantly.

c Suggest and explain how the data might be different on a day in mid-December.

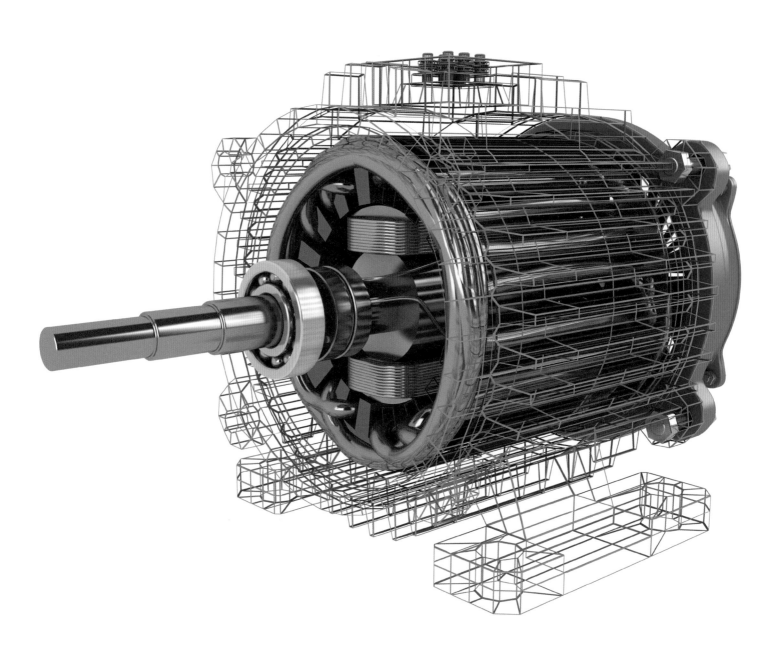

P3 Electric circuits

Why study electricity and magnetism?

Imagine life without electricity – rooms lit by candles or oil lamps; no electric cookers or kettles; no radio, television, computers, or mobile phones; no cars or aeroplanes. Electricity has transformed our lives, but you need to know enough about it to use it safely. More fundamentally, electric charge is one of the basic properties of matter – so anyone who wants to understand the natural world needs some understanding of electricity.

What you already know

- Electric circuits are drawn with standard symbols for lamps, batteries, and meters.
- Electric current is a flow of charge.
- Electric current transfers energy from the battery to components in the circuit.
- Electric current is not used up in a circuit.
- The voltage of a battery is a measure of the 'push' it gives to the charge in the circuit.
- The power rating of a device is measured in watts, and power = voltage × current.
- Electrical resistance affects the size of the current in a circuit. Resistance is measured in ohms.
- Magnets attract and repel other magnets.
- There is a magnetic field near a wire carrying a current. This can be used to make an electromagnet.
- In power stations, a moving magnet induces a voltage that drives a current through the National Grid.

The Science

An electric current is a flow of electric charge. A useful model of an electric circuit is to imagine the wires full of charges, being made to move around by the battery. The size of the current depends on the voltage of the battery and the resistance of the circuit.

The magnetic field due to a current interacts with any other magnetic field that is present. This interaction causes motors to spin.

Ideas about Science

Models are used in science to help explain ideas. We cannot see what is happening in an electric circuit, so we use models to help explain and predict observations. As ideas develop, the limitations of simple models become clear.

Applications of the fundamental ideas of electricity and magnetism have enhanced our lives in many ways. As with all new technologies, we must assess the risks before fully embracing them.

A: A closed loop

Find out about

- how simple electric circuits work
- models of electric circuits
- how to measure electric current
- the relationship between electric current and charge

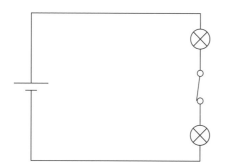

When you open the switch in this electric circuit, both lamps go off.

The diagram in the margin shows a simple **electric circuit**. If you make a circuit like this, you can quickly show that:

- if you make a break *anywhere* in the circuit, *everything* stops.

This suggests that 'something' has to go all the way around an electric circuit to make it work. This 'something' is **electric charge**.

You will also notice that:

- both lamps come on immediately when the circuit is completed. And they go off immediately if you make a break in the circuit.

This suggests that electric charge moves around the circuit very fast. Even with a large electric circuit and long wires, the lamps come on with no delay. But there is another possible explanation. Perhaps there are already tiny particles with electric charge in all the components of the circuit – in the wires, bulb filaments, and batteries. Closing the switch allows these charges to move. They all move together, so the lamps light immediately, even if the charges do not move very fast.

The diagram below shows a model of a simple electric circuit. The power source is the hamster in the treadmill. As the treadmill starts to turn, it pushes the peas along the pipe. If the pipe is full of peas all the time, then they will start moving everywhere around the circuit – immediately. The paddle wheel at the bottom will turn as soon as the hamster starts to run.

The turning paddle wheel could be used to lift a mass. The hamster loses energy (it gets tired), and the mass gains energy. The hamster does **work** on the treadmill to make it turn and set the peas moving, and the moving peas do work on the paddle wheel.

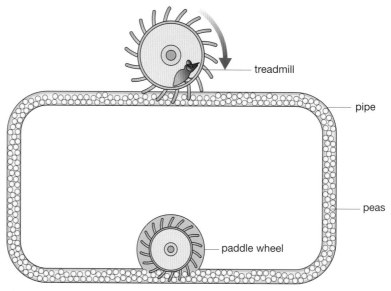

Electric circuit model.

Key words

➤ electric circuit
➤ electric charge
➤ work
➤ electric current

An electric circuit model

A model is a way of thinking about how something works. This diagram shows a useful scientific model of an electric circuit.

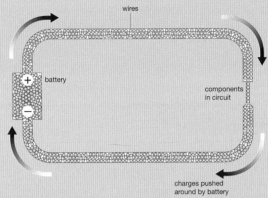

This model shows an electric current as a flow of charges.

The key ideas are:

● Charges are present throughout the circuit all the time.

● When the circuit is a closed loop, the battery makes the charges move.

● All of the charges move around at the same time.

What does the battery do?

The battery makes the charges move. Chemical reactions inside the battery have the effect of separating electric charges. Positive charges collect at one terminal of the battery, and negative charges at the other. If you connect the battery to a circuit, the charges at the terminals set up an electric field in the wires. This makes charges in the wire drift slowly along. Even though the charges move slowly, they all begin to move at once, as soon as the battery is connected. So the moving charges have an effect immediately.

The flow of charge is continuous, all around the circuit. Charge also flows through the battery itself.

Electric current

Charges are present in all materials. In materials that conduct electricity, the charges are free to move. In our model, an **electric current** is a flow of charges moving around a closed loop of conducting material, pushed by the battery.

You cannot see a current, but you can observe its effects. The current through a torch bulb makes the fine wire filament heat up and glow. The bigger the current through a bulb, the brighter it glows (unless the current gets too big and melts the filament, which breaks the circuit).

To measure the size of an electric current we use an **ammeter**. It measures the current in amperes, or amps (A) for short. The reading shows how much charge goes through the ammeter every second.

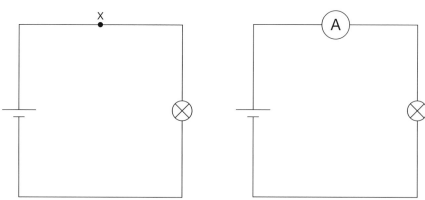

To measure the current at point X, you make a gap in the circuit at X and put in the ammeter, so that the current flows through it.

Electric current I measures how quickly the charges pass any point in the circuit. It is the amount of charge passing each second. Electric charge Q is measured in coulombs (C).

$$1 \text{ ampere} = 1 \text{ coulomb/second}$$

So you can work out the amount of charge passing a point in a length of time:

$$\text{charge (C)} = \text{current (A)} \times \text{time (s)}$$

$$Q = It$$

Worked example: Calculating charge

Calculate the amount of charge that passes through an ammeter in a minute when the reading on the meter is 0.2 A.

Step 1: Write down what you know, with the units. Convert to standard units.

current I = 0.2 A
time t = 1 min = 60 s

Step 2: Write down the equation you will use to calculate the charge.

charge = current × time
$Q = It$

Step 3: Substitute the quantities into the equation and calculate the charge. Include the units in your answer.

Q = 0.2 A × 60 s
Q = 12 C

Answer:

charge = 12 C

Key words

➤ ammeter
➤ series circuit

Current around a circuit

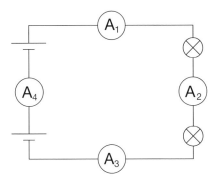

The ammeters measure the current. It is the same all the way around a series circuit.

If you use an ammeter to measure the size of the electric current at different points around a circuit, you get a very important result.

The current is the same at all points around a simple circuit – even between the batteries.

This is always the case for a single-loop electric circuit. This is a **series circuit**. The components are connected one after the other in one loop.

Current is not used up to make the lamps light. This may seem surprising. But current is the movement of charges in the wire, all moving around together like dried peas in a tube. No charges are used up. The current at every point around the circuit must be the same.

Something *is* being used up. It is the energy in the chemical store of the battery. This is getting less all the time. The battery is doing work to push the charge through the filaments of the light bulbs, and this heats them up so they glow. Radiation from the glowing lamps (light and infrared) transfers energy to the surroundings, increasing their thermal energy store. So the circuit constantly transfers energy from the battery, to the bulb filaments, and then on to the surroundings. The current enables this energy transfer to happen. But the current itself is not used up.

Questions

1 Look at the hamster electric circuit model at the beginning of this section.

   a What corresponds to:

      i the battery?

      ii the electric current?

      iii the size of the electric current?

   b Suggest one thing in a real electric circuit that might correspond to the paddle wheel.

   c Suggest something to model a switch.

2 How would you change the hamster electric circuit model to explore what happens in a series circuit with two identical lamps? Use the model to explain:

   a why both lamps go on and off together when the circuit is switched on and off

   b why both lamps light immediately when the circuit is switched on

   c why both lamps are equally bright.

3 The current though a lamp is 0.4 A. Calculate the charge that passes through the lamp in 3 minutes.

B: Controlling the current

Find out about

- how the battery voltage and circuit resistance control the current
- what causes resistance
- the links between battery voltage, resistance, and current

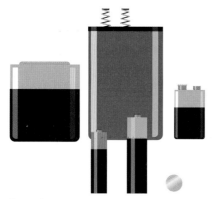

The front three batteries are marked 1.5 V, but are different sizes. The three at the back are marked 4.5 V, 6 V, and 9 V.

The scientific model of an electric circuit imagines a flow of charge around a closed conducting loop, pushed by a battery. This movement of charge around the circuit is an electric current.

The size of the current is determined by two factors:

- the **voltage** of the battery
- the **resistance** of the circuit components.

Battery voltage

Batteries come in different shapes and sizes. They are usually labelled with their voltage, measured in volts (V), for example, 1.5 V, 4.5 V, 9 V. As well as looking at the label on a battery, we can also measure the voltage across a component in a circuit using a **voltmeter**.

To understand what voltage means, look at the following diagrams. They show the same lamp connected first to a 4.5 V battery and then to a 1.5 V battery.

With a 4.5 V battery, this lamp is brightly lit.

With a 1.5 V battery, the same lamp is lit, but very dimly.

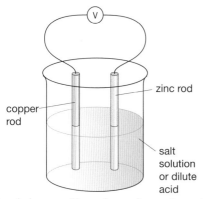

A simple battery. The voltage depends on the metals and the solution you choose.

The bigger the current through a lamp, the brighter it will be (up to the point where it 'blows'). The lamp above is brighter with the 4.5 V battery than with the 1.5 V battery because the current is bigger with the 4.5 V battery. You can think of the voltage of a battery as the amount of 'push' it gives to the charges in the circuit. The bigger the voltage, the bigger the 'push' – and the bigger the current as a result.

A battery's voltage depends on the choice of chemicals inside it. To make a simple battery, all you need are pieces of two different metals in a beaker of salt solution or acid. The voltage of this battery quickly drops, however. The chemicals used in commercial batteries are chosen to provide a steady voltage for several hours of use.

Resistance

The size of the current in a circuit also depends on the resistance that the components in the circuit provide to the flow of charge. The battery 'pushes' against this resistance. You can see the effect of this if you compare two circuits with different resistors. **Resistors** are components designed to control the flow of charge.

Changing resistance changes the size of the current. The bigger the resistance, the smaller the current.

Key words

➤ voltage
➤ resistance
➤ voltmeter
➤ resistor

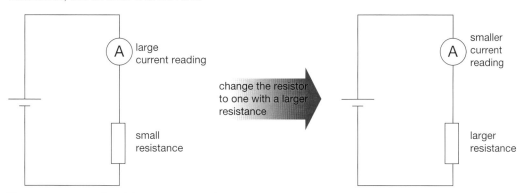

The current is smaller if the resistance is larger.

What causes resistance?

Everything has resistance, not just special components called resistors. Connecting wires are good conductors – they have a very small resistance. Other kinds of metal wire have a larger resistance. The filament of a light bulb has a lot of resistance. This is why it gets hot and glows when there is a current through it. A heating element, such as that in an electric kettle, is a resistor.

All materials get hot when current flows through them. In metals, the moving charges are free electrons. As they move through a wire, they collide with the fixed arrangement, or lattice, of ions in the wire. These collisions make the ions vibrate a little more, so the temperature of the wire rises.

The resistance of some metals is lower because the electrons move relatively quickly or because there are more free electrons.

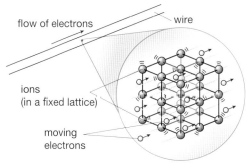

This diagram shows why the temperature of a wire rises when a current flows through it.

Key relationship in an electric circuit

The size of the electric current I in a circuit depends on the battery voltage V and the resistance R of the circuit.

- If you make V bigger ⬆, I increases ⬆.
- If you make R bigger ⬆, I decreases ⬇.

Measuring resistance

The key relationship on the previous page, between battery voltage, resistance, and current, means that we can measure and define resistance. The first step is to explore the relationship between voltage and current in more detail. Keiko, a student, did this by measuring the current through a coil of wire in circuits with different batteries.

Keiko connected a coil of resistance wire to a 1.5 V battery and an ammeter. She noted the current.

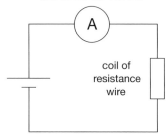

She then added a second battery in series. She noted the current again.

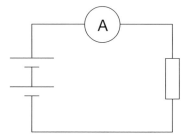

Keiko repeated this with 3, 4, 5, and 6 batteries, to get a set of results:

Finally, she drew a graph of current against battery voltage:

Number of 1.5 V batteries	Battery voltage (V)	Current (A)	voltage current (V/A)
1	1.5	0.075	20
2	3.0	0.150	20
3	4.5	0.225	20
4	6.0	0.300	20
5	7.5	0.375	20
6	9.0	0.450	20

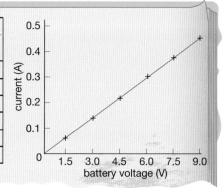

- For some materials $\dfrac{\text{voltage}}{\text{current}}$ is a constant value.
- The graph of current against voltage is a straight line.

These two facts show that the current in the circuit is proportional to the battery voltage. This result is known as *Ohm's law*.

The value $\dfrac{\text{voltage}}{\text{current}}$ *is* the resistance.

The units of resistance are called **ohms (Ω)**.

This is how to calculate resistance:

$$\text{resistance } R \text{ of a conductor } (\Omega) = \frac{\text{voltage } V \text{ across the conductor (V)}}{\text{current } I \text{ through the conductor (A)}}$$

Rearranging this equation gives $I = \dfrac{V}{R}$. You can use this to calculate the current in a circuit, if you know the battery voltage and the resistance of the circuit.

Worked example: Using the relationship $I = V/R$

Calculate the current that will pass through a 15 Ω resistor when the voltage across the resistor is 6 V.

Step 1: Write down what you know, with the units.

resistance $R = 15\ \Omega$
voltage $V = 6\ V$

Step 2: Write down the equation you will use to calculate the current.

$$current\ I = \frac{voltage}{resistance}$$

$$I = \frac{V}{R}$$

Step 3: Substitute the quantities into the equation and calculate the current. Include the units in your answer.

$$I = \frac{6\ V}{15\ \Omega}$$

$$I = 0.4\ A$$

Answer:

current = 0.4 A

Ohm's law

Ohm's law says that the current through a conductor is proportional to the voltage across it, provided its temperature is constant. The law applies only to some types of conductor, such as metals. If Ohm's law is true for a component across a range of currents and voltages, the component is called a **fixed resistor**.

Electric current causes heating in a component, which complicates matters. For example, the current through a lamp is not proportional to the battery voltage. The graph of current against voltage is curved. The reason is that bulb filament heats up, and its resistance increases with temperature.

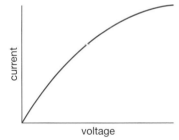

If you plot current against voltage for a lamp, the value of I/V decreases. The filament heats up, so its resistance increases.

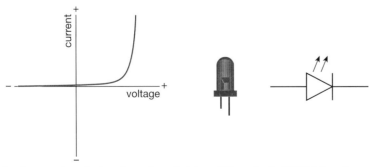

Graph of current against voltage for a light-emitting diode (LED). Like all diodes, an LED conducts current only in one direction. The diode lights when a minimum voltage is reached, and then has a fairly steady brightness.

Questions

1 Look back at the hamster electric circuit model at the beginning of P3.1A.
   How would you change the model to show the effect of:
   a a bigger battery voltage?
   b an increase in resistance? (You might be able to think of two different ways of doing this.)
   In each case, does the model correctly predict the effect these would have on the current?

2 Suggest two different ways in which you could change a simple electric circuit to make the current bigger.

3 In Keiko's investigation:
   a how many 1.5 V batteries would she need to use to make a current of 0.6 A flow through her coil?
   b what is the resistance of her coil, in ohms?

4 In a simple series circuit, a 9 V battery is connected to a 45 Ω resistor.
   a Calculate the electric current in the circuit.
   b What would happen to the current if the voltage were doubled to 18 V?
   c What would happen to the current if the voltage were 9 V and the resistance were doubled to 90 Ω?

A: Branching circuits

Find out about

● the advantages of parallel circuits
● combining resistors in a circuit

In this portable DVD player, the battery runs several components. It is connected to the motor that turns the DVD, the head that reads the disk, and the circuits that decode and amplify the sound and picture signals.

This circuit board from a computer contains a complex circuit, with many components.

Key words

➤ parallel circuit
➤ equivalent resistance

Often, we want to run two or more components from the same battery. One way to do this is to put them all in a single loop, in series, like the circuits in P3.1. All of the moving charges have to pass through each component.

The diagram below shows another way to connect components to a battery. In this circuit, the two lamps are connected in **parallel**. Each lamp now works independently of the other. If one burns out, the other will stay lit. This makes it easy to spot a broken one and replace it.

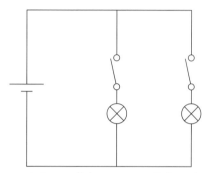

If you connect components in parallel, you can switch each one on and off independently.

Combinations of resistors

Most electric circuits are more complicated than the ones you have met so far. Circuits usually contain many components connected together. Circuit components may be connected in series or in parallel.

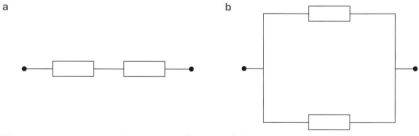

Two resistors connected **a** in series, **b** in parallel.

Two resistors in series have a larger resistance than one on its own. The battery has to push the charges through both of them. The total resistance is the sum of the two separate resistances.

In contrast, connecting two resistors in parallel makes a *smaller* total resistance. There are now two paths that the moving charges can take. Adding a second resistor in parallel does not affect the original path, but adds a second one. It is now easier for the battery to push charges around, so the resistance is smaller.

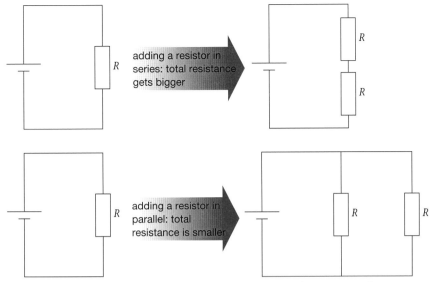

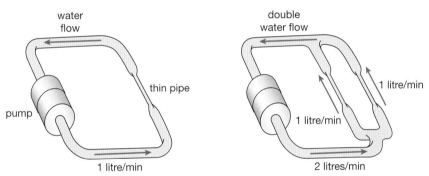

When adding a second resistor, how you connect it into the circuit makes a difference to the resistance.

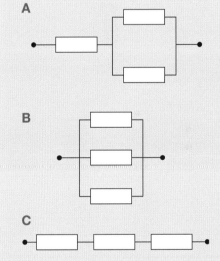

This model shows how the total resistance gets less when a second parallel path is added to a circuit.

Equivalent resistance

Two (or more) resistors in series, of resistance R_1 and R_2, could be replaced by a single resistor. It would need to have a resistance R equal to the sum of R_1 and R_2. This is called the **equivalent resistance**.

$$R = R_1 + R_2$$

Questions

1 When manufacturers make circuits running several components from the same battery, it is much more common to connect them in parallel than in series. Write down three advantages of parallel connections.

2 Look at the first parallel circuit on the opposite page. If you wanted to switch both lamps on and off together, where would you put the switch? Draw two diagrams showing possible positions of the switch.

3 All the resistors in the three diagrams below are identical. List the groups of resistors in order, from the one with the largest total resistance to the one with the smallest total resistance.

A

B

C

4 Resistors are manufactured with a standard set of resistance values. These include 1.1 Ω, 1.2 Ω, 1.3 Ω, 3.6 Ω, 3.9 Ω, 5.1 Ω, 6.2 Ω, and 6.8 Ω, but not 6.3 Ω.

Suggest two different combinations of resistors from the list that would be equivalent to 6.3 Ω.

B: Potential difference

- how voltmeters measure the potential difference
- how height provides a useful model of electrical potential
- how current splits between parallel branches

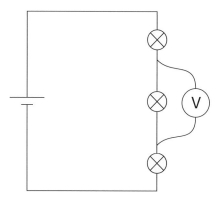

There is a reading on a voltmeter connected across a lamp. It is not measuring the strength of 'push' from the battery – so what is it telling us?

Key words

➤ voltmeter
➤ work
➤ potential difference

You can think of the voltage of a battery as a measure of the 'push' it exerts on the charges in a circuit. But a **voltmeter** also shows a reading in a circuit if you connect it across a resistor or lamp, as shown in the diagram on the left. Resistors and lamps do not 'push'. So the voltmeter reading must be showing something else.

A water-pump model to explain potential difference

A useful picture is to think of the battery as a pump, lifting water up to a higher level. The water then falls to its original level as it flows back to the inlet of the pump. The diagram below shows this for a series circuit with three resistors (or three lamps). The pump does work on the water to raise it to a higher level. This increases the energy in the gravitational store. The water then does **work** on the three water wheels as it falls back to its original level. If we ignore energy losses, the amount of work done on the water wheels is the same as the amount of work done by the pump.

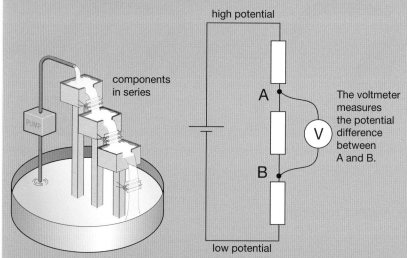

The water-pump model for potential difference.

In the electric circuit, the battery does work on the electric charges, to lift them up to a higher 'energy level'. They then do work (and transfer energy) in three stages as they fall back to their starting level. A voltmeter measures the difference in 'level' between the two points it is connected to. This is called the **potential difference** between these points. Potential difference (p.d.) is measured in volts (V).

The voltage of a battery is the potential difference between its terminals. You could put a battery with a larger voltage into the circuit above. There would be a bigger potential difference across its terminals. The potential difference across each lamp (or resistor) would also now be bigger. In the water-pump model, this would be like using a stronger pump to lift the water up through a greater height. The three downhill steps would then also be bigger, so that the water ends up back at its starting level.

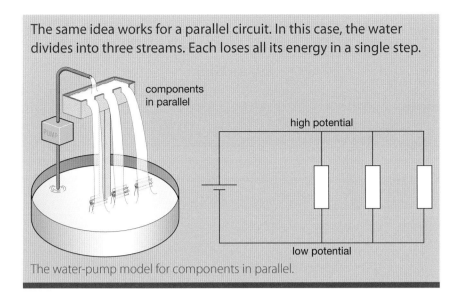

The same idea works for a parallel circuit. In this case, the water divides into three streams. Each loses all its energy in a single step.

components in parallel

high potential

low potential

The water-pump model for components in parallel.

Voltmeter readings across circuit components

The water-pump model helps us to predict voltmeter readings across resistors in different circuits. If several resistors are connected in parallel to a battery, the potential difference across each is the same. It is equal to the battery voltage.

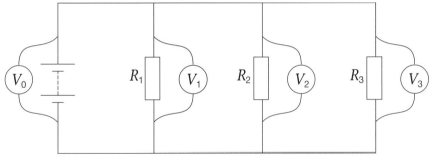

All of these voltmeters will have the same reading, even if R_1, R_2, and R_3 are different. $V_0 = V_1 = V_2 = V_3$.

However, if the resistors are connected in series (as on the right), the sum of the potential differences across them is equal to the battery voltage. This is exactly what you would expect from the water-pump picture on the previous page.

In this series circuit, the potential difference across each resistor depends on its resistance. The biggest voltmeter reading is across the resistor with the biggest resistance. Again this makes sense: more work has to be done to push charge through a big resistance than through a smaller one.

The potential difference measures the work done, or energy transferred, by the charge as it passes through the component in the circuit.

$$\text{potential difference (V)} = \frac{\text{work done (energy transferred) (J)}}{\text{charge (C)}}$$

$$V = \frac{W}{Q}$$

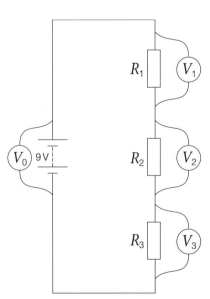

The sum of the voltages across the three resistors is equal to the battery voltage. $V_0 = V_1 + V_2 + V_3$.

Worked example: Calculating potential difference

A current of 300 mA passes through a 2 W lamp in a circuit for 2 minutes. Calculate the energy transferred by the lamp, the charge that passed, and hence calculate the potential difference across the lamp.

Step 1: Write down what you know, with the units.

power $P = 2$ W $= 2$ J/s
current $I = 300$ mA $= 0.3$ A
time $t = 2$ min $= 120$ s

Step 2: Calculate the energy transferred as you did in P2.1B.

energy transferred = power × time
$W = Pt$
$W = 2$ J/s × 120 s $= 240$ J

Step 3: Calculate the charge that passed, as in P3.1A.

charge = current × time
$Q = It$
$Q = 0.3$ A × 120 s
$Q = 36$ C

Step 4: Write down the equation you will use to calculate the potential difference.

$$\text{potential difference} = \frac{\text{energy transferred}}{\text{charge}}$$
$$V = \frac{W}{Q}$$

Step 5: Substitute in the values from **step 2** and **step 3** to calculate the potential difference. Include the units in your answer.

$$V = \frac{240 \text{ J}}{36 \text{ C}}$$
$$V = 6.7 \text{ V}$$

Answer:

potential difference = 6.7 V

Currents in the parallel branches

In the parallel circuit in the middle of the previous page, the potential difference across resistors R_1, R_2, and R_3 is exactly the same for each. It is equal to the potential difference across the battery. But the *current* through each resistor is not necessarily the same. It depends on their resistances. The current through the biggest resistor will be the smallest. There are two ways to think of this.

1 Imagine water flowing through a pipe. The pipe then splits in two, before joining up again later. If the two parallel pipes have different diameters, more water will flow every second through the pipe with the larger diameter. This wider pipe has less resistance than the narrower pipe to the flow of water. So the current through it is larger.

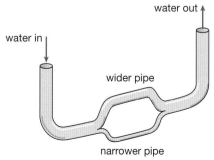

More water flows each second through the wider pipe. It has less resistance to the water flow.

2   Think of two resistors connected in parallel to a battery as making two separate circuits that share the same battery. The current in each loop is independent of the other. The smaller the resistance in a loop, the bigger the current. Some wires in the circuit are part of both loops, so here the current will be biggest. The current here will be the sum of the currents in the loops.

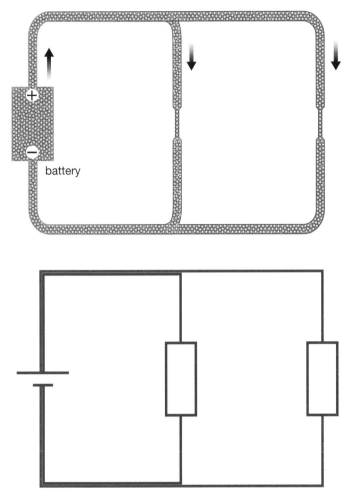

A parallel circuit like this behaves like two separate simple-loop circuits.

Questions

1   A small motor is rated as 8 W. It is connected to a 12 V supply. Calculate the charge that will pass through the circuit in 1 minute.

2   Imagine removing the red resistor from the circuit above, leaving a gap. Explain what would happen to:
   a the current through the purple resistor
   b the current from (and back to) the battery.

C: Variable resistors, diodes, and sensors

Find out about

● using variable resistors to control current
● using sensors to control circuits

Each of these sliders adjusts a variable resistor.

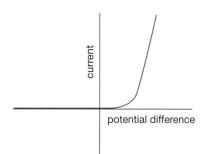

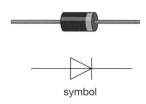

symbol

The resistance of a diode is high when connected one way in the circuit, but low when connected in the other direction.

Key words

➤ variable resistor
➤ diode
➤ sensor
➤ light-dependent resistor (LDR)
➤ thermistor
➤ potential divider

Variable resistors

Sometimes we want to vary the current in a circuit, for example, to change the volume on a radio. A **variable resistor** is used to control the current. Its resistance can be steadily changed by turning a dial or moving a slider.

The circuit diagram below shows the symbol for a variable resistor. As you change its resistance, the brightness of the lamp changes, and the readings on both ammeters go up or down together. The variable resistor controls the size of the current everywhere around the circuit loop. (Is this what the circuit model in P3.1A would predict?)

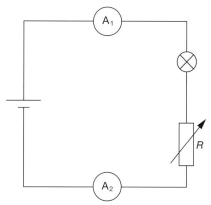

A variable resistor controls the current in a series circuit.

Diodes

Diodes have extremely high resistance when connected one way in the circuit, but a low resistance in the other direction. So they allow current to flow in one direction but not the other. They are used in many electronic circuits.

Sensors

Many electrical devices use **sensors** to detect changes in the surroundings. They might detect changes in light level or temperature. Some of these sensors are a kind of variable resistor.

A **light-dependent resistor (LDR)** is a sensor whose resistance is large in the dark but gets smaller as the light falling on it gets brighter. An LDR can be used to measure the intensity (brightness) of light, or to switch another device on and off as the light gets brighter or dimmer. For example, it could be used to switch an outdoor light on in the evening and off again in the morning.

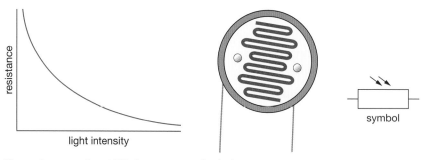

The resistance of an LDR decreases as the light intensity increases.

A **thermistor** is another sensor. Its resistance changes rapidly with temperature. The most common type has a lower resistance when it is hotter.

Thermistors are used in thermometers, or to switch a device on or off as the temperature changes. For example, a thermistor circuit could switch an immersion heater on when the temperature of the water in a tank falls, and switch it off when the water is hot.

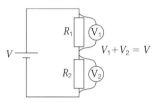

The resistance of a thermistor decreases as the temperature increases.

Potential dividers

Circuits with two resistors in series are often used in devices, particularly in electronics. You saw in P3.2B that the sum of the potential differences across two resistors in series is equal to the battery voltage. The resistors divide up the battery voltage into two parts. This kind of circuit is called a **potential divider**. The two parts are often unequal. The bigger resistance has a bigger potential difference across it.

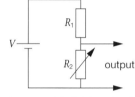

Two resistors in series make a potential divider.

A potential divider circuit provides a variable voltage supply.

A battery provides a fixed voltage. Sometimes we want a power supply with a voltage that we can change by turning a control knob. We can use a potential divider to supply a variable voltage like this.

If the resistance of the variable resistor R_2 (above right) is turned down to zero, then the potential difference across the output leads will be zero. The potential difference across the fixed resistor R_1 will be equal to the battery voltage. But if the resistance of R_2 is turned up, it takes a larger share of the total potential difference across it. The potential difference across the output leads will increase.

In a light-intensity meter, the reading on a voltmeter shows the brightness of the light falling on the LDR. The circuit includes a potential divider.

A light-intensity meter circuit uses an LDR in series with a fixed resistor. In the dark, the resistance of the LDR is large – much bigger than the resistance of R_2. So the reading on the voltmeter is very small, close to zero.

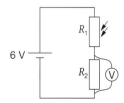

A simple light-intensity meter.

But in bright light, the resistance of the LDR is very small. Now the resistance of R_2 is much bigger than the resistance of the LDR. So the potential difference across R_2 is almost all of the battery voltage – and the reading on the voltmeter is close to 6 V.

Questions

1 Diodes were invented at the beginning of the 20th century and were an important component in early radios. Some diodes were also called 'valves'. Explain how diodes behave in the same way as valves in the heart.

2 **a** Describe and explain the reading on the voltmeter in the circuit below when the thermistor is:
   i cold   **ii** hot.
   b Explain how the circuit could be used as an electrical thermometer.

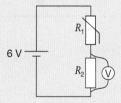

A thermistor in a potential divider circuit.

3 You are asked to plot a graph of the current through an LDR as the voltage across it varies. Draw a circuit that uses a potential divider to give a variable voltage. Show where you would place the ammeter and voltmeter to take your readings.

A: Electrical power

Find out about

- how the power produced in a component depends on current and voltage
- energy conservation and transformers in the National Grid

Key word

➤ power

An electric circuit is a device for doing work of some kind, as you saw in P2.1. The circuit transfers energy that was stored in the battery to the components, and then on to the surroundings.

The rate of energy transfer is the **power** of the circuit. You know that the unit of power is the watt (W). One watt is equal to one joule per second.

Measuring the power of an electric circuit

Imagine you have a simple battery and lamp circuit. You want to double, and treble, the power. You could do this in two ways:

- Add a second lamp, and then a third lamp, in parallel with the first. Look at the circuits down the left-hand side of the diagram. The potential difference is the same, but the current supplied by the battery doubles and trebles. *The power is proportional to the current.*

- Add a second lamp, and then a third, in series with the first. Look at the circuits across the top of the diagram. Now you need to add a second battery, and then a third, to keep the brightness of the lamps the same each time. The current is the same, but the potential difference of the battery doubles and trebles. *The power is proportional to the potential difference.*

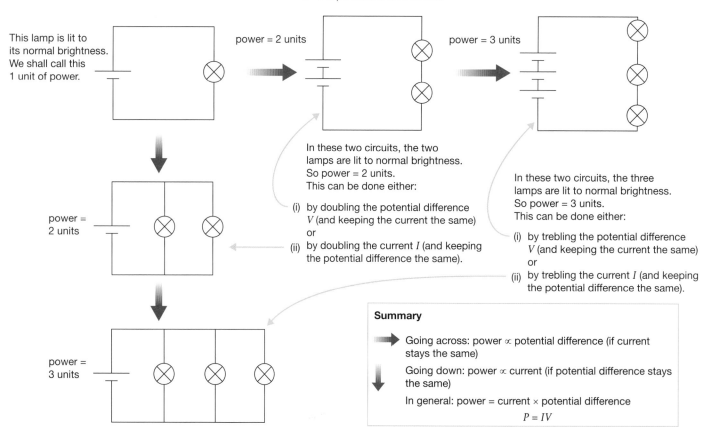

This lamp is lit to its normal brightness. We shall call this 1 unit of power.

power = 2 units

power = 3 units

power = 2 units

power = 3 units

In these two circuits, the two lamps are lit to normal brightness. So power = 2 units. This can be done either:

(i) by doubling the potential difference V (and keeping the current the same) or

(ii) by doubling the current I (and keeping the potential difference the same).

In these two circuits, the three lamps are lit to normal brightness. So power = 3 units. This can be done either:

(i) by trebling the potential difference V (and keeping the current the same) or

(ii) by trebling the current I (and keeping the potential difference the same).

Summary

➡ Going across: power ∝ potential difference (if current stays the same)

⬇ Going down: power ∝ current (if potential difference stays the same)

In general: power = current × potential difference
$$P = IV$$

The power depends on both the current and the voltage.

The rate at which energy is dissipated in an electric circuit (the power P) depends on both the current and the potential difference:

$$\text{power (W)} = \text{current (A)} \times \text{potential difference (V)}$$
$$P = IV$$

Look back at the explanation of resistance and heating in P3.2B. If the battery voltage is increased, the electric field in the wires gets bigger. So the electrons move faster and when they collide with ions in the metal wire, more energy is transferred in the collision. They also collide more often. Increasing the voltage makes collisions between electrons and the lattice of ions both more energetic and more frequent.

In P2.1B, you used the power rating of a device to calculate how much work W is done (how much energy is transferred) in a given period of time:

$$\text{work done (energy transferred) (J)} = \text{power (W)} \times \text{time (s)}$$
$$W = Pt$$

The power of the electric motor in this tube train is much greater than the power of the strip lights. Both the voltage and the current are bigger in the train motor.

Potential difference and energy

On this page are two equations involving power. We can combine the two equations by substituting 'power = current × potential difference' into the second one:

$$\text{energy transferred (J)} = \text{current (A)} \times \text{potential difference (V)} \times \text{time (s)}$$

In P3.1A you used the equation: charge (C) = current (A) × time (s). So we can also write:

$$\text{energy transferred (J)} = \text{potential difference (V)} \times \text{charge (C)}$$
$$W = VQ$$

This links back to the definition of potential difference in P3.2B:

$$V = \frac{W}{Q}$$

Current and power

How does the power dissipated by a component depend on the current in a circuit? To answer this, think about the rate of energy transfer by a resistance R when a current I passes through it.

The potential difference V across the resistance is $I \times R$.

The power $P = I \times V$.

So $P = I \times I \times R = I^2R$.

$$\text{power (W)} = (\text{current})^2 (A^2) \times \text{resistance } (\Omega)$$

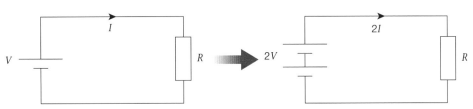

Doubling the battery voltage V doubles the current I. So the power is four times as big, because $P = IV$.

Worked example: Calculating rate of energy transfer

An electric motor is advertised as '12 V, 1400 mA'. What would you expect the rate of energy transfer to be?

Step 1: Write down what you know, with the units.

potential difference $V = 12$ V
current $I = 1400$ mA = 1.4 A

Step 2: Write down the equation you will use to calculate the rate of energy transfer.

rate of energy transfer = power
$P = IV$

Step 3: Substitute the quantities into the equation to calculate the rate of energy transfer. Include the units in your answer.

$P = 1.4$ A $\times$ 12 V
$P = 16.8$ W

Answer:

power = 16.8 W

Key words

➤ National Grid
➤ transformer

Power transmission

Energy is transferred from power stations to our homes through the **National Grid**. In P2.2C we stated that that transmitting electricity at a high voltage and low current was more efficient.

The diagram on page 66 shows that in part of the Grid, the power is transmitted at 132 kV. If the current is 400 A, the power transmitted is about 53 000 kW.

When a current passes through a power line, some energy will be dissipated, because the power line has resistance. This worked example calculates the power lost from every kilometre of power line when 400 A passes through it.

Worked example: Calculating the rate of energy loss from a power line

An electric power line has a resistance of 0.2 Ω per km. It carries a current of 400 A. Calculate the rate at which energy is transferred to the surroundings from 1 km of cable.

Step 1: Write down what you know, with the units.

current $I = 400$ A
resistance $R = 0.2$ Ω

Step 2: Write down the equation you will use to calculate the rate of energy transfer.

energy transferred = power $P = I^2R$

Step 3: Substitute the quantities into the equation and calculate the rate of energy transfer. Include the units in your answer.

$P = (400$ A$)^2 \times 0.2$ Ω
$P = 32\ 000$ W

Answer:

power = 32 000 W

Transmitting power at a lower voltage needs a much higher current. A higher current would result in much greater power losses from the transmission cables, because power $= I^2R$.

Transformers

In P2.2C you saw that **transformers** step up the voltage that is output from the power station, and step it back down to 230 V for use in homes.

A transformer that steps the voltage up from 25 kV to 132 kV must at the same time reduce the current, because $P = IV$. The power output cannot be greater than the power input, because energy cannot be created.

Transformers are used throughout the National Grid to ensure that electricity is transmitted as efficiently as possible.

Questions

1 In circuits **a** and **b**, resistor R_1 has a high resistance and resistor R_2 has a low resistance. If the circuits are switched on for a while, which resistor will get hotter in each circuit? Explain your answers.

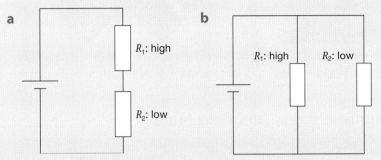

2 In circuit A below, a battery is connected to a resistor with a low resistance. In circuit B, the resistor has a high resistance. The two batteries are identical. Which will go 'flat' first? Explain your answer.

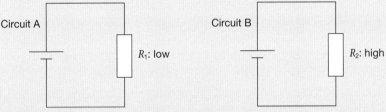

3 A filament lamp is marked as 150 W and is connected to a 230 V supply. Calculate the current in the circuit.

4 A 50 MW power station produces power with an output voltage of 25 kV.
   a Calculate the current in the cables leaving the power station.
   b The cables have a resistance of 0.2 Ω per km. Calculate the power loss per km at the current that you calculated in part **a**.

5 The transformer in a power adapter for a computer takes the mains voltage 230 V and reduces it to 15 V and a current of 4 A.
   a Calculate the power output from the transformer.
   b Assuming energy is conserved, calculate the current input to the transformer.

A: Magnetic forces

Find out about

- magnetic fields
- some uses of magnets and electromagnets

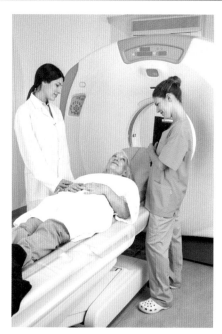

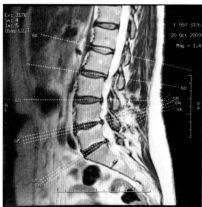

Magnetic resonance imaging (MRI) scanners use magnetic fields and radio waves to create the most detailed images yet of the human body.

Magnets and magnetic fields have many uses in everyday life, from keeping the fridge door closed to driving the coil in your headphones.

Changing magnetic fields produce the music in headphones.

A strip of magnetic material on the back of a credit card stores information that is read when the card is swiped.

Magnetic fields and field lines

From experimenting with magnets you will know that like magnetic poles repel and opposite magnetic poles attract. A **magnetic field** is the region around a magnet where another magnet will experience a force of attraction or repulsion. The field gets weaker as you go further away from the magnet.

A plotting compass needle is a small, light magnet that is free to move. It shows us the field around a bar magnet.

We can use a plotting compass to help us draw field lines around a magnet. The arrows show the direction of the force acting on the north pole of a second magnet placed in the magnetic field. The closer the field lines, the stronger the force. A magnet's field is strongest close to its poles.

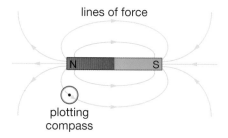

A plotting compass shows the field lines around a bar magnet.

Iron filings scattered around two magnet poles are another way of showing the field lines.

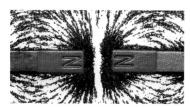

The pattern of iron filings around these two magnets shows that the two north poles are **repelling** each other.

The pattern of iron filings around these two magnets shows that the north and south poles are **attracting** each other.

The Earth's magnetic field

A compass needle is a magnet that can move, so it aligns itself with the **Earth's magnetic field** unless there is another magnet nearby to affect it. Scientists believe that the magnetic field of the Earth is due to the large amount of solid and molten iron at its core.

The end of a magnet that is attracted to the North Pole of the Earth is called the north-seeking end, often labelled N.

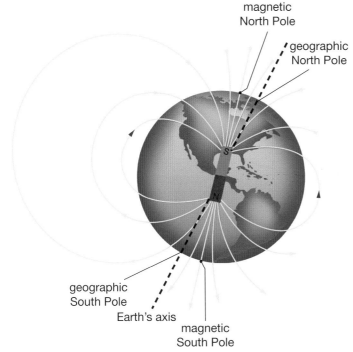

The pattern of the Earth's magnetic field is similar to that of a bar magnet. Perhaps confusingly, the North Pole of the Earth is in fact a magnetic south pole. It attracts north-seeking poles of magnets in the Earth's magnetic field.

Magnetic materials

Some materials, including iron and steel, are called magnetic materials. To make a magnet, you leave a magnetic material in the field of a magnet. When you take the material out of the magnetic field, it retains its magnetism. It has become a **permanent magnet**.

The bar magnets shown in the photographs are examples of permanent magnets. Early permanent magnets were made of iron or steel. Stronger magnets were later developed using alloys of iron, nickel, and cobalt.

More recently scientists have used powders containing iron oxide to make ceramic magnets which can be used to coat plastics. These developments meant magnets could be used in lots of new ways. In 1982 materials scientists developed an alloy of neodymium (chemical symbol Nd) that could be used to make very strong, very compact magnets. These have many applications. They are used in the motors of cordless tools, high-quality headphones, and magnetic fasteners.

Key words

➤ magnetic field
➤ repel
➤ attract
➤ Earth's magnetic field
➤ permanent magnet

A magnetic compass aligns itself with the Earth's magnetic field, helping walkers and orienteers find their way.

Neodymium magnets are much stronger and more compact than traditional magnets. They are used for magnetic clasps for jewellery and in magnetic toys.

The magnetic field of the bar magnet has induced a magnetic field in the steel pins. The opposite magnetic poles of the pins attract each other. The pins will remain magnetised for a short time after the bar magnet has been removed.

Not all steel is magnetic. Some steel becomes magnetised if you place it close to a permanent magnet, but later loses its magnetism. Pins and nails can be magnetised in this way. We call this **induced magnetism**. Sometimes steel becomes magnetised by the Earth's magnetic field over a long period.

Electromagnets

In 1819, the Danish physicist Hans-Christian Oersted had a magnetic compass on his desk near to an electrical circuit. He noticed that the needle of the compass moved every time he switched on the electric current. He investigated this further, and showed that there was a link between electricity and magnetism.

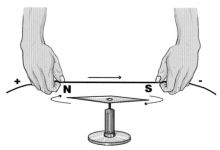

If you hold a wire carrying a small electric current above a compass needle, the needle moves when the electric current is switched on.

When there is an electric current in a wire, there is a magnetic field in the region around the wire. The compass needle is a magnet. It experiences a force near to the wire because it is in the magnetic field caused by the electric current.

The magnetic field around a wire is circular. The magnetic field gets weaker as you get further away from a wire. This is shown by drawing the field lines further apart. The direction of the field depends on the direction of the electric current. The greater the current in the wire, the stronger the magnetic field.

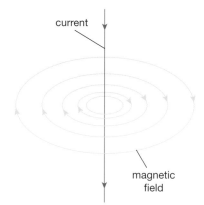

The magnetic field around a wire gets weaker further away from the wire.

Key words

➤ induced magnetism
➤ solenoid
➤ electromagnet

Winding a wire to make a coil makes the magnetic field stronger. This is because the fields of each turn of the coil add together. A coil like this is called a **solenoid**. The magnetic field can be strengthened further by putting an iron core inside the coil to make an **electromagnet**. It has the advantage that you can switch it on and off, unlike a permanent magnet.

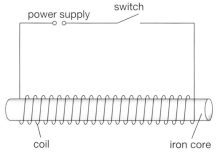

A coil of wire wound around an iron core makes an electromagnet.

A scrap metal yard uses large electromagnets to separate out metal that contains iron.

Using electromagnets

Electromagnets have many uses because they can be switched on and off. Security guards can operate a magnetic door latch elsewhere in the building by pressing a button, and scrap merchants can pick up and move heavy scrap metal using electromagnets. There are electromagnets in motors and generators.

In the nineteenth century the electric telegraph relied on electromagnetic effects to send signals across great distances. Some of those effects are still used in today's telephone systems.

In this bell telegraph from 1855, electromagnets were used to send the signal and to ring the bell.

Questions

1 Describe three uses of magnets other than those in the photographs in this section.

2 Electromagnets have revolutionised communications, from the first electric telegraph to mobile phones. Describe two ways in which your life would be different if there were no electrical methods of communication.

A: Electromagnetic forces

HIGHER TIER ONLY

Find out about

- the force on a current-carrying wire in a magnetic field
- why an electric motor spins

Electric **motors** make things move. Motors come in all shapes and sizes. Tiny motors less than 0.9 mm long with an output of 20 µW (microwatts) are used in medical devices and cameras. Huge motors used to propel ships have power outputs of 100 MW.

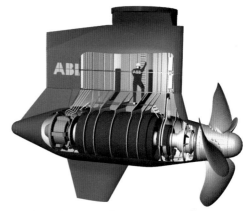

Large electric motors drive the propellers of huge ships.

This tiny electric motor provides controlled movement in small spaces.
© Namiki Precision Jewel Co., Ltd.

The motor effect

You saw in P3.4 that if you place a permanent magnet, such as a compass needle, in the magnetic field near a wire that is carrying an electric current, it experiences a force. The force is caused by the magnetic field of the magnet interacting with the magnetic field around the current-carrying wire.

In a motor, we keep the magnet fixed and allow the wire to move instead.

The diagram below shows one way of doing this. The two long parallel wires, and the wire 'rider' that is laid across them, are made of copper wire with no insulation. The 'rider' is sitting in the magnetic field between the two flat magnets on the metal holder. If you switch on the power supply, the 'rider' slides sideways. The force acting on it is at right-angles to the magnetic field of the magnet and also at right-angles to the electric current. This is the **motor effect**, which is the principle behind all electric motors.

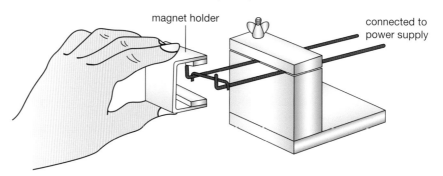

Demonstrating the motor effect. When the current is switched on, the rider moves sideways.

The current and the magnetic field of the magnet must be at an angle for the motor effect to work. If we hold the magnets so that the magnetic field is parallel to the wire rider (and to the current), the wire does not experience a force.

Key words

➤ motor
➤ motor effect
➤ Fleming's left-hand rule

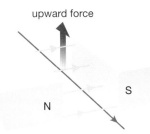

The force on the wire is at right-angles to both the magnetic field lines and the electric current.

You can predict the direction of the force from the direction of the current and the direction of the magnetic field. **Fleming's left-hand rule** is a useful way of working this out.

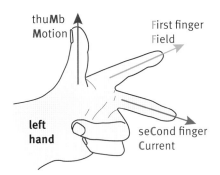

Fleming's left-hand rule shows the direction of motion of a current-carrying wire due to the force in a magnetic field.

The strength of the force on the wire is proportional to:

● the strength of the magnetic field
● the current in the wire
● the length of the wire.

Calculating the force

The strength of a magnetic field is measured in units called tesla (T). The symbol for magnetic field is B. The Earth's magnetic field strength is about 50 μT (5×10^{-5} T) in the UK. It is stronger at the poles, and weaker at the Equator.

You can calculate the force F using this equation for a wire perpendicular to the magnetic field:

force (N) = magnetic field strength (B) × current (A) × length of wire (m)

$$F = BIl$$

Turning a coil

We can set up a coil of wire in a magnetic field so that the magnetic forces make it turn when a current flows. The diagram below shows a square coil of wire in a magnetic field. There is no force on the two ends of the coil, because here the current is parallel to the magnetic field lines. However, there are forces on the two sides of the coil, because here the currents are at right-angles to the magnetic field lines.

The forces are at right-angles to both the field and the current. The currents in the two sides of the coil are in opposite directions, so the force on one side acts upwards and the force on the other side acts downwards. The effect of these forces is to make the coil rotate around the dotted line.

If the coil is made with several turns of wire, this makes the turning forces stronger.

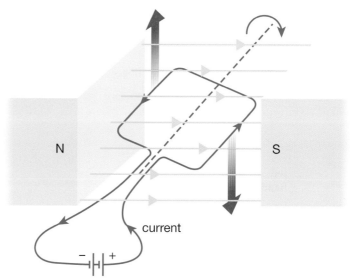

current

When current flows in the flat coil of wire, the magnetic forces have a turning effect on it.

An electric motor

The coil in the diagram above would turn through 90°, then stop. What if we could reverse the direction of the current in the coil at this point? This would reverse the direction of the force on each side – and keep it turning for a further half-turn. If we could then reverse the current direction again, we could make the coil turn continuously. This is how a simple electric motor works.

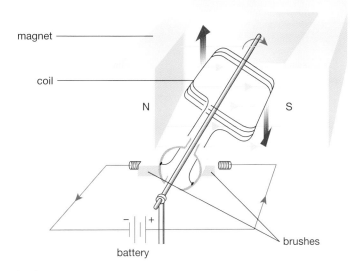

A simple electric motor.

Questions

1 Look at the diagram on the opposite page of the flat coil between the magnets. Explain why there is no rotating force on the coil when it is vertical.

2 A student is doing an experiment to measure the force of a magnetic field on a wire. She tries to measure the force on a 5 cm length of wire when there is a current of 3 A passing through it, at right-angles to a magnetic field of strength 0.2 T.
   a Calculate the size of the force.
   b Explain whether the student needs to take into account the magnetic effects of the Earth in her experiment.

Science explanations

P3 Electric circuits

Electricity is essential to modern-day life. In this chapter you have gained an understanding of electric charge, current, voltage, and resistance in a circuit. You have seen how this allows us to use electricity safely, and how it enables power to be generated and distributed.

You should know:

- that electric current is the rate of flow of charges
- how electric circuits work, and about models that help us understand electric circuits
- that current is not used up as it goes around a circuit, but does work on the components it passes through, transferring energy from the battery to the other components
- that the voltage is also called the potential difference (p.d.)
- that the potential difference across a component relates to the work done by electric charge as it passes through a component
- that the components in a circuit resist the flow of charge, and how the current depends on the battery voltage and the circuit resistance
- about components with a variable resistance, including lamps, diodes, thermistors, and light-dependent resistors
- about the p.d. across and the current through resistors connected in series and in parallel
- about the power (energy per second) transferred by an electric circuit
- **H** about the force on a current-carrying wire in a magnetic field and why a motor spins.

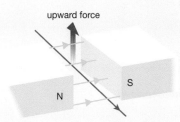

The force on the wire is at right-angles to both the magnetic field lines and the electric current.

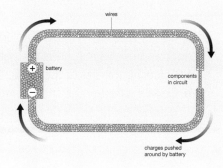

This model shows an electric current as a flow of charges.

Ideas about Science

Scientists use models to help explain their ideas. Models are particularly useful for describing and explaining observations of electric circuits.

You should be able to:

- identify the main features of a model that represents an electric circuit
- suggest how this model can be used to explain observations
- use the model to make predictions
- identify limitations of the model.

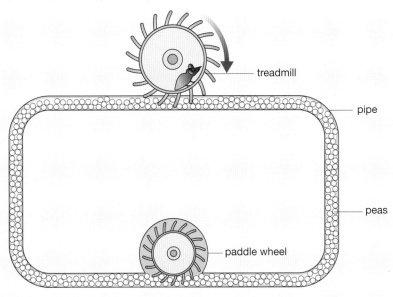

- treadmill
- pipe
- peas
- paddle wheel

Electric circuit model.

H Since Oersted's discovery of the link between electricity and magnetism, physicists and engineers have exploited these effects to give us many new technologies.

You should be able to:

- give some examples of applications of electromagnetism that have made a positive impact on people's lives
- suggest some applications of electromagnetism that have had unintended consequences.

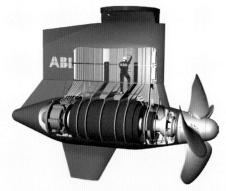

Large electric motors drive the propellers of huge ships.

P3 Review questions

1 Look at the models of electric circuits in this chapter. Copy and complete the following table.

Model	What corresponds to ...		
	the battery?	electric current?	the resistors or lamps?
'peas in a pipe'			
'water in a pipe'			

2 In a simple, single-loop electric circuit, the current is the same everywhere. It is not used up. How does each of the models in question **1** help to account for this?

3 Imagine a simple electric circuit consisting of a battery and a lamp. For each of the following statements, say if it is true or false, and explain why.

A Before the battery is connected, there are no electric charges in the wire. When the circuit is switched on, electric charges flow out of the battery into the wire.

B Collisions between the moving charges and fixed ions in the bulb filament make it heat up and give out light.

C Electric charges are used up in the bulb to make it light.

4 An electric lamp operates at 230 V with a current of 0.25 A.

a Calculate the charge that passes though the lamp when it runs for 1 hour.

b Calculate the resistance of the lamp filament when it is operating normally.

c Calculate the power rating of the lamp.

d Explain why the resistance might be less if it were measured when connected to a 12 V supply.

5 You are given four 4 Ω resistors. Draw diagrams to show how you could connect all four together to make a resistance of:

a 16 Ω **b** 1 Ω **c** 10 Ω **d** 4 Ω.

(Note that there is more than one possible answer to **c** and **d**.)

6 In shops, you can buy batteries labelled 1.5 V, 4.5 V, 6 V, or 9 V. But you cannot buy batteries labelled 1.5 A, 4.5 A, 6 A, or 9 A. Explain why not.

7 Peter has a sensor labelled LDR.

   a What do the letters LDR stand for?

   b What does an LDR detect?

   c What does Peter need to measure to work out the resistance of the LDR in a circuit?

   d Draw a circuit diagram to show how he could measure the quantities in your answer to part **c**.

   e Peter repeats the experiment the next day. He gets a different value for the resistance. Suggest a reason why.

8 Describe how you could make a simple tool to help a dressmaker pick up dropped pins.

9 An electric motor is constructed from a coil of wire that rotates in a magnetic field. Suggest three ways in which the motor can be made more powerful.

10 Aasha is using a rectangular coil to make a motor. It has 20 turns of wire. It has two sides 8 cm long and two shorter sides that are 4 cm across.

   a Explain whether she should place the axle parallel to the longer sides or the shorter sides.

   b The coil is placed in a magnetic field of strength 0.2 T. The field is perpendicular to the 8 cm sides. Calculate the force on one side of the coil when a current of 0.3 A passes through the coil.

P4 Explaining motion

Why study motion?

People have always been interested in how things move, and why they move the way they do. Motion plays a big part in our everyday lives, and to understand the natural world we live in we need to be able to explain and predict how objects move. An understanding of motion has allowed humans to travel to the Moon, faster than sound. It also allows us all to travel more safely every day. Engineers continue to make advances in technology based on their understanding of how things move, from space travel to high-speed performance cars and vehicles that drive themselves.

What you already know

- Speed is calculated by the distance travelled divided by time.
- The slope of a distance–time graph shows how the speed of a moving object changed.
- Forces arise due to interactions between objects.
- Force is measured in newtons.
- On a diagram, arrows are used to represent the direction and size of the forces on an object.
- Unbalanced forces on an object can change its shape or its motion.
- Gravity, magnetism, and electrostatic forces all act without contact.
- The weight of an object is due to the gravitational force between the Earth and the object.
- The turning effect of a force is called a moment.

The Science

Scientists who studied motion in the past asked the question: 'Can all the motion we see be explained by a few simple rules that apply to everything?' Remarkably, the answer is 'yes'. These rules (or laws) are so exact and precise that they can be used to predict the motion of an object very accurately. A key idea in the laws of motion is that an unbalanced force acting on an object changes its motion.

Ideas about Science

A scientific explanation cannot be deduced by just looking at data. It needs someone to think creatively to explain the observations. Many people had tried to describe and explain how things move. To write his laws of motion, Sir Isaac Newton built on the ideas of those who had come before. But making the link between an apple falling to the ground and the Moon orbiting the Earth required a leap of imagination.

A: Forces and interactions

Find out about

- how forces arise when two objects interact
- contact forces and forces acting at a distance
- how interactions get things moving

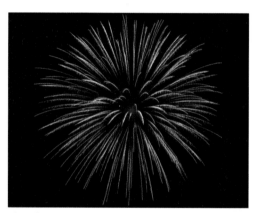

The chemical reaction inside the firework produces forces that send the burning fragments out equally in all directions.

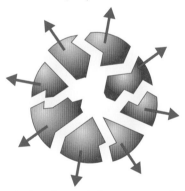

An exploding firework. For every moving spark, there is another spark moving in exactly the opposite direction.

Key words

- ➤ force
- ➤ interaction
- ➤ interaction pair
- ➤ contact force
- ➤ friction
- ➤ action at a distance

What is a **force**? You may know that exerting a force on an object can push, pull, turn, or twist the object. But what causes the force?

Where do forces come from?

When a firework explodes, sparks move out from the centre. The starburst in the photo is symmetrical. For every moving spark, another spark moves in the opposite direction. In the same way, forces always come in pairs.

The diagram shows Sophie and Sam standing on an ice rink. When Sophie gives Sam a push, both of them move.

Sophie can't make Sam move without moving backwards herself, however hard she tries. When Sophie exerts a pushing force on Sam, Sam exerts an equal and opposite force on Sophie – not by pushing, but just by being there as something to push against. If Sam pushed Sophie, she would exert an equal and opposite force on him.

The same is true with pulling forces. If Sophie and Sam stand a distance apart on the ice holding a rope and one of them pulls, they both start to move towards each other.

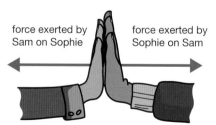

force exerted by Sam on Sophie

force exerted by Sophie on Sam

Forces always arise in pairs. Sophie pushes Sam, and experiences a force herself in return.

These important facts about forces form Isaac Newton's third law of motion.

Newton's third law of motion

Forces always arise from an **interaction** between two objects. Forces always come in pairs. The two forces in an **interaction pair** are:

- the same kind of force
- equal in size
- opposite in direction.

This is always true, even if a large, strong person pushes a small person.

Another important thing to notice is that:

- the two forces in an interaction pair act on different objects.

In this example, one force of the pair acts on Sam and the other on Sophie.

Contact forces

Forces caused by two objects touching are called **contact forces**. Contact forces exist only while the objects actually touch. When the objects separate, the contact forces stop, although the two objects may keep moving.

Friction is a contact force between two surfaces when they slide – or try to slide – over each other. Both objects experience a force. The two forces are equal and opposite. Friction acts in the direction that prevents the object sliding. Friction is caused by the roughness of surfaces. Even surfaces that seem smooth are rough when you look at them under a microscope.

Forces acting at a distance

Forces can be caused by an interaction without objects touching. This is called **action at a distance**. Here are some examples.

Magnetism

The two ring magnets in the diagram are repelling each other. Both supporting threads are at an angle, because both magnets experience a force. When magnets attract, both experience a force. If you hold a fridge magnet close to the door, the magnet experiences a force towards the door, and the door experiences a force towards the magnet.

Gravity

An apple falls from a tree because of the force exerted on it by the Earth, pulling it downwards. But gravity is an attraction between two objects. The apple also exerts an equal and opposite force on the Earth! This does not have any visible effect, because the Earth is so massive.

Electrostatic forces

The girl in the photo has electrically charged hair. Each charged hair repels another charged hair so that both hairs stay as far apart as possible.

Action-at-a distance forces act even when the two interacting objects are far apart. They get weaker as the distance between the objects increases.

As one object slides (or tries to slide) across the other, the bumps and hollows on each surface cause a force that resists motion.

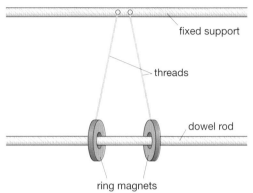

These two ring magnets are repelling each other. Both magnets are being pushed away.

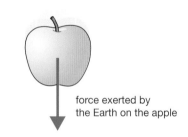

force exerted by the Earth on the apple

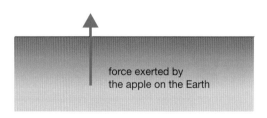

force exerted by the apple on the Earth

The forces in a gravitational interaction always come in pairs.

Each electrically charged hair repels another electrically charged hair.

Interactions make things move

What makes things move the way they do? To start something moving, you exert a force on it. This sets up an interaction pair of forces. Here are some examples.

Rockets

A rocket pushes out hot gases as its fuel burns. The rocket engine exerts a large force on these gases. The other half of this interaction pair is the force exerted on the rocket by the escaping gases. This pushes the rocket in the opposite direction.

The photograph shows the launch of the *Apollo 11* mission to land the first humans on the Moon. The interaction pair of forces is shown on the photo.

Rockets carry with them everything they need to make the burning gases they push out. This means that they can work anywhere, even in space.

Jet engines

A jet engine works by drawing air in and pushing air and exhaust gases out at high speed from the back. The other force in the interaction pair pushes the engine forward. Jet engines need to draw air in, so they cannot work in space.

How does a car get moving?

To make a car move, the engine makes the wheels turn. This causes a forward force on the car. To understand how, think first about a car trying to start on ice. If the ice is very slippery, the wheels will just spin. The car will not move at all. The spinning wheels produce no forward force on the car. Now imagine a car on a muddy track. It throws up a shower of mud as it tries to get going.

You can see that the wheels are causing a backward force on the ground. This makes the mud fly backwards. When the force is small, mud moves. The other force of the interaction pair is the forward force on the car. It is equal in size. It is too small to get the car moving.

With a hard surface and good tyres, the friction between the tyre and the road surface stops the wheel slipping. The wheel exerts a very large backward force on the road. The other force of the interaction pair is the same size, so there is a large forward force which gets the car moving.

Walking

When you walk, you push back on the ground with each foot in turn. The ground then pushes you forward. You are not usually aware of this. When you walk across a floor, it does not feel as though you are pushing backwards on it. You only become aware of the importance of this interaction when the surface is slippery, such as ice, and there is not enough friction. Because you cannot push back on ice, it is unable to move you forward.

force exerted on the rocket

force exerted on the hot gases

A huge force (thrust) is needed to push a rocket upwards. It is provided by the hot exhaust gases from the burning fuel.

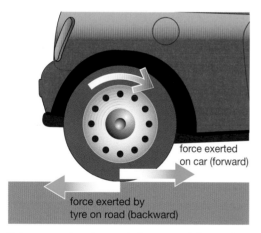

force exerted on car (forward)

force exerted by tyre on road (backward)

If the tyre grips the road, the second force of the interaction pair results in a large forward force on the axle. This pushes the car forward.

If friction didn't exist, walking would be impossible and wheels would not move. In the diagram, the roughness of the boot and the floor is exaggerated. It shows that, when you walk, pushing back with your foot causes a backward force on the ground and a forward force on your foot.

Friction between the foot and the floor results in a pair of opposite forces. The arrows show the directions of the forces. In reality, the bumps and hollows in the two surfaces are tiny.

Questions

1 Here are some examples of forces.

A A child pulls a parent's hand and the parent's hand pulls the child.

B Jack pushes the handle of a buggy and the buggy handle pushes on Jack.

C An electrically charged balloon on a string is attracted to the wall and Leila pulls the string away.

D Amy pushes a wheelbarrow forward and the friction between the wheelbarrow and the ground pushes it backward.

E Because of gravity, a rock is attracted towards the Earth and the Earth is attracted towards the rock.

a Which of the examples are interaction pairs of forces? (Use the things that are always true about interaction pairs to help you decide.)

b For the examples that are not interaction pairs of forces, explain how you know.

2 **a** List three everyday situations in which we try to reduce friction.

b List three everyday situations in which we try to make friction as large as possible.

3 Use the ideas on the four pages in this section to write short explanations of the following observations.

a We can reduce the friction between two moving surfaces by putting oil on them.

b It is easier to push a box across the floor when it is empty than when it is full.

4 How could you modify the apparatus with the ring magnets to show that attraction forces between magnets arise in pairs? Sketch how you would set it up, and write down what you would expect to see.

5 Maya swims a length of the pool. Using the ideas on these four pages, describe how an interaction pair of forces moves her forward.

6 Sketch a matchstick figure walking. Mark and label the interaction pair of forces on the foot in contact with the ground.

Icy surfaces are difficult to walk on. Your foot cannot get a grip to push back on the surface, so the surface does not push you forwards.

B: More about forces

Find out about

- friction: its size and direction
- the normal contact force
- the gravitational force and weight
- how to add the forces acting on an object

Friction – a responsive force

How big is the friction force between two surfaces, and what does it depend on? Think about the forces involved as Jack tries to push a large box along a level floor.

The size of the friction force depends on the size of Jack's pushing force, up to a certain limit. If Jack's push is below this limit, friction matches it exactly. The two forces cancel each other out and the box does not move. But if Jack's force is above this limit, the box will move. So what determines this limit? It depends on the weight of the box, and on the roughness of the two surfaces in contact.

friction = 25 N

Jack pushes the box with a force of 25 N. It does not move. The friction force exerted by the floor on the box is 25 N. This exactly balances Jack's push.

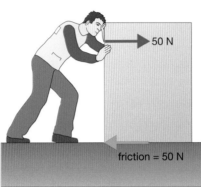

friction = 50 N

Jack then pushes harder, with a force of 50 N. The box still does not move. The friction force exerted by the floor on the box is now 50 N. Again, this balances Jack's push.

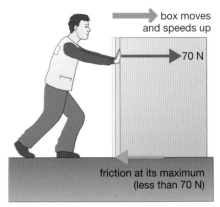

box moves and speeds up

friction at its maximum (less than 70 N)

Jack pushes harder still, exerting a force of 70 N. The box starts to move. 70 N is bigger than the maximum friction force for this box and floor surface.

Normal contact force

If you hold a tennis ball at arm's length and let it go, it immediately starts to move downwards. There is a force acting on the tennis ball due to gravity.

But if you put a tennis ball on a table so that it does not roll around, it does not fall. The force of gravity has not suddenly stopped or been switched off. There must be another force that balances it. The only thing that can be causing this is the table. The table must exert an upward force on the ball that balances the downward force of gravity.

a falling

b sitting on a table

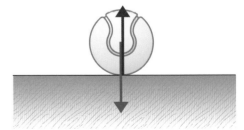

The forces acting on a tennis ball.

Key words

➤ normal contact force
➤ weight
➤ mass

How can a table exert a force?

Although it may seem strange, tables can and do exert forces. To understand how, imagine an object, such as a school bag, sitting on the foam cushion of a sofa. The bag presses down on the foam, squashing it a bit. Because foam is springy, it pushes upward on the bag, just like a spring. Like a spring, the more it is squeezed, the harder it pushes back. So the bag sinks into the foam until the push of the foam on it exactly balances the downward pull of gravity on it.

The same thing happens, though on a much smaller scale, when the bag sits on a table top. A table top is not so easily squeezed as a foam cushion. But it can be squashed, although this is not visible to the naked eye.

We call the force that a surface exerts when something presses on it the **normal contact force**. 'Normal' here means at 90° to the surface, just as the normal line in optics is at 90° to the interface.

The size of the normal contact force depends on the force that is causing it. The surface distorts just enough to make the normal contact force balance the downward force on the object due to gravity.

There is, of course, a limit to this. If the downward force exerted on a table is bigger than it can take, the table top will break. But up to this limit, the normal contact force matches the downward force.

Walls can push too!

Any surface can exert a normal contact force, not just horizontal ones.

The diagram on the right shows Deborah on roller-skates. When she pushes on the wall, it pushes back on her. She immediately starts to move backwards. Deborah's push squashes the wall where her hands touch it. Although we cannot see any distortion, this part of the wall is compressed. Like a spring, it exerts an equal force back on Deborah's hands.

Gravity – a universal force

The gravitational force doesn't just act between objects on the Earth and the Earth itself. It acts everywhere – it is a universal force that acts between all masses. Just as there is a force between every magnet and every other magnet, there is a force between every mass and every other mass. We only notice the force when one of the masses is very large, like the Earth.

An object's **weight** is the gravitational force of attraction on it, towards the centre of the Earth. It is a force measured in newtons (N).

This may sound strange because, in everyday life, if someone asks you the weight of a bag of sugar, you might give the answer in kilograms. In fact, the amount of sugar – how much 'matter' you have – is the **mass** of the sugar. Mass is measured in kilograms.

Anything with a mass of 1 kg close to the Earth is attracted with a force of approximately 10 N, so we say it weighs 10 N. (The force of gravity at the Earth's surface is actually 9.8 N on every kilogram, but we use the approximation of 10 N in this course.)

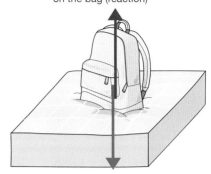

force exerted by the cushion on the bag (reaction)

force exerted by the Earth on the bag (due to gravity)

The bag squeezes the foam until the upward force of the foam on the bag exactly balances the downward force of gravity on the bag.

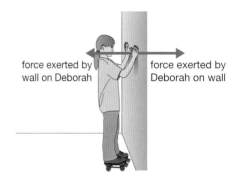

force exerted by wall on Deborah

force exerted by Deborah on wall

Deborah pushes against the wall. The other force in the interaction pair starts her moving away from the wall.

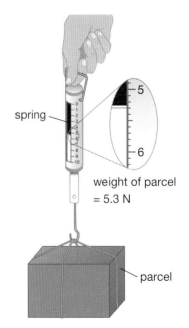

spring

weight of parcel = 5.3 N

parcel

A newtonmeter is used to measure weight. This parcel weighs 5.3 N.

If you have two bags of sugar you have twice the mass, 2 kg, so the weight has doubled. You have 2 × 10 N or 20 N.

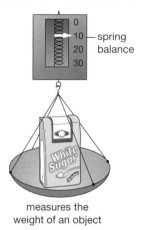

spring
balance

measures the
weight of an object

This 1 kg bag of sugar weighs 10 N.

Gravitational field strength

If the 1 kg bag of sugar is sent to the Moon, or to another planet, there is still 1 kg of sugar. The mass is exactly the same as it was on Earth. But the weight is different. The mass of the Moon is much less than the mass of the Earth. This means an object is attracted to the Moon by a much smaller gravitational force, and 1 kg of sugar weighs less than 10 N there.

The astronaut on the Moon weighs less than he does on Earth.

In P3 you saw how we use the idea of an electric field to explain forces between objects with charge, and a magnetic field to explain forces between magnets. In the same way, we can use gravitational fields to explain forces between objects with mass.

The Earth has a gravitational field. There is an attractive force $F_{gravity}$ between any object in the field and the Earth. The size of the force depends on the object's mass m and the strength of the field. For objects on, or close to, the Earth, the **gravitational field strength** g has a value of about 10 N for each kilogram, which is written 10 N/kg.

The equation for calculating the weight of an object on, or close to, the Earth is:

weight (N) = mass (kg) × gravitational field strength (N/kg)

$$F_{gravity} = mg$$

Worked example: Calculating mass

The weight of an object is 3500 N. Calculate the mass of the object. (g = 10 N/kg)

Step 1: Write down what you know, with the units.

weight $F_{gravity}$ = 3500 N
gravitational field strength g = 10 N/kg

Step 2: Write down the equation you will use to calculate the mass.

weight = mass × gravitational field strength
$F_{gravity}$ = mg

Step 3: Rearrange the equation to make mass the subject. Divide both sides by g.

$$\frac{F_{gravity}}{g} = \frac{m\cancel{g}}{\cancel{g}}$$

$$m = \frac{F_{gravity}}{g}$$

Step 4: Substitute the quantities into the equation and calculate the mass. Include the units in your answer.

$$m = \frac{3500 \text{ N}}{10 \text{ N/kg}}$$

Answer:

mass = 350 kg

Forces have direction and size

You know that the size or **magnitude** of a force is measured in newtons (N). But a force always has a direction as well as magnitude. In physics, a quantity with direction and magnitude is called a **vector**, so force is a vector.

Adding forces

If there is a force acting on an object, but the object is not moving, then there must be another force balancing (or cancelling out) the first one. If the forces acting on an object balance each other, we say they add to zero.

When adding several forces that act on the same object, you must take the direction of each force into account. The sum of all the forces acting on an object is called the **resultant force**. The diagrams show some examples.

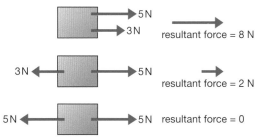

To find the resultant force acting on an object, you add the separate forces. You must take account of their directions.

Key words

➤ gravitational field strength
➤ magnitude
➤ vector
➤ resultant force

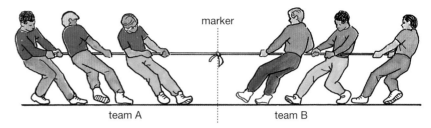

The direction of the resultant force in this tug of war will decide which team wins.

Questions

1 Sketch the first diagram of Jack pushing the box at the beginning of this section. Mark and label the forces acting on *Jack* as he pushes. Use the length of each force arrow to indicate the size of the force.

2 Calculate the weight of these masses close to the Earth's surface (gravitational field strength $g = 10$ N/kg):
 a a 70 kg person
 b a 1200 kg car
 c a 420 g football.

3 The gravitational field strength on the Moon is 1.6 N/kg. Calculate the weight on the Moon of:
 a a 1 kg bag of sugar
 b a 95 kg astronaut.

4 Draw diagrams to show the forces on the block at the bottom of the previous page when:
 a a force of 6 N and a force of 8 N give a resultant force of 14 N to the right
 b a force of 6 N and a force of 8 N give a resultant force of 2 N to the left
 c a force of 2 N, a force of 4 N, and a force of 5 N give a resultant force of 3 N to the left.

5 In the tug of war above, the people in team A are pulling with forces of 300 N, 450 N, and 250 N, and the people in team B are pulling with forces of 300 N, 350 N, and 400 N.
 a Calculate the resultant force. (Remember to state the magnitude *and* the direction.)
 b Which is the winning team?

6 A bag is hanging from a string. The string must be exerting an upward force on the bag, equal to the downward force of gravity on it.

 Suggest how the string exerts this upward force. (Use the ideas on the pages in this section to suggest an explanation.)

A: Describing motion

Speed

One question to ask about the motion of an object is, 'How fast is it moving?'. You can answer this by measuring, or calculating, its speed. To find the speed of an object, you measure the time t it takes to travel a known distance s or the distance it travels in a known time. You can then calculate its **average speed** v.

To calculate speed, remember that if the speed of the object is doubled:

- it will travel twice the distance in the same time
- it will travel the same distance in half the time.

So the equation for calculating the average speed in metres per second is:

$$\text{average speed (metres per second, m/s)} = \frac{\text{distance travelled (metres, m)}}{\text{time (seconds, s)}}$$

$$v = \frac{s}{t}$$

Find out about

- how to calculate the speed of a moving object
- units for measuring speed
- displacement and velocity
- acceleration

Key word

➤ average speed

Worked example: Calculating speed

A car travels 780 m in 1 minute. Calculate its average speed.

Step 1: Write down what you know, with the units. Convert to standard units

Step 2: Write down the equation you will use to calculate the average speed.

Step 3: Substitute the quantities into the equation and calculate the speed. Include the units in your answer.

Answer:

distance s = 780 m
time t = 1 minute = 60 s
average speed = $\dfrac{\text{distance}}{\text{time}}$
$v = \dfrac{s}{t}$
$v = \dfrac{780 \text{ m}}{60 \text{ s}}$ = 13 m/s

average speed = 13 m/s

Worked example: Calculating distance travelled

The people in the photo are running with an average speed of 3 m/s. How far will they travel in 2 minutes?

Step 1: Write down what you know, with the units. Convert to standard units.

Step 2: Write down the equation that links distance, time, and average speed.

Step 3: Rearrange the equation to make distance the subject.

Multiply both sides by t.

Step 4: Substitute the quantities into the equation and calculate the distance. Include the units in your answer.

Answer:

average speed = 3 m/s
time = 2 minutes = 120 s
average speed = $\dfrac{\text{distance}}{\text{time}}$
$v = \dfrac{s}{t}$
$v \times t = \dfrac{s}{\cancel{t}} \times \cancel{t}$
$s = v \times t$
$s = 3 \text{ m/s} \times 120 \text{ s}$
$s = 360 \text{ m}$

distance = 360 m

An average walking speed is about 1.5 m/s.

An average running speed is about 3 m/s.

Movement	Typical speed (m/s)	Typical speed (km/h)
light breeze	7	
gale force wind	20	
sound	330	
walking	1 to 1.5	
running	3	
cycling	7	
car at about 30 mph	13	
car at about 70 mph	30	
high-speed train		300
passenger aircraft cruising		900

Some typical speeds in metres per second and kilometres per hour.

Different units for measuring speed

This car speedometer measures speed in kilometres per hour (km/h). The car is travelling at 100 km/h.

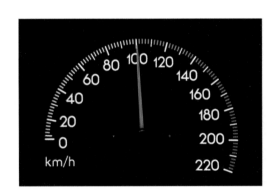

Worked example: Changing units

Change 100 km/h to metres per second, m/s.

Step 1: Write down what you know.

speed v = 100 km/h

Step 2: Write down the unit conversions you will need.

1 km = 1000 m

1 h = 3600 s (because 1 minute = 60 s and 1 h = 60 minutes = 60 × 60 s)

Step 3: Write down the equation for speed.

average speed = $\dfrac{distance}{time}$

$v = \dfrac{s}{t}$

Step 4: Substitute the quantities into the equation.

$v = \dfrac{100 \times 1000 \text{ m}}{3600 \text{ s}} = \dfrac{100\,000 \text{ m}}{3600 \text{ s}}$

Step 5: Work out the value. Include the units in your answer.

v = 27.77 m/s

Answer:

speed = 28 m/s
(to 2 significant figures)

Instantaneous speed or average speed?

The **instantaneous speed** of an object is the speed at which it is travelling at a particular instant. To estimate the instantaneous speed of an object, you measure its average speed over a very short time interval. The shorter you make this time interval, the less likely it is that the speed has changed much while you are measuring it. On the other hand, if you make it very short, it is harder to measure the distance and the time accurately.

A car's speedometer measures its average speed over a short time interval, giving a good indication of the instantaneous speed.

Key words

➤ instantaneous speed
➤ displacement
➤ velocity
➤ scalar
➤ acceleration

When an athlete runs a race, her speed changes throughout the race. The diagram below shows an athlete's position at 1-second intervals during a race. She ran 100 m in 12.5 s. Her average speed was 8 m/s.

But she didn't run at 8 m/s for the whole race. Sometimes she ran more quickly; sometimes she ran more slowly. This is why we call this value the *average speed*.

She made a dash for the finish line, and at this point her instantaneous speed was about 10 m/s, which is faster than her average speed.

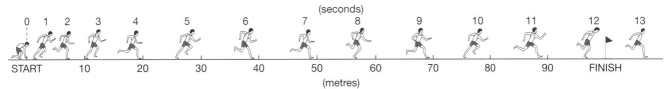

How an athlete's speed changes as she runs a race.

Distance and displacement

A group of walkers follow the route shown on the map in the margin. The distance along the trail is 6 km. When they finish their walk, they have walked a distance of 6 km, but their final position is 2 km east of the starting point. This is called their **displacement**. The displacement is the straight-line distance and direction from the starting point. It has magnitude and direction, so displacement is a vector.

Speed and velocity

People often use the words 'speed' and '**velocity**' to mean the same thing, but the velocity of an object also tells you the direction in which it is moving. It has magnitude and direction, so velocity is a vector. A cyclist pedalling at 8 m/s along a road in a westerly direction has a speed of 8 m/s, but his velocity is 8 m/s west.

Quantities such as speed and distance, which have magnitude but no direction, are called **scalar** quantities.

Acceleration
Calculating acceleration from speed and time

In everyday language, if the speed of an object is increasing, we say that it is accelerating. Drivers are often interested in the **acceleration** of their car. For a high-performance car this might be stated as '0 to 60 miles per hour (mph) in 6 seconds'.

If the acceleration is uniform, which means it stays the same during the 6 seconds, then in the first second the car speeds up from 0 to 10 mph. In the second second it speeds up from 10 mph to 20 mph, and so on, until in the sixth second it speeds up from 50 mph to 60 mph. Its acceleration is 10 mph/s.

In situations like this, where the direction of motion does not matter, we can use the equation:

$$\text{acceleration} = \frac{\text{change in speed}}{\text{time taken for the change}}$$

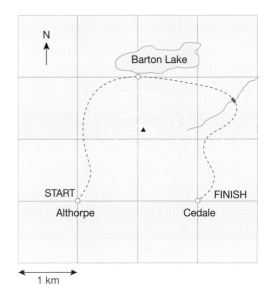

The distance from start to finish is 6 km. But the displacement at the finish is 2 km east of the start.

Synoptic link

You can learn more about the practical techniques for investigating acceleration in P8G *Measuring acceleration*.

A more complete definition of acceleration that applies to all situations is:

$$\text{acceleration (m/s}^2) = \frac{\text{change in velocity (m/s)}}{\text{time taken for the change (s)}}$$

You can see that the velocity is given here in units of metres per second, which gives the acceleration in units of m/s², or '(metres per second) per second'.

The symbol equation for calculating acceleration is:

$$a = \frac{v - u}{t}$$

where **a** is the acceleration and **t** is the time taken. **v – u** is the change in velocity (or speed). The symbol for the velocity at the start is **u**. The symbol for the velocity at the end is **v**.

Worked example: Calculating acceleration 1

A car accelerates from 10 m/s to 30 m/s (23 mph to 68 mph) in 8 s. Calculate the average acceleration in m/s².

Step 1: Write down what you know, with the units.

initial speed u = 10 m/s
final speed v = 30 m/s
time t = 8 s

Step 2: Write down the equation you will use to calculate the acceleration.

$$\text{acceleration} = \frac{\text{change in speed}}{\text{time taken}}$$

$$a = \frac{v - u}{t}$$

Step 3: Substitute the quantities into the equation.

$$a = \frac{30 \text{ m/s} - 10 \text{ m/s}}{8 \text{ s}} = \frac{20 \text{ m/s}}{8 \text{ s}}$$

Step 4: Calculate the acceleration. Include the units in your answer.

$$a = 2.5 \text{ m/s}^2$$

Answer:

acceleration = 2.5 m/s²

Calculating acceleration from speed and distance

If an object accelerates over a known distance, and you know the initial (starting) speed and the final speed, what is its acceleration? You don't know the time taken, so you cannot use the equation above, but there is another useful equation:

$$(\text{final speed})^2 - (\text{initial speed})^2 = 2 \times \text{acceleration} \times \text{distance travelled}$$
$$v^2 - u^2 = 2as$$

The cheetah is the fastest land mammal. It also has the largest acceleration, which can be as much as 13 m/s².

A large acceleration can be an exciting experience.

Worked example: Calculating acceleration 2

A bicycle accelerates from 1 m/s to 9 m/s, over a distance of 500 m. What is its acceleration?

Step 1: Write down what you know, with the units.

initial speed u = 1 m/s
final speed v = 9 m/s
distance travelled s = 500 m

Step 2: Write down the symbol equation that includes initial and final speed, acceleration, and distance.

$v^2 - u^2 = 2as$

Step 3: Substitute the quantities into the equation.

$(9 \text{ m/s})^2 - (1 \text{ m/s})^2 = 2 \times a \times 500 \text{ m}$
$81 \text{ (m/s)}^2 - 1 \text{ (m/s)}^2 = a \times 1000 \text{ m}$
$80 \text{ (m/s)}^2 = a \times 1000 \text{ m}$

Step 4: Divide both sides by 1000 m.

$$\frac{80 \text{ (m/s)}^2}{1000 \text{ m}} = \frac{a \times \cancel{1000 \text{ m}}}{\cancel{1000 \text{ m}}}$$

Step 5: Calculate the acceleration. Include the units in your answer.

$a = \dfrac{80 \text{ (m/s)}^2}{1000 \text{ m}} = 0.08 \text{ m/s}^2$

Answer:

acceleration = 0.08 m/s²

Questions

1   A cheetah runs 600 m in 20 s. Calculate its speed.

2   A racing cyclist has a speed of 14 m/s. How long will it take him to travel 280 m?

3   Copy the table of typical speeds from page 122, with columns for m/s and km/h, and calculate the missing values.

4   Look at the example of the athlete on page 123.
    a Calculate her average speed over the first 20 m of the race.
    b During which time interval do you think she was running fastest? Explain your answer.

5   State whether the following measurements are speeds, velocities, distances, or displacements.
    a 50 cm   **b** 2 km north   **c** 8 m/s
    d 20 km/h east   **e** −0.5 m/s

6   A high-performance car can accelerate from 0 to 27 m/s (0 to 60 mph) in 6 s. Calculate the average acceleration of the car in m/s².

7   A cheetah accelerates at 13 m/s². Calculate the time taken to accelerate from stationary to 16 m/s.

8   An aircraft has a take-off speed of 30 m/s. Calculate the length of runway required if the average acceleration is 2.0 m/s².

9   A rollercoaster has an acceleration of 9 m/s². It accelerates from rest. Calculate its speed when it has travelled 35 m.

B: Picturing motion

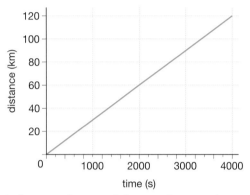

A distance–time graph for a car journey along the motorway.

You can use a graph to analyse Vijay's bicycle ride.

Synoptic link

You can learn more about the gradients of graphs in the *Maths skills* section at the end of the book.

You can find a lot of information about the motion of an object in a graph. A graph provides information about a moving object at any instant in time. From the shape and **slope** of the graph, we can work out how the object moved.

Distance–time graphs

A **distance–time graph** shows the distance a moving object has travelled at every instant during its motion. The graph on the left is a distance–time graph for a car travelling along a motorway. You can read off the graph the distances the car has travelled after 1000 s, 2000 s, 3000 s, and 4000 s.

The distance increases steadily so we say the speed of the car is constant. The constant slope, or **gradient**, of the distance–time graph indicates a steady speed.

The graph below shows a bicycle ride taken by Vijay. The graph has four sections: A, B, C, and D. In each section the slope of the graph is constant. This means that Vijay's speed is constant during that section of the ride.

But the slope of each section is different. The steeper the slope, the faster the bicycle is going, because it is covering a larger distance in the same time.

In section C the graph is horizontal, so the distance travelled is not changing. It stays at 35 m. Vijay has stopped. This is what a horizontal section of a distance–time graph means.

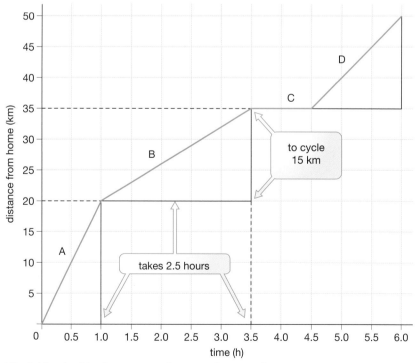

Vijay's bicycle ride shown on a distance–time graph.

Worked example: Calculating speed from a distance–time graph

Calculate Vijay's speed in km/h for the first two sections of his ride, A and B.

Step 1: Write down what you know, with the units. Convert to standard units.

A: time = 1 h   distance travelled = 20 km
B: time = 2.5 h   distance travelled = 15 km

Step 2: Write down the equation you will use to calculate the speed.

$$speed = \frac{distance}{time} = slope \text{ (or gradient) of the graph}$$

Step 3: Substitute the quantities into the equation and calculate the speed. Include the units in your answer.

A: speed $\frac{20 \text{ km}}{1 \text{ h}} = 20$ km/h

B: speed $= \frac{15 \text{ km}}{2.5 \text{ h}} = 6$ km/h

Step 4: Look at your two answers – do they make sense?

Yes, the shallower slope has the slower speed.

Real-life distance–time graphs

This distance–time graph for Vijay's journey is not very realistic. In a real journey, the speed would change gradually.

Look at the distance–time graph on the right. It shows a car journey. The slope tells you the speed of the car. If the slope gets steeper, the car is speeding up, or accelerating. If the slope is getting less steep, then the car's speed is decreasing. This is sometimes called **deceleration**.

Displacement–time graphs

If an object moves in a straight line, we can draw a **displacement–time graph** of its motion. The graph shows how the size of the object's displacement changes with time. If the direction of motion reverses, the distance continues to increase, but the displacement decreases because the object is moving back towards the starting point.

The graphs below show the motion of a ball thrown vertically upwards from the moment it leaves the hand until the moment it arrives back again.

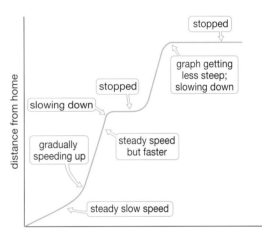

A more realistic distance–time graph.

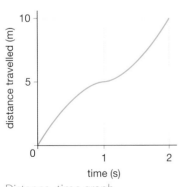

Distance–time graph.

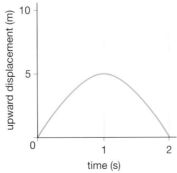

Displacement–time graph.

Two graphs showing the motion of a ball thrown up in the air.

Key words

➤ slope
➤ distance–time graph
➤ gradient
➤ deceleration
➤ displacement–time graph

Key words

➤ speed–time graph
➤ velocity–time graph

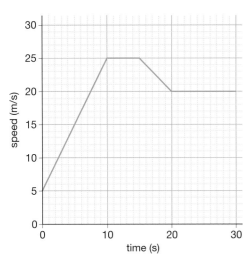

Speed–time graph for a car on a track.

Speed–time graphs

A **speed–time graph** shows the speed of a moving object at every instant during its journey. Look at the speed–time graph below for Vijay's bicycle ride. A steady speed is shown by a straight horizontal line.

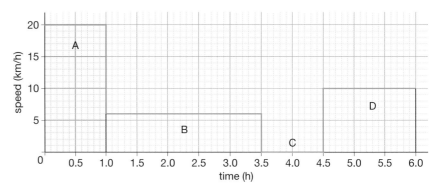

Speed–time graph of Vijay's bicycle ride.

A more realistic speed–time graph would not have sudden changes of speed. There would be smoother, more gradual changes from one speed to another.

The speed–time graph in the margin is for a car on a track. It shows that the car is initially accelerating, then travels at a steady 25 m/s for 5 seconds before slowing to a new steady speed of 20 m/s.

Worked example: Calculating acceleration from a speed–time graph

From the speed–time graph for the car on a track in the margin, calculate the acceleration of the car in the first 10 s.

Step 1: Mark on the line the points the question is asking about.

Step 2: Mark on the graph the changes in values.

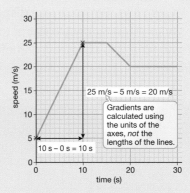

25 m/s – 5 m/s = 20 m/s

Gradients are calculated using the units of the axes, *not* the lengths of the lines.

10 s – 0 s = 10 s

Step 3: Write down the equation to calculate the gradient.

$$\text{acceleration} = \frac{\text{change in speed}}{\text{time taken}}$$

Step 4: Substitute in the values from the graph. Calculate the acceleration, including the units.

$$\text{acceleration} = \frac{20 \text{ m/s}}{10 \text{ s}} = 2 \text{ m/s}^2$$

Answer:

$$\text{acceleration} = 2 \text{ m/s}^2$$

Velocity–time graphs

On a speed–time graph, the speed is always positive. On a **velocity–time graph**, the object can move away from the start (in a positive direction) or back towards the start (in a negative direction).

Look at the graph below. It shows the motion of Zoe's skateboard up and then down a slope. At the start Zoe begins travelling up the slope at 10 m/s. She gradually slows down until her velocity is zero. Notice that the graph has a negative slope – her acceleration is negative. For a moment she is stationary. Then she starts to roll back down the slope. Her velocity has changed to the opposite direction – it is negative – and she speeds up as she rolls back down.

Zoe rides her skateboard up a ramp.

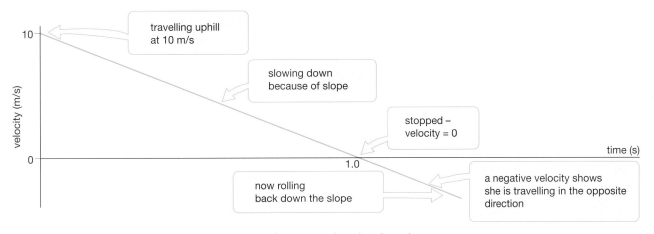

Velocity–time graph. The negative velocity means that Zoe on her skateboard is travelling in the opposite direction to her original motion.

Finding the distance from speed–time graphs

Look at the speed–time graph of Vijay's bicycle ride on the previous page.

$$\text{average speed} = \frac{\text{distance}}{\text{time}}$$

In section A:

$$20 \text{ km/h} = \frac{\text{distance}}{1 \text{ h}}$$

$$20 \text{ km/h} \times 1 \text{ h} = \frac{\text{distance}}{1 \text{ h}} \times 1 \text{ h}$$

so: $\qquad \text{distance} = 20 \text{ km/h} \times 1 \text{ h} = 20 \text{ km}$

> **H** Notice that on the graph, this distance is the area of the shaded rectangle.
>
> The distance travelled is the area of the enclosed shape formed by the time axis and the graph line. So you can find the distance by calculating the area. The same method works for velocity–time graphs.

Worked example: Calculating the distance travelled from a velocity–time graph

In the graph showing the motion of the car on the race track, what is the distance travelled between 0 s and 10 s?

Step 1: Mark on the line the points the question is asking about.

Step 2: Shade the area under this portion of the graph.

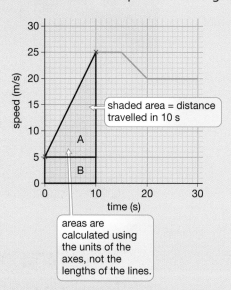

shaded area = distance travelled in 10 s

areas are calculated using the units of the axes, not the lengths of the lines.

Counting the squares:
number of whole squares + number of 'more than half' squares in triangle **A** = 100
number of squares in rectangle **B** = 50
total number of squares = 150
area of each square = 1 s × 1 m/s = 1 m
therefore distance = 150 × 1 m = 150 m

Step 3: Calculate the area of the shaded area. You can do this by:

- counting the squares in the shaded area, *or*
- finding the area of the triangle and the rectangle that make up the shape. Include the units in your answer.

area of triangle **A** = $\frac{1}{2}$ base × height
$= \frac{1}{2}$ × 10 s × 20 m/s = 100 m
area of rectangle **B** = base × height
= 10 s × 5 m/s = 50 m
therefore distance = 100 m + 50 m = 150 m

Answer:

distance = 150 m (Both methods give the same answer.)

Questions

1 Look at the distance–time graph of Vijay's bicycle ride on page 126.
  a Calculate his speed in section D.
  b Vijay cycled more slowly in the uphill section. Which section was uphill?

2 Look at the two graphs showing the motion of the ball thrown in the air at the bottom of page 127.
  a Describe how the slope of both graphs changes over the first second of the ball's motion. What does this mean is happening to its speed? Is this what you would expect?
  b What is the speed of the ball after 1 s of its motion? Explain how you can tell this from the graphs.

  c How high does the ball go?
  d Explain why the displacement–time graph turns down after 1 s, whereas the distance–time graph continues to go up.

H 3 Use the speed–time graph of Vijay's bicycle ride to calculate the distance travelled in:
  a section B
  b section D
  c the whole journey.

4 From Zoe's skateboard graph calculate:
  a the acceleration as she travels up the slope
  H b how far up the slope she travels.

C: Free fall

In 2012, skydiver Felix Baumgartner fell from the stratosphere to Earth. We can use a graph as a mathematical model to describe his motion. The velocity–time graph shows the first 25 s of his fall. The graph is a straight line, showing that he had a uniform acceleration. This means that he picked up speed steadily from the moment he fell. You can calculate his acceleration using data from the graph.

What was Felix's acceleration in the first 25 s?

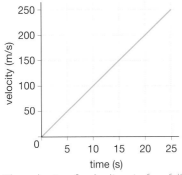

$u = 0$ m/s
$v = 250$ m/s
$t = 25$ s
$a = \dfrac{v - u}{t} = \dfrac{250 \text{ m/s}}{25 \text{ s}}$
$a = 10$ m/s^2

The velocity of a skydiver in free fall.

Find out about
- the motion of falling objects

Key words
➤ free fall
➤ air resistance

If there are no other forces acting, any falling object will fall with the same acceleration of 10 m/s^2 (or almost 10 m/s^2). This is called the acceleration of **free fall**.

You saw in P4.1B that near the surface, the Earth has a gravitational field strength of about 10 N/kg. Objects in this field that do not have any other forces acting on them have an acceleration towards the centre of the Earth of 10 m/s^2.

You will learn more about why this happens later in this chapter.

The multi-flash photograph on the right shows a ball in free fall. The time interval between flashes is constant. As the ball falls, it moves further between one flash and the next. Its speed increases. It accelerates.

If you drop an object that is light relative to its size, such as a cupcake case, it does not continue to fall with an acceleration of 10 m/s^2. The reason is that **air resistance** has a big effect on it. Air resistance is a force that slows down anything moving through the air. Felix Baumgartner fell from the top of the atmosphere where there is very little air to have any effect.

A falling ball gets steadily faster as it falls.

Skydivers lie horizontally to increase their air resistance and reduce their acceleration.

Questions

(Acceleration of free fall = 10 m/s^2; assume negligible air resistance.)

1 A stone is dropped down a deep well. It is heard hitting the water after 3 s.
   a How fast is it falling when it hits the water?
   b How deep in the well is the surface of the water?

2 Julie drops an ice-cream over a balcony 7.2 m above the ground. Calculate the speed of the ice-cream when it hits the ground.

P4.3 What is the connection between forces and motion?

A: Resultant forces

Find out about

- free-body diagrams
- balanced forces and equilibrium
- scale drawings of vector diagrams

Key words

➤ free-body force diagram
➤ vector diagram
➤ equilibrium
➤ balanced forces

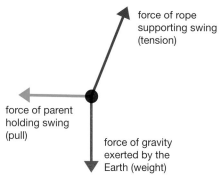

A picture showing the three forces on a child on a swing and a free-body force diagram of the same situation.

You saw in P4.1B that to decide whether an object will start to move, you need to add together all the forces acting on it. It is useful to start with a diagram showing all the forces on the object.

Free-body force diagrams

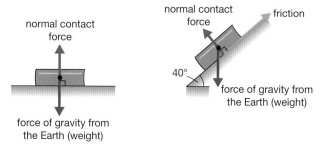

A diagram showing the forces on a book. The book is resting on a table, but will slide if the table is tipped far enough.

In the first diagram of the book on the table there are two forces. When the table is tipped, a friction force acts to stop the book sliding down the table.

It is often easier to think about the forces on one object. It is also easier to draw if you replace the object by a large dot and then draw the labelled arrows. If the drawing doesn't look balanced, then either the object will start to move or you have forgotten a force!

A **free-body force diagram** is a diagram showing all the forces acting on an object. Notice that in a free-body force diagram:

- no forces acting on other objects (no other interaction pair forces) are shown
- the forces are shown by straight arrows
- the arrows start in the object or on its surface
- all the force arrows are labelled
- the arrows touching the object all represent forces – there are no arrows showing velocity, for example
- there is no need to draw the object – a large dot can be used to represent it.

In the picture on the left there are three forces on the child and swing:

- the force of gravity downwards
- the force of the parent pulling the swing to the left
- the tension in the rope of the swing.

You can think about the forces by drawing a free-body force diagram.

Resultant force

From P4.1B you know that the resultant force is the sum of all the forces acting on an object, taking into account their directions.

If you know what forces are acting on an object, you can use a **vector diagram** to find the resultant. In a vector diagram:

- lines with arrow heads represent the forces
- the end of one force is the start of the next force
- the lines are in the directions of the forces
- the lengths of the lines represent the sizes of the forces
- the resultant force is shown by a double arrowhead.

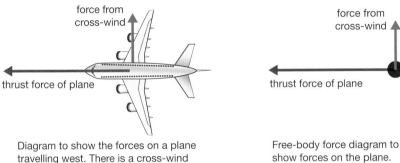

Diagram to show the forces on a plane travelling west. There is a cross-wind from the south.

Free-body force diagram to show forces on the plane.

Vector diagram. To find the resultant force, the two forces are added 'tip to tail'. The resultant force is shown with a double arrowhead.

A vector diagram of the forces acting on a plane. To find the resultant force, you add the forces, taking account of their sizes and directions.

Balanced forces

What will happen to the book on the tilted table?

If the table is smooth, so there is little friction, there is a large resultant force down the slope. A small friction force will mean the resultant force is less. But if the friction force is large enough to balance the other two forces, then the resultant force is zero, so the book is in **equilibrium**. This means there are **balanced forces** on the book.

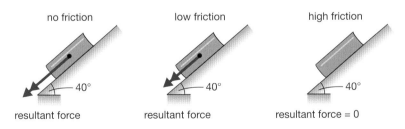

The resultant force on the book.

The forces on Anna are balanced: her weight, the tension in the rope, and the normal reaction on each foot.

Key word

➤ scale diagram

Using vector diagrams

If you draw a **scale diagram** to represent the vectors, you can work out the size and direction of the resultant force.

Worked example: Drawing a scale diagram to find the resultant force

The diagram below shows the forces when two tugs tow a ship. Draw a scale diagram to find the resultant force R and the direction, angle θ.

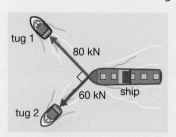

Step 1: Choose a suitable scale to represent the forces on the page.

scale : 1 cm represents 10 kN

Step 2: Draw an arrow to represent the 60 kN vector.

60 kN represented by 6 cm (line AB)

Step 3: Draw an arrow to represent the 80 kN vector, at right-angles to 60 kN and starting from its tip.

80 kN represented by 8 cm (line BC)

Step 4: Draw an arrow from A to C. This is the resultant vector. Mark it with a double arrowhead.

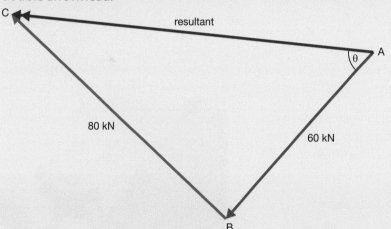

Step 5: Measure the length of AC and work out what size force this represents.

AC = 10 cm

10 cm represents 100 kN

resultant force = 100 kN

Step 6: Measure the angle between AB and AC.

angle θ = 53°

Questions

1 Draw a free-body force diagram for:
   a a person standing on the floor
   b a ball hanging from a string.

2 Draw a free-body force diagram of Anna in the rock climbing photo. (Sketch a simple matchstick figure.)

H 3 For the tug boats towing the ship, the 80 kN force is increased to 100 kN, and the angle between the tow ropes remains at 90°. Draw a scale diagram to determine the new direction of the resultant force.

B: Momentum

Momentum is a useful quantity for exploring the change in an object's motion. The momentum of an object is its mass multiplied by its velocity. The units of momentum are kilogram metre per second (kg m/s).

$$\text{momentum (kg m/s)} = \text{mass (kg)} \times \text{velocity (m/s)}$$

$$\text{momentum} = mv$$

Investigating momentum

You can investigate changing the mass of an object and what happens to its velocity using small carts. The carts all have the same mass and have low-friction wheels. You can vary the mass by putting carts on top of each other.

In this experiment, two carts experience forces of exactly the same size. We start with two stationary carts, one of which is spring-loaded. When the spring is released, the forces on the two carts are equal and opposite, and they move apart at the same speed.

The diagrams show what happens to the velocity when the mass of one cart is changed.

Find out about

- momentum
- the link between change of momentum, force, and time
- conservation of momentum

Key word

➤ momentum

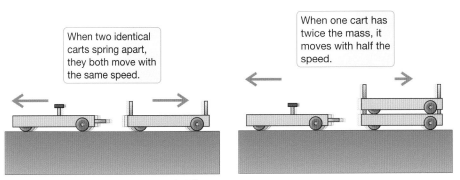
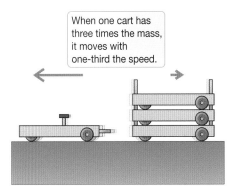

When two identical carts spring apart, they both move with the same speed.

When one cart has twice the mass, it moves with half the speed.

When one cart has three times the mass, it moves with one-third the speed.

What happens when two carts of different masses spring apart.

In each interaction above, mass × velocity (which is the momentum) is the same for both the carts involved. This makes momentum a useful and important quantity for understanding motion. As velocity is a vector quantity, momentum is too. In calculations, the *direction* of the momentum is important as well as the size.

The faster an object is moving, the more momentum it has. At the same speed, a heavy object has more momentum than a lighter object.

The momentum of a cruise ship is large because of its large mass.

Worked example: Calculating momentum

A whale has a mass of 5000 kg and travels at 2 m/s. Calculate its momentum.

Step 1: Write down what you know, with the units. Convert to standard units.

mass = 5000 kg
velocity = 2 m/s

Step 2: Write down the equation you will use to calculate momentum.

momentum = mass × velocity

Step 3: Substitute the quantities into the equation to calculate the momentum. Include the units in your answer.

momentum = 5000 kg × 2m/s
= 10 000 kg m/s

Answer:

momentum = 10 000 kg m/s

Key words

➤ duration
➤ conservation of momentum

Newton's second law: force and change of momentum

In any interaction, such as the three collisions between pairs of carts on the previous page, the following quantities are the same size for each object:

- the change of momentum $mv - mu$
- the resultant force F acting on each object
- the time t for which this force acts (the **duration** of the interaction).

This is the link between them:

change of momentum (kg m/s) = resultant force (N) × time for which it acts (s)

$$mv - mu = Ft$$

The change of momentum is always in the direction of the resultant force.

Using the change of momentum equation

We can use the change of momentum equation to calculate the force applied in an interaction. For example, when a footballer takes a free kick, his foot exerts a force on the ball.

This force lasts for only a very short time, the time for which the foot and the ball are in contact. After that, the player's foot can no longer affect the motion of the ball. The kick has not given the ball some 'force' but it has given it some momentum.

Taking a free kick. The interaction between the footballer's foot and the ball causes a change of momentum.

HIGHER TIER ONLY

Worked example: Calculating the force

A football has a mass of 0.45 kg. A free kick gives it a speed of 30 m/s. The ball is in contact with the foot for 0.05 s. What is the average force on the ball?

Step 1: Write down what you know, with the units. Convert to standard units.

mass m = 0.45 kg
initial velocity u = 0 m/s
final velocity v = 30 m/s
contact time for kick t = 0.05 s

Step 2: Write down the equations you will use to calculate the force.

change of momentum = resultant force × time
$mv - mu = Ft$

Step 3: Substitute the values you know into the equation.

0.45 kg × 30 m/s – 0.45 kg × 0 m/s = F × 0.05 s
13.5 kg m/s = F × 0.05 s

Step 4: Rearrange the equation to make F the subject. Divide both sides by 0.05 s.

$$\frac{13.5 \text{ kg m/s}}{0.05 \text{ s}} = \frac{F \times 0.05 \text{ s}}{0.05 \text{ s}}$$

Step 5: Work out the average force. Include the units in your answer.

$$F = \frac{13.5 \text{ kg m/s}}{0.05 \text{ s}} = 270 \text{ N}$$

Answer:

average force = 270 N

The momentum of each vehicle depends on its mass and its velocity.

Questions

1   What is the momentum of a skier of mass 50 kg moving at a speed of 5 m/s?

2   Which has the greatest momentum?
    A a lorry of mass 2800 kg and velocity 13 m/s (30 mph)
    B a car of mass 900 kg and velocity 13 m/s
    C a motorbike of mass 220 kg and velocity 31 m/s (70 mph)

3   Calculate the change of momentum produced by:
    a a force of 40 N acting for 3 s
    b a force of 200 N acting for 0.5 s
    c a force of 3 N acting for 50 s.

4   A model car with mass 1 kg and velocity 2 m/s hits another stationary car with mass 1 kg and the two stick together and continue moving.
    a What is the total momentum before the collision?
    b What is the total momentum after the collision?
    c What is their velocity after the collision?

Conservation of momentum

In all collisions, as long as no other forces are acting on the objects, the total momentum is the same before and after the collision. This is an important principle called the **conservation of momentum**.

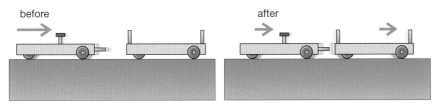

before   after

Conservation of momentum. The total momentum of the two carts after the collision is the same as the momentum of the moving cart before the collision.

C: Newton's laws of motion

Find out about

- Newton's first law
- Newton's second law
- Newton's third law
- the ideas of Newton, Aristotle, and Einstein
- circular motion

Isaac Newton's laws of motion enable us to predict and explain the motion of objects. So far you have learnt about the second and third laws. The first law is about objects that are stationary, or moving with a steady speed.

Moving with a steady speed

These diagrams show a player pushing a curling stone. He gives it momentu.m. What happens when he lets go depends on the surface.

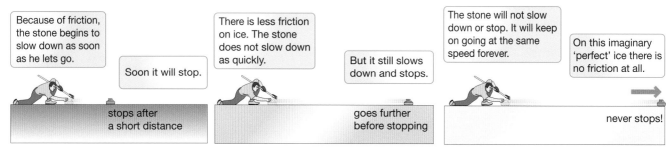

| Because of friction, the stone begins to slow down as soon as he lets go. | Soon it will stop. | There is less friction on ice. The stone does not slow down as quickly. | But it still slows down and stops. | The stone will not slow down or stop. It will keep on going at the same speed forever. | On this imaginary 'perfect' ice there is no friction at all. |

stops after a short distance

goes further before stopping

never stops!

Smooth floor.　　　　Ice.　　　　Perfectly smooth ice.

On perfectly smooth ice, with no friction, once the player has let the stone go there would be no resultant force on it. The stone would travel at a constant velocity. An object moving at a constant velocity does not need a force to keep it moving.

Newton's first law

When the resultant force on an object is zero, its motion remains unchanged. If it is stationary it will stay stationary, and if it is moving it will carry on moving at the same speed in the same direction.

It may seem strange that no resultant force is needed to maintain a steady speed, because in the real world there is always friction. A **driving force** is needed to keep an object moving. The driving force balances the **counter force**. Friction and air resistance are examples of counter forces.

Forces on a bicycle

When you pedal a bicycle the tyre pushes back on the ground, and the force from the ground pushes the bicycle forward. The force from the ground is the driving force. Air resistance and friction at the axles cause a counter force in the opposite direction to your motion. The worked example opposite shows what happens.

Key words

➤ driving force
➤ counter force

Worked example: Identifying the forces on a moving object

Draw free-body force diagrams of the forces on a bicycle when it is:

1. *starting off (from stationary)*
2. *accelerating*
3. *travelling at a steady speed*
4. *slowing down (stopped pedalling)*

1. Starting off: there is a very small counter force due to friction; the driving force is bigger.

counter force   driving force

2. Accelerating: the air resistance increases so the counter force is larger.

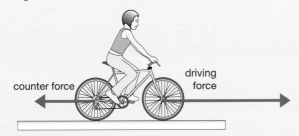

counter force   driving force

3. Steady speed: the counter force exactly balances the driving force, so there is no acceleration.

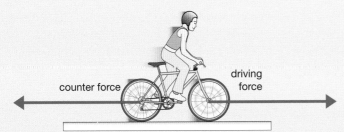

counter force   driving force

4. Slowing down: there is no driving force when the cyclist stops pedalling. There is still a counter force which slows her down as she free-wheels.

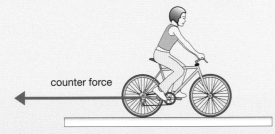

counter force

Notice that when the bicycle is slowing down, it is still moving forwards, but the resultant force is in the opposite direction. People sometimes forget this. Remember that a force does not cause motion; it causes a *change* of motion.

There is a story that an apple falling on Newton's head gave him the idea that the force of gravity makes things fall.

Theories of motion

The link between force, time, and change of momentum was proposed by Isaac Newton in 1687 in his famous book, *Philosophiæ Naturalis Principia Mathematica (The Mathematical Principles of Natural Philosophy)*. Instead of the word 'momentum', Newton wrote about an object's 'amount of motion' and how a force acting for a time could change it. The way he uses the term makes it clear that he was talking about the quantity we now call momentum.

Newton started from the ideas of the Greek scientist Aristotle and the Italian scientist Galileo. Aristotle thought, wrongly, that things move to their natural place and then stop. (So rocks fall down and stop, while flames move up and stop.) He did not test his ideas with experiments. Galileo did careful experiments. He correctly thought that objects that move would continue to move if there were no force – but he wrongly thought they move in circles, because he knew the Earth was a sphere.

Newton realised that objects moving in a straight line continue to move in a straight line. He used his imagination to picture what would happen if there were no friction, as using well as using careful observation, to improve on the work of other scientists.

Newton's **hypothesis** has been supported by many observations and measurements since then. There are all kinds of examples of motion we can study, from the motion of everyday objects to the motion of the planets and stars. We now accept Newton's idea as a reliable **theory** (rule) for explaining and predicting the motion of anything, except very small objects (at the scale of atoms) and very fast-moving objects (approaching the speed of light).

One of Newton's most creative ideas was to realise that the force of gravity that makes things fall is also the force that keeps the Moon in its orbit. This insight led to Newton's statement of the universal law of gravitation.

Newton's laws of motion

Law 1: If the resultant force acting on an object is zero, the momentum of the object does not change.

Law 2: If there is a resultant force acting on an object, the momentum of the object will change. The size of the change of momentum is equal to the resultant force × the time for which it acts. The change is in the same direction as the resultant force.

Law 3: When two objects interact, each experiences a force. The two forces are equal in size, but opposite in direction.

These laws apply to all objects and to every situation (apart from objects at the subatomic level or those moving at speeds near the speed of light).

Albert Einstein started from Newton's ideas and thought about what would happen if things moved as fast as light. He realised that Newton's laws would not apply at that speed and using his imagination and creativity he developed the *theory of relativity*.

We cannot solve our problems with the same thinking we used when we created them

—Albert Einstein

Moving in a circle

Another way of expressing Newton's first law of motion is to say that:

- objects continue to move in a straight line unless there is a resultant force on them.

It follows from this that an object moving in a circle must have a resultant force acting on it.

The tension in the string keeps the ball moving in a circle.

A force to change direction

Maya has a ball on the end of a string, and she swings it round in a circle. The force changing the direction of the ball is the **tension** in the string. If the string breaks, the ball continues in a straight line – along a **tangent** to the circle.

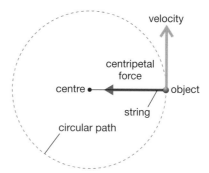

When an object moves in a circle, the direction of the velocity of the object is always at a tangent to the circle. The force is always at right-angles to the direction of the velocity of the object.

The direction of the force is along the string towards Maya's hand, which is along the radius of the circle. So the force that keeps the ball moving in a circle is at right-angles to the direction of motion. This force is called the **centripetal force**.

If Maya makes the ball go faster, the centripetal force needed increases, so the tension in the string increases.

> **H** The ball is moving at constant speed, but, because its direction is changing, its velocity is changing.

Moving in orbit

The force of the Sun's gravity on the planets changes the direction of their velocity to keep them in orbit.

There is no string between a planet and the Sun, but the force of gravity attracts the planet towards the Sun. This provides the centripetal force to keep it in orbit. When a planet is closer to the Sun the gravitational attraction is larger, so it moves faster.

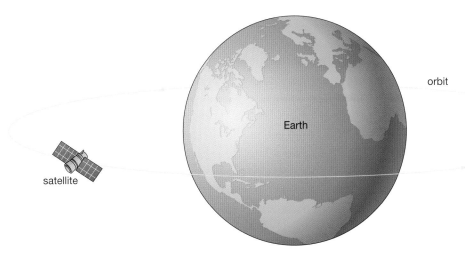

orbit

Earth

satellite

The force of gravity keeps a satellite in orbit around the Earth.

Questions

1 Draw free-body force diagrams showing the weight and counter force on a skydiver:
   a starting to fall
   b accelerating
   c falling at a steady speed
   d slowing down (because the parachute has opened).

2 Give an example of a situation in which the resultant force on a moving object is zero. Explain how the motion of this object demonstrates Newton's first law of motion.

3 Give an example of a situation in which the resultant force on a moving object is not zero. Explain how this is an example of Newton's second law of motion.

4 The Moon is in orbit around the Earth.
   a In what direction is the force on the Moon to keep it in orbit?
   b What causes this force?

5 A satellite orbits the Earth in 23 hours. To change the orbit time to 24 hours, explain whether it should be moved closer to the Earth or further away.

D: Mass and inertia

Find out about

- inertia
- inertial mass
- how force, mass, and acceleration are connected

In P4.1B you learnt that mass is the amount of matter in something and that gravity is a force of attraction between masses. This means, for example, that objects with larger mass have larger weight. Another property of mass is that larger masses need larger forces to change their motion, in other words, to accelerate them. This resistance to change of motion is called **inertia**.

Inertial mass

If you could take an object far away from other objects with mass – out in deep space – how could you tell how large its mass was? It would have no weight and its size would not be a guide because large objects can have very little mass (e.g., balloons). The answer is: if you pushed it with a known force, then an object with large mass would accelerate less than an object with small mass. This property is called **inertial mass** to make it clear that it is not defined by how gravity affects an object.

The unit for measuring force, the newton, is defined using acceleration:

One newton is the force that accelerates a mass of one kilogram by one metre per second every second.

Newton's second law

In P4.3B, Newton's second law stated that a force will change the momentum of an object. This is expressed by the equation:

$$mv - mu = Ft$$

This can be rearranged:

$$F = \frac{m(v - u)}{t}$$

In many situations the mass does not change when a force changes the momentum of an object. So if the mass is constant:

$$F = \frac{m(v - u)}{t} = m\frac{(v - u)}{t}$$

And because the change in velocity in a time interval is the acceleration, we can write this as:

$$F = ma$$

force = mass × acceleration

So this equation is another way of writing Newton's second law – if the mass does not change.

Large aircraft have masses greater than 300 000 kg. A large force needs to act for a significant time for the aircraft to accelerate to take-off speed.

Worked example: Calculating acceleration

The resultant force on an aircraft of mass 500 000 kg during take-off is 550 kN. Calculate the acceleration of the aircraft.

Step 1: Write down what you know, with the units. Convert to standard units.

mass m = 500 000 kg

force F = 550 kN = 550 000 N

Step 2: Write down the equation you will use to calculate the acceleration.

force = mass × acceleration

$F = ma$

Step 3: Rearrange the equation to make a the subject.

Divide both sides by m.

$\dfrac{F}{m} = \dfrac{\cancel{m}a}{\cancel{m}}$

$\dfrac{F}{m} = a$

Step 4: Substitute the quantities into the equation and calculate the acceleration. Include the units in your answer.

$a = \dfrac{550\,000 \text{ N}}{500\,000 \text{ kg}}$

$= 1.1 \text{ m/s}^2$

Answer:

acceleration = 1.1 m/s^2

Key words

➤ inertia
➤ inertial mass

HIGHER TIER ONLY

Inertial mass and gravitational mass

It doesn't matter how we measure mass – by finding the force need to accelerate it or by measuring the gravitational force on it – the value for the mass is always the same.

Questions

1 A car of mass 900 kg accelerates at 2 m/s^2. Calculate the resultant force on the car.

2 A shopper pushes a trolley of mass 30 kg. The resultant force on the trolley is 6 N. Calculate the acceleration.

3 A high-performance car with a mass of 1500 kg has an acceleration of 4.5 m/s^2. Calculate the resultant force that is needed to produce this acceleration.

4 A large aircraft has a take-off speed of 280 km/h and can achieve lift-off in about 80 s. Estimate the resultant force needed to achieve take-off.

5 Astronauts in the International Space Station need to monitor their body mass while in obit. Explain why they cannot use a pair of bathroom scales for this.

E: Travelling safely

Find out about
- human reaction time and stopping distances
- collisions
- car safety features and risk

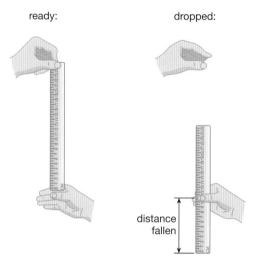

ready: dropped:

distance fallen

Measuring reaction time.

Over 35 million vehicles use UK roads. The total number of people killed or seriously injured on UK roads has fallen steadily since 1979 to about 23 000 in 2013. This is due to improved cars, roads, and driving. What factors affect safety?

Reaction times

When the car in front stops, how long does it take a driver to react? A simple way to measure your **reaction time** is to catch a falling ruler, as shown on the left. You can then measure how far it fell before you caught it. If the ruler fell 11 cm (0.11 m), your reaction time works out as 0.15 s. This is a fairly typical time, but will be increased if a person is tired, unwell, has taken drugs or alcohol, or is just distracted and not concentrating.

Synoptic link

You can learn more about measuring reaction times in P8C *Measuring time*.

Stopping distances

In an emergency stop, how far does a car travel before stopping completely? In the *Highway Code*, this stopping distance is described as the sum of two distances.

Thinking distance is the distance travelled between the driver seeing a hazard and applying the brakes. It depends on the driver's reaction time and the speed of the car.

$$\text{thinking distance} = \text{speed} \times \text{reaction time}$$

When the speed doubles, the thinking distance is doubled.

Braking distance is the distance travelled while braking to a stop. The deceleration depends on:

- the friction, which depends on road conditions such as the road surface and whether it is wet or dry, and the condition of the tyres and brakes
- the mass of the car, passengers, and luggage.

The braking distance depends on (speed)^2. You will learn more about this in P4.4A.

Stopping distance is the distance travelled between the driver seeing a hazard and the car being stationary.

$$\text{stopping distance} = \text{thinking distance} + \text{braking distance}$$

Car safety features

When a car travels at 100 km/h, the driver and passengers are also travelling at that speed. If the car comes to a sudden stop in a collision, the occupants experience a very rapid deceleration. A large force is needed to produce the large change in momentum. This sudden change in their momentum could cause serious injury.

Worked examples: Road safety

Key words

➤ reaction time
➤ thinking distance
➤ braking distance
➤ stopping distance

At 13 m/s (30 mph), in the Highway Code, *the thinking distance is given as 9 m.*

1 *What is the reaction time?*

Step 1: Write down what you know, with the units. Convert to standard units.

speed v = 13 m/s

distance travelled s = 9 m

Step 2: Write down the equation that relates speed, distance, and time.

$$v = \frac{s}{t}$$

Step 3: Rearrange the equation to make time t the subject.

$$vt = \frac{st}{t}$$

• multiply both sides by t.

$$vt = s$$

• divide both sides by v.

$$\frac{vt}{v} = \frac{s}{v}$$

$$t = \frac{s}{v}$$

Step 4: Substitute the quantities into the equation and calculate the time. Include the units in your answer.

$$t = \frac{9 \text{ m}}{13 \text{ m/s}} = 0.69 \text{ s}$$

Answer:

time = 0.69 s

2 *What is the thinking distance at 26 m/s (60 mph)?*

Step: Use proportional reasoning.

Thinking distance depends on speed.
Speed is twice as large, so
thinking distance × 2 = 2 × 9 m = **18 m**

3 *The braking distance at 13 m/s is 14 m. Estimate the braking distance at 26 m/s.*

Step: Use proportional reasoning.

Braking distance depends on (speed)².
speed × 2 gives braking distance × 4
braking distance = 4 × 14 m = **56 m**

This crash dummy, Hybrid 111, has experienced many crashes. It is packed with sensing equipment to record forces on different areas, such as the head, chest, and neck. Each dummy costs more than £100 000 to build.

Crumple zones

Look at the diagram below. Which car would be safer in a collision?

a   b

Would you be safer in car **a** or car **b**?

Change of momentum reasoning

In a collision, the car suddenly stops. Its momentum is then zero. The size of the average force exerted on the car during the collision depends on the time the collision lasts:

> change of momentum = average force × time for which it acts

For the same change of momentum, the bigger the time, the smaller the average force. If a collision takes place over 0.5 s instead of 0.05 s, the force is only one-tenth of the size.

This is why cars are fitted with front and rear **crumple zones**, with a rigid box in the middle. The crumple zones are designed to crumple gradually in a collision. This makes the duration of the collision longer, so the average force exerted on the car is less.

The occupants of the car were moving at the same speed as the car and are suddenly brought to a stop. A force exerted on their bodies (by whatever they come into contact with) causes this change of momentum. The longer the time it takes to change a passenger's speed to zero, the smaller the average force they will experience.

So you are safer in car **a**.

Force and acceleration reasoning

Consider the time the collision lasts and the deceleration that takes place.

The size of the force on a car, and on the occupants, is:

$$average\ force = mass \times acceleration$$

$$acceleration = \frac{change\ in\ velocity}{time\ taken\ for\ the\ change}$$

To keep the average force small, the deceleration must be small. So the time for the change must be as large as possible. The answer is the same: car **a** is safer. These are two different ways of explaining the same effect.

Seat belts, crash helmets, and air bags

Some people think that seat belts work by stopping you moving in a crash. In fact, to work, a seat belt has to stretch. As the seat belt stretches the driver moves forward, but more slowly than without a seat belt. This makes the change of momentum take longer, so the average force is less. A crash helmet works in the same way. As the helmet deforms, it increases the time it takes for your head to stop, so the force is less.

Key word

➤ crumple zone

With a seat belt, the top half of your body still moves forward, and you may hit yourself against parts of the car. Air bags increase the time it takes to reduce your momentum, reducing the average force you experience.

Could you save yourself?

Some people think they could survive a car accident without a seat belt, especially if they are travelling in the back seat. When a car travelling at 13 m/s (30 mph) has an impact, without a seat belt the driver hits the steering wheel and windscreen about 0.07 s after the impact. Back-seat passengers hit the back of the front seats at roughly the same time. Your reaction time is typically about 0.14 s, so this would happen before you had time to react. And the force needed to change your speed from 13 m/s to zero in 0.07 s is larger than your arms or legs could possibly exert.

Safety and risk

Car safety features, such as seat belts, are designed to reduce the risk of injury in a car accident. Travel can never be made completely safe. We cannot reduce the risk to zero. But many studies in different countries have shown that wearing seat belts greatly reduces the risk of serious injury. Many countries have laws requiring drivers and passengers to use seat belts.

Questions

1 When you jump down from a wall, it is a good idea to bend your knees as you land. Explain why this reduces the risk of injury.

2 In railway stations, there are buffers at the end of the track. These are designed to stop the train if the brakes fail. The buffers are compressed when the train hits them. Explain how this would reduce the forces acting on the train and on the passengers.

3 Look at the pictures on the left.
   a Estimate how long it takes for the driver to move to the position furthest forward.
   b His mass is 70 kg. His speed before the collision was 14 m/s. Calculate the average force that the belt exerts.

4 A recent survey found that 95% of front-seat passengers wear seat belts. But only 69% of adult back-seat passengers wear a seat belt, though 96% of child back-seat passengers do.
   a Suggest why a few front-seat passengers do not wear a seat belt, despite the evidence that it reduces the risk of death.
   b Suggest why a higher proportion of children wear seat belts.

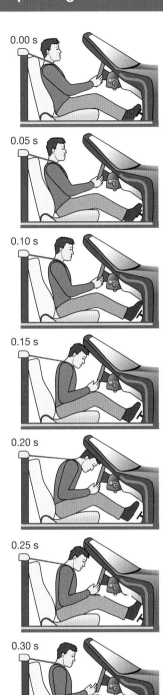

0.00 s
0.05 s
0.10 s
0.15 s
0.20 s
0.25 s
0.30 s

The pictures show what happens to a driver wearing a seat belt in a collision. Notice how the seat belt stretches.

A: Work done

Find out about

- how to calculate the work done by a force
- the link between work done on an object and the energy transferred
- using energy ideas to predict the motion of objects

When you push a trolley it speeds up. Its kinetic energy increases. You are doing work.

When you push something and start it moving, your push transfers energy to the kinetic store of the moving object. The energy of a moving object is called **kinetic energy**.

Work

In physics, the word '**work**' has a special meaning. When a force makes something move, it transfers energy to the moving object. We say the force 'does work'.

When you push a trolley you do more work if:

- it is hard to push
- you have to push it a long way.

The amount of work W a force does depends on:

- the size of the force F
- the distance s the object moves in the direction of the force.

The equation for calculating the amount of work done by a force is:

work done by a force (J) = force (N) × distance moved in the direction of the force (m)

$$W = Fs$$

We can use this to find the amount of energy transferred by a force, because:

amount of energy transferred = amount of work done by the force

Energy and work are both measured in joules (J). A force of 1 N applied over a distan.ce of 1 m does 1 J of work, and transfers 1 J of energy.

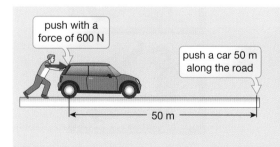

push with a force of 600 N

push a car 50 m along the road

50 m

Worked example: Calculating work done

Calculate how much work is needed to push a car 50 m along a road using a force of 600 N.

work done = force × distance moved in direction of force

= 600 N × 50 m

work done = 30 000 J

Key words

➤ kinetic energy
➤ work
➤ proportional

Not working

When you push an object but cannot get it to move, you feel that you are doing work! However, from the physics point of view, you are not doing work because the force you are applying is not moving anything. Holding a heavy object also feels like work, but the force you are applying is not making it move, so you are not doing any work.

Calculating kinetic energy

The equation for calculating the kinetic energy (KE) of a moving object is:

kinetic energy (J) = ½ × mass (kg) × (speed (m/s))^2

$$KE = \tfrac{1}{2}mv^2$$

Worked example: Calculating kinetic energy

1 *Calculate the kinetic energy of an 800 kg car travelling at 13 m/s (30 mph).*

Step 1: Write down what you know, with the units. Convert to standard units.

> mass m = 800 kg
> speed v = 13 m/s

Step 2: Write down the equation you will use to calculate the kinetic energy.

> kinetic energy = ½ × mass × (speed)^2
> KE = $\tfrac{1}{2}mv^2$

Step 3: Substitute the quantities into the equation and calculate the kinetic energy. Include the units in your answer.

> KE = $\tfrac{1}{2}$ × 800 kg × (13 m/s)^2
> = 400 kg × 169 (m/s)^2

Answer:

> **KE = 67 600 J**

2 *Calculate the kinetic energy of the same car travelling at twice the speed, 26 m/s (60 mph).*

Step 1: Substitute the quantities into the equation and calculate the kinetic energy. Include the units in your answer.

> KE = $\tfrac{1}{2}$ × 800 kg × (26 m/s)^2
> = 400 kg × 676 (m/s)^2

Answer:

> **KE = 270 400 J**

3 *Compare the kinetic energy of the car at 13 m/s and at 26 m/s.*

Step 1: Write down what you know, with the units.

> v = 13 m/s   KE = 67 600 J
> v = 26 m/s   KE = 270 400 J

Step 2: When you are asked to compare numbers, look for patterns in the data – for example, compare the ratios.

> ratio of speeds: $\dfrac{26\ m/s}{13\ m/s} = 2$
>
> ratio of KE: $\dfrac{270\ 400\ J}{67\ 600\ J} = 4$

Answer:

> When the speed *doubles*, the kinetic energy *quadruples*.

The kinetic energy of a moving object is **proportional** to its mass, but depends on its speed squared.

This is why the braking distance of a car depends on (speed)^2.

> work done by the force of the brakes = decrease in kinetic energy

> braking force × braking distance = ½ × mass × (speed)^2

Synoptic link

You can learn more about braking distance in P4.3E *Travelling safely.*

Making things speed up: changing their kinetic energy

When Dillon does work pushing a trolley along a level floor, the trolley speeds up. He transfers stored energy from his body to the trolley, where it is stored as kinetic energy.

If the trolley had no friction, the work done would equal the increase in kinetic energy. A real trolley always has friction, so some energy is dissipated through heating the wheels and surroundings. The energy transferred to the kinetic store of the trolley will be less than the work done on it.

Lifting things: gravitational potential energy

When you lift a bag into the car boot you do work against the weight of the bag. You are transferring stored energy from your body to increase the gravitational store of the bag and of the Earth, also called the **gravitational potential energy (GPE)** of the bag. The increase is equal to the amount of work you have done.

work done = force × distance moved in the direction of the force, so:

GPE = work done in lifting load

work done = weight × vertical height difference

You know that weight = mass × gravitational field strength, so you can calculate a change in **GPE** from the equation:

gravitational potential energy (J) = mass (kg) × gravitational field strength (N/kg) × vertical height difference (m)

$$GPE = mgh$$

Notice that it is the *vertical* height difference that matters when you lift something. If you slide a suitcase up a ramp, the gain in gravitational potential energy is the same as if you lift it vertically.

I have to exert an upward lift force of just over 300 N to lift the suitcase.

1m

weight = 300 N

Worked example: Calculating gravitational potential energy

A suitcase has a mass of 30 kg. Calculate the increase in gravitational potential energy when you lift it 1.2 m up into the boot of a car. (gravitational field strength = 10 N/kg)

Step 1: Write down what you know, with the units. Convert to standard units.

mass m = 30 kg
height h = 1.2 m
gravitational field strength g = 10 N/kg

Step 2: Write down the equation you will use to calculate GPE.

$GPE = mgh$

Step 3: Substitute the quantities into the equation and calculate the GPE. Include the units in your answer.

$GPE = 30\ kg \times 10\ N/kg \times 1.2\ m$
$GPE = 360\ J$

Answer:

increase in GPE = 360 J

Doing work by lifting: increasing the gravitational potential energy of weights.

Conservation of energy

When something falls through a height difference, or slides down a ramp, the amount of gravitational potential energy stored in the system decreases, and the kinetic energy of the moving object increases. If friction is small enough to be ignored:

decrease in gravitational potential energy = increase in kinetic energy

And the opposite happens when you lift an object:

increase in gravitational potential energy = decrease in kinetic energy

This doesn't depend on the shape of the path the object follows. For example, as a rollercoaster goes around the track, gravitational potential energy is changing to kinetic energy (on the down slopes) and kinetic energy is changing to gravitational potential energy (on the up slopes).

If the slope has a complicated shape, it is very difficult to work out how fast the rollercoaster is going at the bottom of the slope using ideas of force and momentum. It is much easier to use the principle of conservation of energy that you met in P2.1C.

Worked example: Calculations using conservation of energy

Calculate the speed of this rollercoaster at the bottom of the ride (assuming there are no friction forces).

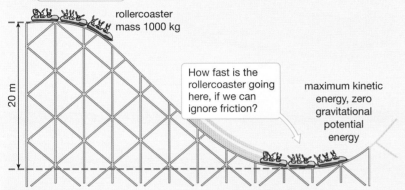

maximum gravitational potential energy, zero kinetic energy

The rollercoaster is stationary here.

rollercoaster mass 1000 kg

20 m

How fast is the rollercoaster going here, if we can ignore friction?

maximum kinetic energy, zero gravitational potential energy

On a down slope, gravitational potential energy decreases and kinetic energy increases. On an up slope, gravitational potential energy increases and kinetic energy decreases.

Step 1: Write down what you know, with the units.	mass m = 1000 kg height h = 20 m gravitational field strength g = 10 N/kg
Step 2: Use the principle of conservation of energy.	If friction is small enough to ignore, energy is conserved. decrease in GPE = increase in KE
Step 3: Write down the equation you will use to calculate the GPE.	GPE = mgh
Step 4: Substitute the quantities into the equation and calculate the GPE.	GPE = 1000 kg × 10 N/kg × 20 m GPE = 200 000 J
Step 5: Write down the equation for kinetic energy and use the values you have to calculate the speed at the bottom.	decrease in GPE = increase in KE KE = $\frac{1}{2}mv^2$ KE = GPE = 200 000 J so $\frac{1}{2}mv^2$ = 200 000 J $\frac{1}{2}$ × 1000 kg × v^2 = 200 000 J 500 kg × v^2 = 200 000 J $\frac{500 \text{ kg} \times v^2}{500 \text{ kg}} = \frac{200\,000 \text{ J}}{500 \text{ kg}}$ v^2 = 400 (m/s)² v = 20 m/s
Answer:	speed = 20 m/s

Questions

1 Esme has a mass of 55 kg. How much work does she do to go upstairs, a vertical height gain of 2.5 m?

2 A mother is pushing a child along in a buggy *at a steady speed*. She is doing work. Energy stored in her body is being transferred.
   a What force is she working against?
   b Where is the energy stored after the transfer?

3 Which of the following has more kinetic energy:
   A a car of mass 500 kg travelling at 20 m/s *or*
   B a car of mass 1000 kg travelling at 10 m/s?

4 a Repeat the calculation opposite for a rollercoaster that is only half as heavy (weight 5000 N).
   b What do you notice about its speed at the bottom? How would you explain this?

B: Power

Find out about

- the power output when work is done
- the link between mechanical power output and the power of electrical appliances

Key word

➤ power

In P2.1B you learnt that **power** is the rate at which an electrical appliance transfers energy. But it is not only electrical appliances that transfer energy.

The power of machines

Two cars may have the same mass and top speed, but one may accelerate from 0 to 100 km/h in a shorter time. It has a greater power output.

Two high-performance cars have the same top speed. They have the same mass, 1900 kg, and when they both accelerate from 0 to 100 km/h (or 28 m/s), they do the same work.

But compare their power outputs. The first car takes 2.5 s while the second takes 3.4 s to reach 100 km/h. So the first car has a greater power output – it does the work in a shorter time.

Power is the rate at which work is done in a system.

$$\text{power} = \frac{\text{work done}}{\text{time taken}}$$

The work done is the same as the energy transferred, so this equation is the same as the one you have already met in P2.1B:

$$\text{power} = \frac{\text{energy transferred}}{\text{time taken}}$$

The unit of power is the watt, W. 1 W = 1 J/s.

Human power

You can estimate your own power by running upstairs. Time yourself and measure your mass and the height of the stairs. Here's how to calculate your power.

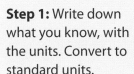

Estimating human power. These are the measurements you need to make.

Worked example: Calculating power

A girl with mass of 60 kg runs up 12 m of stairs in 15 s. Calculate her power.

Step 1: Write down what you know, with the units. Convert to standard units.

mass m = 60 kg
height h = 12 m
gravitational field strength g = 10 N/kg
time t = 15 s

Step 2: Write down the equation you will use to calculate the power.

$$\text{power } P = \frac{\text{energy transferred}}{\text{time taken}} = \frac{mgh}{t}$$

Step 3: Substitute the quantities into the equation and calculate the power. Include the units in your answer.

$$P = \frac{60 \text{ kg} \times 10 \text{ N/kg} \times 12 \text{ m}}{15 \text{ s}} = \frac{7200 \text{ J}}{15 \text{ s}} = 480 \text{ W}$$

Answer: power = 480 W

Questions

Gravitational field strength = 10 m/s^2

1 A motor is used to pull crates a distance of 12 m with a force of 890 N in 22 s. Calculate its output power.

2 a How long will it take a crane with power output of 25 kW to lift a 5000 kg mass through 20 m?
b How far will it lift a 1000 kg mass in 10 s?

3 For each of the two cars described on the opposite page, calculate:
a the kinetic energy at 28 m/s
b the output power when accelerating to this speed.

4 A lift in the Shanghai tower went up 557 m at a speed of 18 m/s.
a How long did it take?
b Calculate the power required if it was lifting 2000 kg.

Shanghai tower in China is one of the tallest buildings in the world. It has some of the world's fastest lifts, rising 557 m at a maximum speed of 18 m/s. They can carry a load of 2000 kg.

Science explanations

P4 Explaining motion

Forces and motion form the basis of our understanding of how the world works. In this chapter you have seen how a few simple rules (or laws) explain every example of motion we observe. These laws are so exact and precise that they can be used to predict the motion of an object very accurately.

You should know:

- about the interaction pair of forces that always arise when two objects interact, including examples of how gravitational, electrostatic, magnetic, and contact forces produce a force on each object
- that vehicles, and people, move by pushing back on something, and this interaction causes a forward force to act on them
- about the normal contact force on an object that arises because it pushes down on a surface
- that the resultant force on an object is the sum of all the individual forces acting on it, taking their directions into account
- the relationship between mass and weight
- how to calculate the average speed of a moving object, and the values of some typical everyday speeds
- what is meant by distance, displacement, speed, velocity, and acceleration
- how to draw and interpret distance–time, speed–time, and velocity–time graphs
- how to calculate the acceleration of an object
- the acceleration of free fall and how to calculate values of everyday accelerations
- how to find acceleration from the gradient of a velocity–time graph
- **H** that when a resultant force acts on an object, it causes a change in momentum
- how to use scale drawings of vector diagrams to find the resultant force on an object when two or more forces act
- how to calculate momentum and the change in momentum due to a force
- that many vehicle safety features increase the duration of an event (such as a collision), to reduce the deceleration and average force for the same change of momentum
- **H** that if there is no resultant force on an object, its momentum does not change – it either remains stationary or keeps moving at a steady speed in a straight line
- the relationship between inertial mass, force, and acceleration
- how to measure reaction time
- factors that affect the stopping distance of a moving vehicle
- about the work done when a force moves an object and how to calculate the work done, which is equal to the energy transferred
- that when work is done on an object, energy is transferred to the object and when work is done by an object, energy is transferred from the object to something else
- about kinetic energy, how to calculate it, and that doing work on an object can increase its kinetic energy by making it move faster
- about gravitational potential energy and how to calculate the change in gravitational potential energy as an object is raised or lowered.

Ideas about Science

In addition to understanding forces and motion, you need to understand how scientific explanations are developed. The list below links these ideas about science with some examples from the chapter.

In developing scientific explanations you should be able to do the following.

- Identify statements that are data and statements that are explanations. For example, the statement 'The acceleration of a falling object has a constant value' is data; the statement 'When a constant force acts on an object it causes a constant acceleration' is an explanation.

- Identify where creative thinking is involved in the development of an explanation. For example, the idea of an interaction pair of forces says that when you push on a wall, the wall pushes back. This is not an obvious idea, but Isaac Newton suggested this as his third law of motion: action and reaction are equal and opposite.

- Give good reasons for accepting or rejecting a scientific explanation. For example, Aristotle believed that heavier objects always fall faster than light objects. A good reason for rejecting this would be a slow-motion film of objects falling in a vacuum – they fall at the same speed.

- Understand that when a prediction agrees with an observation, this increases confidence in the explanation on which the prediction is based (although it does not *prove* it is correct). For example, Newton's laws of motion have correctly predicted the behaviour of many moving objects.

- Understand that when a prediction disagrees with an observation, this indicates that either the prediction or the observation is wrong. It decreases confidence in the explanation on which the prediction is based. For example, observations do not support Aristotle's ideas about motion.

You should be able to relate examples of the way forces affect motion to technological developments, and the benefits and risks of these developments. In thinking about how science and technology impact on society, you should be able to:

- identify examples of risks from early transport systems and how science is used to reduce those risks; for example, early cars did not have crumple zones or seat belts

- interpret information about the size of given risks and suggest reasons why people are willing to accept some risks, but not others; for example, some people choose to cycle in cities, while others do not

- discuss public regulation of risk and explain why the regulation may be controversial in some situations; for example, when seat belts were first introduced many people objected to being told to use them.

P4 Review questions

1 A tin of beans on a kitchen shelf is not falling, even though gravity is acting on it. The shelf exerts an upward force, which balances the force of gravity. Explain in a short paragraph how it is possible for a shelf to exert a force. Draw a sketch diagram if it helps your explanation.

2 *Philae* is a small spacecraft that landed on Comet 67P in November 2014. The mass of the spacecraft was 100 kg. The gravitational field strength of the comet was estimated to be 10^{-3} N/kg. The gravitational field strength on the Earth is 10 N/kg.

  a Calculate the weight of *Philae* when it was on Earth.

  b Calculate the weight of *Philae* when it landed on the comet.

  c Explain why the spacecraft weighs much less on the comet.

3 Think about the following situations.

  i Amjad on his skateboard, throwing a heavy ball to his friend (main objects to consider: Amjad and the ball)

  ii a furniture remover trying to pull a piano across the floor, but it will not move (main objects to consider: the furniture remover and the piano)

  iii a hanging basket of flowers outside a café (main objects to consider: the basket and the chain it is hanging from)

  For each situation:

  a Sketch a diagram (looking at it from the side).

  b Sketch separate free-body force diagrams for each of the main objects in the situation.

  c On these separate diagrams, draw arrows to show the forces acting on that object. Use the length of the arrow to show how big each force is.

  d Write a label beside each arrow to show what the force is.

4 a The winner of a 50 m swimming event completes the distance in 80 s. What is his average speed?

  b How far could Leonie cycle in 10 minutes if her average speed is 8 m/s?

  c The average speed of a bus in city traffic is 5 m/s. How much time should the timetable allow for the bus to cover a 6 km route?

5 a A bus leaves a bus stop and reaches a speed of 15 m/s in 10 s. Calculate its acceleration.

  b A car accelerates at 3 m/s^2 for 8 s. By how much will its speed have increased?

6 A sports car accelerates from 0 to 222 km/h while travelling 400 m.

  a Convert 222 km/h to m/s.

  b Calculate the average acceleration of the car.

7 The car in question **6** is reported to accelerate from 0 to 240 km/h in 12.8 s, and from 0 to 320 km/h in 28 s. Suggest why the increase from 240 km/h to 320 km/h takes longer than the increase from 0 to 240 km/h.

8

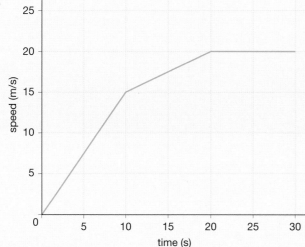

The graph shows a simplified picture of how the speed of a car changed during the first 30 s of a journey.

a Explain how you can tell that the graph is not a true picture of the journey.

b Describe the journey, giving as much detail as you can about each stage.

H **c** Calculate the distance travelled during the 30 s.

H

9 What is the momentum of:

a a hockey ball of mass 0.4 kg moving at 5 m/s?

b a jogger of mass 55 kg running at 4 m/s?

c a van of mass 10 000 kg travelling at 15 m/s?

d a car ferry of mass 20 000 000 kg moving at 0.5 m/s?

10 A jet engine takes in air, which is heated and compressed and then pushed out (discharged) at a much greater speed. This give the engine thrust.

Every second the engine takes in 40 kg of air at a speed of 100 m/s. This air is discharged at 450 m/s.

a Calculate the momentum of the air that is taken in.

b Calculate the momentum of the air when it is discharged.

c Calculate the change in momentum of the air every second.

d What is the thrust of the engine in kN?

11 A weightlifter raises a bar of mass 50 kg until it is above her head – a total height gain of 2.2 m.

a How much gravitational potential energy has it gained?

b How much more work must she do to hold it there for 5 s?

c She drops the weight from a height of 1 m. How fast will it be moving when it hits the floor?

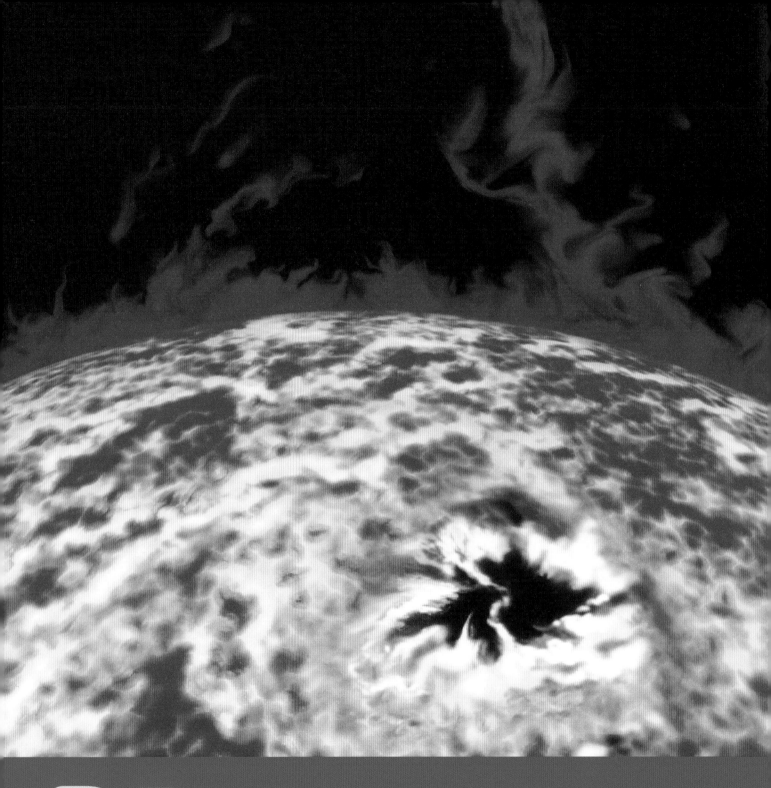

P5 Radioactive materials

Why study radioactive materials?

People make jokes about radioactivity. If you have hospital treatment with radiation, they may say you will 'glow in the dark'. Radiation can be very dangerous, but people may worry about radioactivity when they don't need to.

What questions should we ask if we are offered hospital treatment that involves ionising radiation?

What you already know

- Some materials naturally emit gamma rays.
- Gamma rays are ionising radiation.
- Ionising radiation can damage living cells.
- Nuclear power stations produce radioactive waste.
- Contamination by a radioactive material is more dangerous than a short period of irradiation.

The Science

The discovery of radioactivity changed ideas about matter and atoms. The nuclear model of the atom helped scientists explain many observations – including radioactivity, and why stars are so hot and bright. Having a model for how the atom behaves enables scientists to make and test predictions. It has led to technological advances in how scientists use ionising radiation.

Ideas about Science

Radioactive materials are used in many applications. To make decisions about how they are used we need to assess the balance of risks and benefits.

A: Why are some materials radioactive?

Find out about

- radioactive decay
- what makes an atom radioactive
- types of radiation

Uranium ore. Uranium is used as a fuel in nuclear power stations.

This scientist is measuring the radioactivity of the fruit from plants grown with radioactive water. The radioactive isotope is being used as a tracer.

What do these elements have in common?

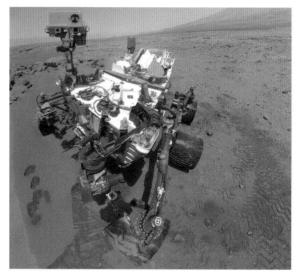

Curiosity, the Mars Science Laboratory, is powered by plutonium. Energy from the element's radioactive decay is used to power the rover and keep its systems within a certain temperature range.

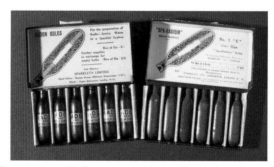

Radon is a radioactive gas. Radium is a radioactive metal. In the early 1900s, people used these bulbs to make drinking water radioactive. They thought it was good for their health.

The **elements** in the photographs on this page are all **radioactive**. If you hold a Geiger counter near them you will hear it click.

When radioactivity was first discovered, people did not know that the radiation was **ionising** and could damage or kill living cells. They thought that it was natural and healthy. Manufacturers made all kinds of products using radioactive materials. When the danger was recognised, the products were banned. Safety rules for using radioactive materials were introduced.

Some radioactive elements occur naturally, and others are man-made. Some man-made radioactive materials are waste products, such as waste from nuclear power stations. Many man-made elements are produced because they are useful. For example, the plants in the photograph have been watered with water that contains radioactive hydrogen. This allows the scientist to work out how the hydrogen is used in the plant to make other substances.

Changes inside the atom

Many elements have more than one type of atom. For example, some carbon atoms are different from the usual type of carbon atom. In most ways they are identical to other carbon atoms, but they are radioactive. All types of carbon atom can:

- make up coal, diamond, or graphite
- combine with oxygen, when carbon-containing substances burn, to form carbon dioxide
- form part of complex molecules that are found in plants and animals.

Radioactive decay

The main difference between the different types of carbon atom is that most carbon atoms do not change. They are stable. But radioactive carbon atoms randomly give out energetic radiation. Each atom does this only once. What is left afterwards is not carbon, but a different element (nitrogen).

The process is called **radioactive decay**. It is not a chemical change; it is a change *inside* the atom.

What makes an atom radioactive?

At the core of every atom is its nucleus. In some atoms, the nucleus is **unstable**. The atom decays to become more stable. It emits energetic radiation and the nucleus changes. The energy released in this process is used in *nuclear reactors*, in *nuclear medicine*, and in *nuclear weapons*.

Four types of radiation are emitted, called **alpha**, **beta**, **gamma**, and **neutron**.

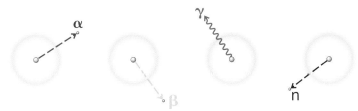

It is the unstable nucleus of an atom that makes it radioactive and that emits the radiation.

Radioactive decay happens in the nucleus of an atom. It is not affected by any physical or chemical changes that happen to the atom.

A cut diamond sitting on a lump of coal. Each of these is made of carbon atoms. Some of the atoms are radioactive.

Key words

- ➤ element
- ➤ radioactive
- ➤ ionising radiation
- ➤ radioactive decay
- ➤ unstable
- ➤ alpha
- ➤ beta
- ➤ gamma
- ➤ neutron

Radiation	What it is
alpha (α)	small, high-speed particle with +2 charge
beta (β)	much smaller, higher-speed particle with −1 charge
gamma (γ)	high-energy electromagnetic radiation
neutron (n)	small, high-energy particle with 0 charge

Making gold

When radioactive platinum decays it turns into a new element – gold. A good way to make money?

No. The price of gold is only half the price of platinum.

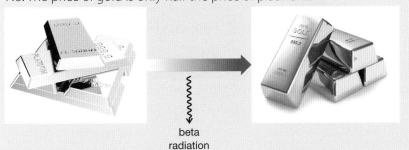

beta radiation

Questions

1 How can you test to find out if something is radioactive?

2 Why is ionising radiation dangerous?

3 What part of the atom does the radiation come from?

4 Name the four different types of radiation from radioactive materials.

B: What is an atom?

Find out about

- models of the atom
- how alpha-particle scattering shows that the nucleus exists

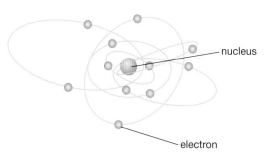

In the nuclear model of the atom, the electrons orbit the central nucleus at different distances.

Dalton's symbols for the elements, together with the masses he calculated. We now know that these substances are not all elements, and the mass values are not all correct, but his work was a great leap forward in understanding atoms.

You often see a diagram of an atom showing it as a miniature 'solar system', with the nucleus at the centre and electrons whizzing round like miniature planets.

In P1.1B we used the **nuclear model of the atom**. It helped us explain how radiation can cause atoms to lose an outer electron and become ionised. But what evidence do we have for that model?

Early models of the atom

People have wondered what matter is made of for thousands of years. Over 2000 years ago some Greek philosophers thought that matter is made of tiny particles which they called *atoms*, from the Greek word *atomon* meaning 'indivisible'. These philosophers did not do experiments; they developed their ideas through creative thinking.

In the early nineteenth century John Dalton, a teacher in Manchester, was doing experiments with gases and reading about the experiments other people were doing. Dalton wanted to explain how a single substance, such as water, could exist as a solid, a liquid, and a gas. He argued that the particles of a substance, such as water, must all be alike:

"In other words, every particle of water is like every other particle of water, every particle of hydrogen is like every other particle of hydrogen, &c."

Dalton went on to use experimental data to show that the particles of different elements had different masses. He suggested that the particles combined and rearranged themselves in chemical reactions.

The next step in understanding came towards the end of the nineteenth century. Scientists were investigating what happened when they applied a high voltage to a gas at very low pressure. J.J. Thomson, working in Cambridge, discovered particles that were negatively charged, much lighter than atoms, and appeared to have come from the metal cathode. He had discovered the electron. Thomson proposed a model that became known as the **plum-pudding model of the atom**.

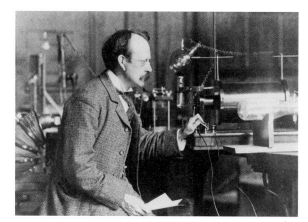

During the nineteenth century new technologies allowed Thomson to set up the high voltages and low gas pressures he needed. He discovered the electron using this apparatus.

Discovering the nucleus

Early in the twentieth century scientists had just discovered the radiation emitted by radioactive materials. Ernest Rutherford was working at Manchester University. He realised that alpha and beta particles were smaller than atoms. He thought they might be useful tools for probing the structure of atoms. So he designed a suitable experiment, and it was carried out by his assistants, Hans Geiger and Ernest Marsden.

Here is his plan for the experiment.

● Start with a metal foil. Use gold, because it can be rolled out very thinly, to a thickness of a few thousand atoms.

● Direct a source of alpha radiation at the foil. Do this in a vacuum chamber, so that the alpha particles are not stopped by air.

● Use a microscope to view what happens. Look through a screen made of a material that emits a flash of light when an alpha particle hits it.

● Work all night, counting the flashes at different angles. This will show how much the alpha radiation is deflected from its path by the thin gold foil.

Results and interpretation

This is what Geiger and Marsden observed.

● Most of the alpha particles passed straight through the gold foil, deflected by no more than a few degrees.

● A small fraction of the alpha particles were reflected back towards the direction from which they had come. They were back-scattered.

This is what Rutherford said:

'It was as if, on firing a bullet at a sheet of tissue paper, the bullet were to bounce back at you!'

Fewer than one alpha particle in 8000 were back-scattered, but this still needed an explanation.

Rutherford realised that there must be something with a lot of mass, or the alpha particles would just push it out of the way. Rutherford assumed the mass was charged. He used a mathematical model to predict how many particles would be deflected at different angles. He assumed the large massive nucleus would be positive, because electrons are negative.

His analysis of the data showed that the nucleus is very tiny, because most alpha particles went straight past without being affected by it. The diameter of the nucleus is roughly $\frac{1}{100\,000}$ times the diameter of the atom. This nucleus contains all the atom's positive charge, and most of its mass.

Rutherford's nuclear model is a good example of a scientist using creative modelling to develop an explanation of the data.

In the plum pudding model the tiny negative electrons are spread throughout a positive atom.

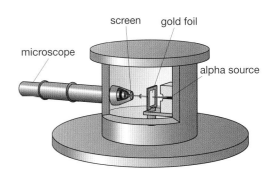

Rutherford's experiment. An alpha particle striking the screen gives a tiny flash of light. The distance from the alpha source to the gold foil was a few centimetres.

Key words

➤ nuclear model of the atom
➤ plum-pudding model of the atom

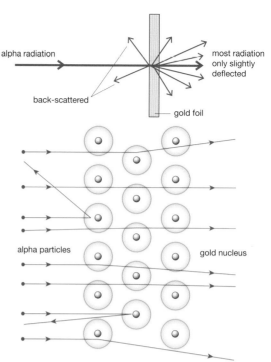

alpha radiation

most radiation only slightly deflected

back-scattered

gold foil

alpha particles

gold nucleus

Questions

1 What sort of charge do the following have?
   a the atomic nucleus
   b alpha radiation
   c electrons

2 List these in order, from least mass to greatest mass: gold atom, alpha particle, gold nucleus, electron.

3 In Rutherford's experiment, describe and explain what happened to alpha particles that were directed:
   a straight towards a gold nucleus
   b slightly to one side of a gold nucleus
   c midway between two nuclei.

4 Suggest how the results would be different if the nucleus:
   a was positive but very large
   b was negative and very small.

5 a Write down the size of a hydrogen atom in nm.
   b Estimate the size of a hydrogen nucleus in nm.

Only alpha particles passing close to a nucleus are deflected much. Those alpha particles are scattered through a large angle, back towards their original path. These diagrams are not to scale. Imagine the lower diagram drawn with the nuclei only $\frac{1}{100\,000}$ times the size of the atoms.

Just how small?

Atoms are not hard spheres like billiard balls, so the diameter of an atom is only an approximate measure of the space it takes up. For this reason we talk about sizes of atoms in **orders of magnitude** – to the nearest power of 10.

The smallest atom, helium, is about 10^{-10} m across.

A potassium atom, with 10 times the mass of the helium atom, is about 5×10^{-10} m across.

Molecules are bigger, with some complex molecules being as much as 100 nm across.

Still searching

Today, scientists are searching for even smaller subatomic particles. They use particle accelerators such as the Large Hadron Collider to smash atoms up. They examine the debris to learn more about subatomic particles.

1804
Dalton's solid atom.

1913
The Bohr–Rutherford 'Solar System' atom, in which electrons orbit around a very small nucleus.

1924
A model of the atom in which the electrons are no longer treated as particles but pictured as occupying energy levels, which give rise to regions of negative charge around the nucleus (charge clouds).

1932
The atom in which the nucleus is built up from neutrons as well as protons.

2000+
The present-day atom in which the protons and neutrons in the nucleus are built up from many kinds of particles.

Atomic models from 1800 to the present. The diameter of an atom is about ten million times smaller than a millimetre. These diagrams are distorted. For atoms at this scale, the nuclei would be invisibly small.

C: Inside the atom

Atoms are small – about $\frac{1}{10\,000\,000}$ mm across. Apart from the orbiting electrons, the rest of the atom is empty space. Most of an atom's mass is concentrated in a tiny core, called a nucleus.

The tiny nucleus in an atom is as small as a pinhead would be in a stadium.

Find out about

- isotopes
- protons and neutrons
- alpha and beta particles

Key words

➤ proton
➤ neutron
➤ isotope
➤ proton number
➤ nucleon number

Isotopes

The tiny nucleus contains two types of particle: **protons** and **neutrons**. The atoms of a particular element all have the same number of protons. For example, all carbon atoms have six protons. But they can have different numbers of neutrons. The word **isotope** is used to describe different atoms of the same element. Carbon-14 and carbon-12 are different isotopes of carbon.

Carbon-14 is radioactive and will emit radiation wherever it is – in diamond, coal, or graphite, or in a compound such as carbon dioxide. You can burn it or vaporise it and it will still be radioactive.

Subatomic particle	Symbol	Mass (kg)	Charge (C)
proton	p	1.7×10^{-27}	$+1.6 \times 10^{-19}$
neutron	n	1.7×10^{-27}	0
electron	e	9.1×10^{-31}	-1.6×10^{-19}

Subatomic particles – the particles that make up atoms.

Describing a nucleus

Scientists use a formula to describe an isotope: the chemical symbol for the element with two numbers in front of it. These are:

- the number of protons (called the **proton number**)
- the total number of particles (protons + neutrons) in the nucleus (called the **nucleon number**).

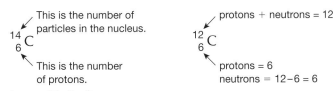

This is the number of particles in the nucleus.

$^{14}_{6}\text{C}$

This is the number of protons.

neutrons = 14−6 = 8
number of neutrons = number of particles in the nucleus − number of protons

protons + neutrons = 12

$^{12}_{6}\text{C}$

protons = 6
neutrons = 12−6 = 6

carbon-12   carbon-14

The nucleus of carbon-12 has six protons and six neutrons. Carbon-14 has 14 particles in its nucleus: six protons and eight neutrons.

α particle = $_2^4$He

An alpha particle has two protons and two neutrons.

Radioactive changes

Some nuclei that are unstable can become more stable by emitting an alpha particle. An alpha particle is made of two protons and two neutrons. It is the same as a helium nucleus.

Other nuclei become more stable when a neutron decays to form a proton. It does this by emitting a beta particle. A beta particle is the same as an electron, but it has come from a neutron in the nucleus. It is not one of the atom's orbital electrons.

Gamma radiation is high-energy electromagnetic radiation. It transfers energy from the nucleus, making it more stable without changing the element.

More rarely, a nucleus becomes more stable by emitting a neutron.

Counting the particles

Scientists use **nuclear equations** to work out what happens during radioactive decay.

Alpha emission

During alpha emission two protons are emitted, so the nucleus has changed to a new element. This process is called **transmutation**. When plutonium-240 decays, uranium-236 is formed.

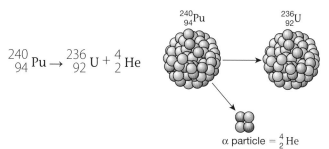

$$_{94}^{240}\text{Pu} \rightarrow \ _{92}^{236}\text{U} + \ _2^4\text{He}$$

Alpha emission. The nucleus emits two protons and two neutrons.

Beta emission

During beta emission the number of protons increases by one, so again a new element is formed. When carbon-14 decays, nitrogen-14 is formed. Nitrogen always has seven protons in the nucleus.

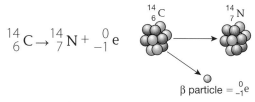

$$_6^{14}\text{C} \rightarrow \ _7^{14}\text{N} + \ _{-1}^0\text{e}$$

During beta emission, the proton number increases by one.

β particle

Beta emission. A neutron in the atom decays to a proton and an electron. The electron is a beta particle.

The emission of either an alpha or a beta particle from an unstable nucleus produces an atom of a different element, called a daughter product or decay product. The daughter product may itself be unstable. There may be a series of changes, but eventually a stable element is formed.

Neutron emission

Neutron emission occurs quite rarely in nature. It mainly occurs during a process called nuclear fission. During neutron emission, the number of protons does not change. The new nucleus is the same element, but a different isotope. Beryllium-13 decays to beryllium-12 by emitting a neutron.

$$^{13}_{4}\text{Be} \rightarrow {^{12}_{4}\text{Be}} + {^{0}_{1}\text{n}}$$

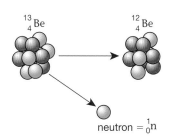

neutron $= {^{1}_{0}\text{n}}$

During neutron emission, the number of neutrons decreases by one.

Questions

1 **a** What is the mass of a proton to the nearest order of magnitude?
   b How many orders of magnitude heavier is the proton than the electron?

2 Consider these isotopes: carbon-12, boron-12, carbon-14, and nitrogen-14.
   a Which two are isotopes of the same element?
   b Which ones have the same number of particles in the nucleus?
   c Do any of them have identical nuclei?
   d A nucleus of carbon-11 has:
      i how many protons?
      ii how many neutrons?

3 Copy the table of isotopes below, and add three extra columns for:
   ● the total number of particles in the nucleus
   ● the number of neutrons in the isotope
   ● the chemical symbol for the isotope.
   Fill in these columns to complete the table.

Isotope	Number of protons	Radioactive?
hydrogen-1	1	
hydrogen-2	1	
hydrogen-3	1	✓
helium-3	2	✓
helium-4	2	
nitrogen-14	7	
uranium-235	92	✓
thorium-231	90	✓

4 Hydrogen-3 decays to helium-3 by beta emission. Write a nuclear equation for the decay.

5 Uranium-235 decays to thorium-231 by alpha emission. Write a nuclear equation for the decay.

6 Nitrogen-16 decays by beta emission. Write a nuclear equation for the decay.

Synoptic link

You can learn more about order-of-magnitude calculations in the *Maths skills* section at the end of the book.

Key words

➤ nuclear equation
➤ transmutation

D: Half-life

Find out about

- the half-life of radioactive materials
- radioactive dating

Key words

➤ random
➤ rate
➤ activity
➤ half-life

Radioactive decay is **random**. You can never tell which nucleus will decay next. Scientists can't predict whether a particular nucleus will decay today, or in 1000 years' time. But in a sample of radioactive material there are billions of atoms. This makes it easier to see a pattern in the decay.

The pattern of radioactive decay

The **rate** at which radiation is emitted from a radioactive material is called its **activity**. The unit for measuring activity is the becquerel (Bq). Activity decreases with time.

- At first there are a lot of radioactive atoms.

- At some (random) time each atom gives out radiation as it decays to become more stable.

- The activity of the material falls because fewer and fewer radioactive atoms remain.

Technetium-99m is a radioactive element used in medical scans. If a sample is injected into a patient at 9.00 a.m. then, on average, by 3.00 p.m. half of the nuclei will have decayed. At 9.00 p.m. half of the remaining nuclei will have decayed, leaving only one-quarter of the original sample. The **half-life** of technetium-99m is 6 hours. The half-life is the time it takes for the activity to drop by half. The table shows that after 24 hours (four half-lives), only one-sixteenth of the original sample remains.

The graph shows how the activity of the sample decreases. After 10 half-lives only about one-thousandth of the original sample remains. For technetium-99m this is only 2.5 days. The 6-hour half-life makes it an ideal isotope for this job. It lasts long enough for doctors to take scans using the decay, but it has almost all gone in a few days.

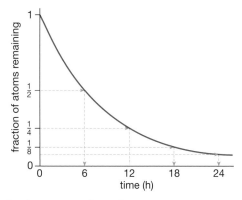

The decay curve for technetium-99m.

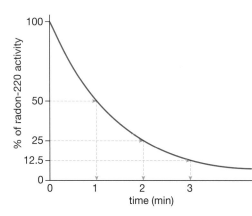

The decay curve for radon-220.

Time	Hours since injection	Number of half-lives	Fraction of original sample remaining
9.00 a.m.	0	0	1
3.00 p.m.	6	1	$\frac{1}{2}$
9.00 p.m.	12	2	$\frac{1}{4}$
3.00 a.m.	18	3	$\frac{1}{8}$
9.00 a.m.	24	4	$\frac{1}{16}$

The radioactive decay of technetium-99m.

Different half-lives

All radioactive materials show the same pattern of decay, but they have different half-lives. This graph shows the pattern of radioactive decay for radon-220. The amount of radiation halves every minute. The half-life of radon-220 is 1 minute.

Some radioactive elements decay slowly over thousands of millions of years. Others decay in milliseconds – less than the blink of an eye.

For a given amount of material, the shorter the half-life, the greater the activity. Neon-17 is the most active radioactive isotope in this table.

There is no way of slowing down or speeding up the rate at which radioactive materials decay.

Radioactive dating

There is carbon in all living things. A small proportion of all carbon is carbon-14. When a living thing dies, it stops exchanging carbon with the environment. The proportion of carbon-14 in all the carbon in its body will get less as the isotope decays. By measuring the proportion of carbon-14 left, scientists can work out the age of organic materials.

Isotope	Half-life
iridium-192	74 days
strontium-81	22 minutes
uranium-235	710 million years
neon-17	0.1 seconds

Half-lives vary greatly for different elements.

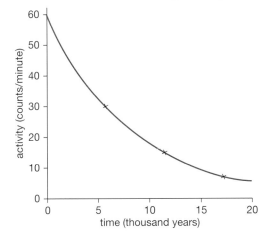

The decay curve for carbon-14.

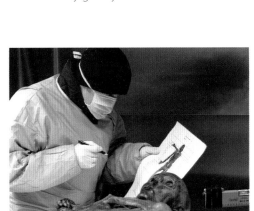

Radiocarbon dating was used to find the age of this mummified body. It was discovered embedded in ice in the Austrian Alps. The evidence suggests the 'Iceman' lived about 5000 years ago.

Questions

1 Look at the decay curve for carbon-14. It shows how the activity changes over time.
   a What is meant by the activity of a radioactive material?
   b Use the graph to explain what is meant by the half-life of carbon-14.
   c Use the graph to estimate the half-life of carbon-14. Show your working.
   d Suggest why radiocarbon dating cannot easily be used to find the age of objects:
      i less than 1000 years old
      ii more than 50 000 years old.

2 How long does it take for a sample of strontium-81 to decay to one-eighth of its original activity?

3 The activity of a neon-17 source is 1120 decays per second. What will the activity be after 0.5 s?

4 The activity of an iridium-192 sample is 9600 decays per second. How long will it take to fall to 2400 decays per second?

A: Properties of radioactive isotopes

Find out about

- properties of alpha, beta, and gamma radiation
- using ionising radiation

Key words

➤ irradiation
➤ contamination

Radioactive isotopes have many uses in industry and medicine. They are quite rare in nature – because most of them have decayed. So scientists have to make radioactive isotopes in nuclear reactors, or in accelerators, and prepare them for use in laboratories and hospitals around the country.

Alpha, beta, or gamma?

The choice of which radiation to use for a job depends on the properties of the radiation. A beam of alpha particles may be the best choice, or it might be beta particles, or gamma rays. To decide, scientists consider the properties described below.

Alpha radiation

Alpha particles are much heavier than beta particles, and they soon collide with molecules in the air. As they collide and cause ionisation, the alpha particles gradually slow down. Eventually, after ionising millions of molecules, they gain two electrons and become helium atoms.

Alpha particles are the least penetrating and are stopped most easily. Alpha particles are the most strongly ionising radiation.

Beta radiation

Beta particles are fast-moving electrons. They are much smaller than alpha particles, so are less likely to collide with other particles. This means they travel further in air and other materials and are less ionising than alpha partcles. When they have slowed down, they are just like any other electrons.

Gamma radiation

Sometimes, after a nucleus emits a beta particle, the protons and neutrons remaining in the new nucleus rearrange themselves to a lower energy state. When this happens the nucleus emits a photon of electromagnetic radiation called a gamma ray. This does not cause a change of element. The photons have more energy than most X-ray photons. They rarely collide with particles, so the radiation is very penetrating. It has only a very weak ionising effect.

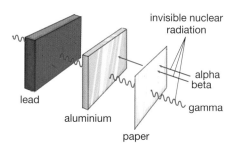

Radiation	Range in air	Stopped by:	Ionisation	Charge
alpha	a few cm	paper or dead cells on the surface of your skin	strong	+2
beta	10–15 cm	thin aluminium	weak	–1
gamma	many metres	very thick lead or several metres of concrete	very weak	no charge

Properties of ionising radiation.

Which isotope?

When choosing an isotope to provide ionising radiation for a particular job, the scientist needs to consider a number of factors, including:

- which isotopes emit the chosen radiation?
- does the isotope need to react chemically with other substances, such as in a plant or in a medical situation?
- what is the half-life of the isotope – does it need to last a long time, or would it be better to have something that decays to a low activity quickly?

There is more about choosing an isotope to provide radiation in medicine in P5.2C.

Sterilisation

As you learnt in P1.1B, ionising radiation has the energy to change molecules in living cells. This property is used to kill bacteria. Gamma radiation is used for sterilising surgical instruments and some hygiene products such as tampons. The products are first sealed from the air and then exposed to the radiation. This passes through the sealed packet and kills the bacteria inside.

Food can be treated in the same way. Irradiating food kills bacteria and prevents spoilage. Only certain types of **irradiated** food are allowed to be sold in the UK. The label must show that they have been treated with ionising radiation. This process is a useful alternative to heating or drying, because it does not affect the taste.

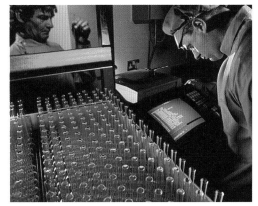
Gamma rays kill the bacteria on and inside these test tubes.

The logo shows that the herbs and spices have been irradiated with gamma radiation from cobalt-60. Gamma rays pass through the glass and kill any bacteria in the jar. Cobalt-60 does not pass into the jar – there is no **contamination**.

Uses of ionising radiation are linked to their properties.

Questions

1 Which type of radiation:
 a is the most penetrating?
 b is the most ionising?
 c has the longest range in air?

2 a Why are packets of surgical instruments sealed before sterilising them?
 b Does gamma radiation make the instruments radioactive? Explain your answer.

3 Smoke detectors used in homes contain a source that emits alpha particles.
 a Explain why these are not dangerous in normal use.
 b What might make them dangerous?
 c Explain whether a source with a long or a short half-life would be better for this use.

4 A scientist tests a radioactive source by placing it 2 cm away from a Geiger counter. She puts sheets of different materials in front of the source and records the count rate. The results are shown in the table. Which type, or types, of radiation does the source emit? Explain your reasoning.

Sheet added	Count rate (counts per second)
none	6.8
paper	4.9
aluminium 3 mm thick	4.7
lead 3 cm thick	0.5

B: Radiation all around

Find out about

- background radiation
- radiation dose and risk

Key words

- ➤ background radiation
- ➤ radiation dose
- ➤ exposure

If you switch on a Geiger counter, you will hear it click. It is picking up **background radiation**, which is all around you. Most background radiation comes from natural sources.

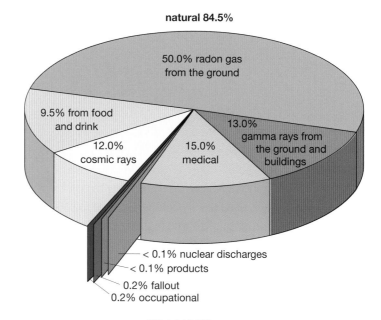

natural 84.5%

50.0% radon gas from the ground

9.5% from food and drink

12.0% cosmic rays

15.0% medical

13.0% gamma rays from the ground and buildings

< 0.1% nuclear discharges
< 0.1% products
0.2% fallout
0.2% occupational

artificial 15.5%

How different sources contribute to the average radiation dose in the UK. The UK average annual dose of radiation is 2.5 mSv.

Radiation dose

Radiation may cause chemical reactions that damage the body. If ionising radiation affects DNA molecules, this may cause the cell to die or to behave abnormally. Cells that behave abnormally can cause cancer.

The **radiation dose** measures the energy transferred when the ionising radiation is absorbed. Dose is related to the possible harm that radiation could do to the body. It is measured in millisieverts (mSv).

The UK average annual dose is 2.5 mSv. For an annual dose of 1000 mSv (400 times larger), three out of 100 people, on average, develop a cancer.

Ionising radiation from outer space is called cosmic radiation. Flying from the UK to Australia gives you a dose of 0.1 mSv, from cosmic rays. That's not much if you go on holiday, but it soon adds up for flight crews making repeated journeys.

What affects the radiation dose?

The dose measures the potential harm done by the radiation. It depends on:

- the amount of radiation – the number of alpha particles, beta particles, or gamma photons reaching the body
- the type of radiation. Alpha is the most ionising radiation, so it can cause the most damage to a cell. The same amount of alpha radiation gives a bigger dose than beta or gamma radiation. But because alpha radiation has a short range in air, it is only a hazard if the source of radiation gets inside the body.

The damage to the body also depends on the type of tissue affected. Lung tissue, for example, is easily damaged by ionising radiation. Radon gas is dangerous because it emits alpha particles. If people breathe the gas in, the tissues of their lungs will absorb alpha radiation.

Is there a safe dose?

There is no such thing as a safe dose. Just one radon atom might cause a cancer, just as a person might get knocked down by a bus the first time they cross a road. The chance of it happening is low, but it still exists. The lower the dose, the lower the risk. But the risk is never zero.

Irradiation and contamination

Exposure to radiation from a radioactive material is called irradiation. Alpha irradiation presents a very low risk because alpha particles:

- travel only a few centimetres in air
- are easily absorbed by air and other materials.

Your clothes will stop alpha particles. So will the outer layer of dead cells on your skin.

Irradiation by beta particles is more risky, because they penetrate a few centimetres into the body. Most gamma rays pass straight through the body without being absorbed. But they have high energy, so if they are absorbed they are dangerous.

If a radiation source enters your body, or gets on skin or clothes, it is called contamination. You become contaminated. If you swallow or breathe in any radioactive material, your vital organs will be exposed to continuous radiation for a long period of time. Sources that emit alpha particles are the most dangerous because alpha particles are the most ionising. Contamination by gamma sources is the least dangerous as most gamma rays will pass straight out of the body.

Radiation protection

Scientists study radiation hazards and give advice to protect against them. They also keep a close eye on the many people who regularly work with radioactive materials – in hospitals, industry, and nuclear power stations. These people are called radiation workers.

Employers must make sure that radiation workers receive a radiation dose 'as low as reasonably achievable'. They have to bear this in mind when considering whether to use better equipment or procedures that can reduce the risks of an activity. They must balance the extra cost against the amount by which the risk is reduced.

To reduce their dose, medical staff take a number of precautions. They:

- use protective clothing and screens
- wear gloves and aprons
- wear special devices to monitor their dose.

The principle also applies to patients who receive radiation treatment. If doctors find that a smaller dose is just as effective as a larger one, then all hospitals are encouraged to use the smaller dose.

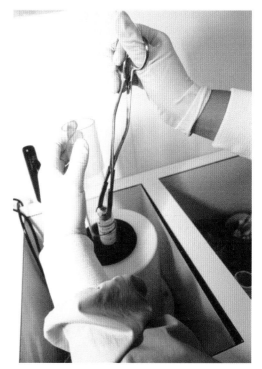

Staff handle radioactive sources with care to reduce the risk of contamination.

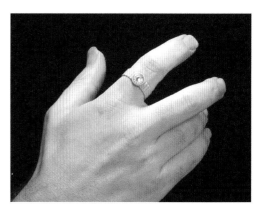

People working with radiation wear a personal radiation monitor that keeps track of their exposure to ionising radiation.

It is difficult to be sure about the harm that low doses of radiation can cause. In the 1970s, Alice Stewart studied the health of people working in the American nuclear industry. Her early results suggested that radiation is more harmful to children and to elderly people. She was criticised for her ideas, and the employers prevented her from studying any more medical records.

Questions

1 Explain the difference between irradiation and contamination.

2 **a** How big a dose of radiation would you get by flying from the UK to Australia?
   b Where do cosmic rays come from?
   c Do cosmic rays cause irradiation or contamination?

3 Imagine that alpha radiation damages a cell on the outside of your body. Why is this less risky than internal damage? Give two reasons.

4 Potassium-40 is a rare naturally occurring radioactive isotope of potassium. It usually decays to calcium (Ca) by emitting a beta particle.
   a Write a nuclear equation for this decay. (Potassium has 19 protons in the nucleus.)
   b Potassium is an important mineral in our diet. We obtain it from vegetables and fruit. What would you say to someone who was concerned that their food might contain radioactive potassium?

5 Explain how each of the precautions that medical staff take help to keep their radiation dose as low as possible.

C: Medical imaging and treatment

Radioactive materials can cause cancer. But they can also be used to diagnose and cure many health problems.

Medical imaging

Jo has been feeling unusually tired for some time. Her doctors decide to investigate whether an infection may have damaged her kidneys when she was younger.

They plan to give her an injection of DMSA. This is a chemical that is taken up by normal kidney cells.

The DMSA has been made using molecules containing technetium-99m (Tc-99m), which are radioactive. This is called labelling. Tc-99m has a half-life of 6 hours. The kidneys absorb normal DMSA and labelled DMSA in exactly the same way.

The Tc-99m is a **tracer**. It gives out gamma radiation from inside the kidneys. Gamma radiation is very penetrating, so nearly all of it passes out of Jo's body and is picked up by a gamma camera. The gamma camera traces where the technetium goes in Jo's body. In the image, parts of the kidney that are working normally appear to glow. Any dark or blank areas show where the kidney isn't working properly.

Jo's scan shows that she has only a small area of damage. The doctors will take no further action.

Glowing in the dark

Jo was temporarily contaminated by the radioactive Tc-99m. For the next few hours, until her body got rid of the technetium, she was told to:

- flush the toilet a few times after using it
- wash her hands thoroughly
- avoid close physical contact with friends and family.

Is it worth it?

There was a small chance that some gamma radiation would damage Jo's healthy cells. Before the treatment, her mother had to sign a consent form, and the doctors checked that Jo was not pregnant.

Jo's mother said: 'We felt the risk was very small. It was worth it to find out what was wrong. Even with ordinary medicines, there can be risks. You have to weigh these things up. Nothing is completely safe.'

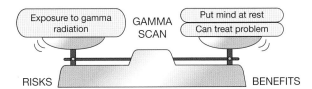

Jo's mother weighed the risk against the benefit.

Find out about

- different uses of radiation
- benefits and risks of using radioactive materials
- limiting radiation dose

Key word

➤ tracer (radioactive)

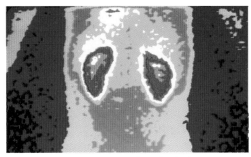

This gamma scan shows that the kidneys are working correctly. The two white areas show that the kidneys have absorbed the radioactive tracer.

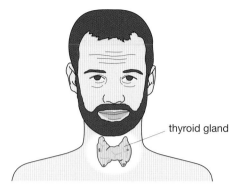

The thyroid gland is located in the front of the neck, below the voice box.

Medical treatment using nuclear radiation

Ionising radiation is used to destroy cancer cells in a range of situations.

Radioactive medicine

Alf has thyroid cancer. First he will have surgery, to remove the tumour. Then he must have **radiotherapy**, to kill any cancer cells that may remain.

He will swallow a medicine containing iodine-131. Iodine-131 decays to an isotope of xenon.

A hospital leaflet describes what will happen.

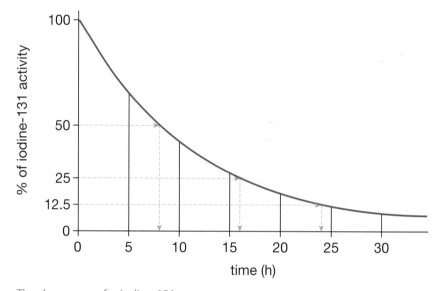

The decay curve for iodine-131.

Radioiodine treatment

You will have to come in to hospital for a few days. You will stay in a single room.

You will be given a capsule to swallow – this contains iodine-131. This form of iodine is radioactive – we call it radioiodine. You cannot eat or drink anything else for a couple of hours.

- The radioiodine is absorbed in your body.
- Radioiodine naturally collects in your thyroid, because this gland uses iodine to make its hormone.
- The radioiodine gives out beta radiation, which is absorbed in the thyroid.
- Any remaining cancer cells should be killed by the radiation.

You will have to stay in your room and take some precautions for the safety of visitors and staff. You will remain in hospital for a few days, until the amount of radioactivity in your body has fallen sufficiently.

Focusing the radiation

Gamma radiation can be targeted on cancer cells from outside the body. Directing narrow gamma beams from several directions to focus on the tumour protects healthy cells from too much radiation.

Key word

➤ radiotherapy

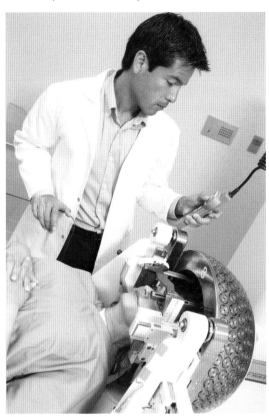

The helmet contains many sources of gamma radiation. The narrow beams of ionising radiation are directed to focus their energy on a tumour. They destroy the cancer tissue by killing the cells.

Questions

1 Look at the precautions that Jo has to take after the scan.
   a Write a few sentences explaining to Jo why she has to do each of them.
   b It would be safe to stand next to Jo but not to kiss her. Use the words 'irradiation' and 'contamination' to explain why.
   c What are the risks and the benefits to Jo of having the treatment?

2 Read the information leaflet about radioiodine. Describe how the risk to Alf's family and other patients is kept as low as possible.

3 Radioiodine has a half-life of 8 days. Explain why this is more suitable than:
   a 8 minutes   b 8 years.

4 Alf has a check-up after 40 days.
   a How many half-lives of iodine-131 is 40 days?
   H b What fraction of the radiation remains after 40 days?

Science explanations

P5 Radioactive materials

In this chapter you have learnt about different types and sources of radiation, and how it can be both useful and dangerous.

You should know:

- why some materials are radioactive and emit ionising radiation all the time
- how ionising radiation can damage living cells
- that atoms have shells of electrons and a nucleus made of protons and neutrons
- that atoms are appoximately 10^{-10} m across
- how ideas about atoms changed as more experimental evidence became available
- about the alpha-scattering experiment and how it showed that the atom has a small, massive, positively charged nucleus
- that all the atoms of an element have the same number of protons
- that isotopes are atoms of the same element with different numbers of neutrons
- how the nucleus changes in radioactive decay
- how to complete nuclear equations for radioactive decay
- what alpha and beta particles and gamma radiation are, and their different properties
- that there is background radiation all around us, mostly from natural sources
- the difference between contamination and irradiation
- how to interpret data on risk related to radiation dose
- that radioactive materials randomly emit ionising radiation all the time, and that the rate of decay is not affected by physical or chemical changes
- that the activity of a radioactive source decreases over time
- what is meant by the half-life of a radioactive isotope
- that radioactive isotopes have a wide range of half-life values
- how to do calculations involving half-life
- about uses of ionising radiation from radioactive materials.

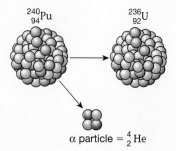

$^{240}_{94}$Pu $\rightarrow$ $^{236}_{92}$U

α particle $= {}^{4}_{2}$He

Alpha emission. The nucleus emits two protons and two neutrons.

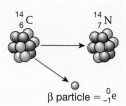

$^{14}_{6}$C $\rightarrow$ $^{14}_{7}$N

β particle $= {}^{0}_{-1}$e

During beta emission, the proton number increases by one.

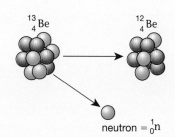

$^{13}_{4}$Be $\rightarrow$ $^{12}_{4}$Be

neutron $= {}^{1}_{0}$n

During neutron emission, the number of neutrons decreases by one.

Ideas about Science

While you develop an understanding of radioactive materials, it is important to appreciate the risks involved and how we make decisions about using science and technology. In discussing these decisions, you should be able to:

- describe some applications of nuclear physics that have made positive differences to people's lives, as well as identifying some of the unintended impacts

- list some uses of radioactive materials and the risks arising from them, and describe some of the ways that we reduce these risks

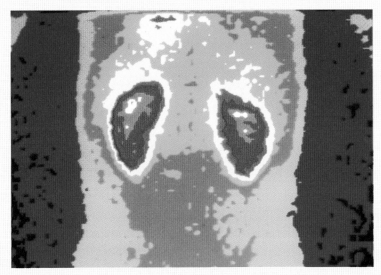

This gamma scan shows that the kidneys are working correctly.
The two white areas show that the kidneys have absorbed the radioactive tracer.

- use data to compare and discuss different risks

- discuss decisions involving risk, taking into account who benefits and who takes the risks

- explain that different decisions may be made depending on social and economic factors

- explain that there is official regulation of some areas of research

- distinguish questions that can be answered using a scientific approach from those that cannot, for example, 'Shall we build a nuclear power station at this site?' Even if there is no scientific reason why not, the final decision still depends on what society wants to do.

P5 Review questions

1 Copy and complete the sentences about radioactivity. Use key words from the chapter.

Ionising radiation is produced by radioactive _____ .
The radiation is produced when an _____ nucleus _____ .
The four types of radiation produced are:
_____, which is made up of particles with two protons and two neutrons;
_____, which is high-energy electrons;
_____, which is uncharged particles;
and _____, which is electromagnetic radiation.

2 a Describe the plum-pudding model of the atom.

   b What did the back-scattering of alpha particles in Rutherford's experiment show about atoms?

   c How is the back-scattering explained by your answer to part b?

   d Explain why Rutherford's experiment led to a change in the model of the atom.

3 Radon-222 has the atomic number 86. It decays, emitting an alpha particle.

   a Write the equation to show this change. Use a Periodic Table to find the product of the decay.

   b Radon is a gas that is emitted from rocks in the ground. Use ideas about contamination and irradiation to explain why the risks from radon gas are far greater if it is breathed in than if radon atoms touch your skin.

4 An isotope has a half-life of 74 days. Its activity is measured at 10 000 decays per second. It emits alpha radiation.

   H a What will its activity be after 148 days?

   b How long will it take for the activity to reach 625 decays per second?

   c For each example below, explain why the isotope would not be suitable and suggest an isotope from the chapter that would be suitable.

      i measuring the age of rocks

      ii a radioactive tracer in the body

5 Iodine-123 is used to investigate problems with the thyroid gland, which absorbs iodine. Iodine-123 is a gamma emitter.

   a Explain why the element iodine is chosen.

   b Explain why it is useful that iodine-123 gives out gamma radiation.

   c Iodine-123 has a half-life of 13 hours. Why would it be a problem if the half-life was:

      i a lot shorter?

      ii a lot longer?

6 Look at the information about sources of background radiation in P5.2B.

   a What is the biggest single source of background radiation? What is the approximate annual dose from that source?

   b What dose would each member of the flight crew receive from cosmic rays if they flew from the UK to Australia and back once a week for a year? Do you think they should be concerned about that? Explain your answer.

7 Read about Alf in P5.2C. Use ideas about risk and benefit to explain why Alf might choose to have radiotherapy, even though it means swallowing radioactive iodine.

8 The table below shows some radioactive isotopes that are used in a range of applications.

For each application listed below, choose the isotope from the table that you think is most suitable. Justify your answer, referring to both the half-life and the radiation emitted.

   a calculating the age of rocks

   b dating an ancient leather belt

   c monitoring the thickness of paper in a factory

   d monitoring uptake of iodine by the thyroid

   e detecting smoke

   f sterilising medical equipment

Isotope	Radiation emitted	Half-life
americium-241	alpha	430 years
carbon-14	beta	5700 years
cobalt-60	gamma	5 years
iodine-123	gamma	13 hours
iodine-131	beta	8 days
strontium-90	beta	29 years
uranium-235	alpha	700 million years

P6 Matter – models and explanations

Why study models and explanations of matter?

It's a familiar idea that everything is made of particles – atoms and molecules. But what evidence do we have for this? Who thought of this idea? What evidence did they have for it?

As recently as the beginning of the twentieth century, a famous Austrian physicist called Ernst Mach didn't think the evidence for atoms was strong enough to be sure that they really existed. 'Have you seen one?' he asked.

However, by the end of the nineteenth century, most scientists were convinced that all matter is made of atoms. Although no one had seen an atom at this time, the particle model explained many properties of matter, both physical and chemical. It was the best possible explanation of what matter really is.

And now we have 'seen' atoms. The photo shows a scanning electron micrograph of a layer of carbon atoms in a substance called graphene, with a single silicon atom embedded in it. For hundreds of years people believed matter was made of atoms, but it took the development of a very powerful new type of microscope before anyone could actually see them.

What you already know

- Matter exists in solid, liquid, and gas states.
- These states, and the changes between them, can be explained in terms of the particles that make up all matter.
- Solids can be extended and compressed by forces. Some elastic materials behave in a regular and predictable way when you stretch and compress them.
- The work done in stretching and compressing an elastic material results in an increase in the energy store of the material.
- The pressure in a liquid increases with depth, and this pressure is what allows objects to float.
- The pressure of the atmosphere acting on us is due to the weight of the air above us.

The Science

In this chapter you will learn more about the properties of solids, liquids, and gases, and how matter is affected when its internal energy is changed. You will study the behaviour of solids under stress, and pressure in gases and fluids. The chapter ends with a study of the origin of the Solar System and of the entire Universe. The particle model underpins our explanations of each aspect of the behaviour of matter.

Ideas about Science

Two models, or major ways of thinking, help us to understand the Universe. These are the concept of energy, which has a role throughout science, and the particle theory of matter. The most important idea about science in this chapter is: 'How are scientific explanations developed?' How did we progress from people thinking objects fall because it is natural for them to do so, and believing all matter to be some combination of earth, air, fire, and water, to our current understanding of matter? Throughout history people have been driven to understand the Universe we live in. The evolution of scientific thinking depends on creativity to think of revolutionary new ideas, careful experimentation, and thorough checking of predictions to test these ideas.

A: Early ideas about matter and energy

Find out about

- mass
- density
- conservation of energy

Key word

➤ density

Two thousand years ago, the Greek philosopher Aristotle thought that all matter was made of four elements: earth, air, fire, and water.

Aristotle wrote that each of the four elements has natural tendencies. Earth is dense and has a tendency to fall. Fire is extremely light and has a tendency to rise. If you shake up a mixture of air, earth, and water, they settle with the dense earth at the bottom and the very light air at the top.

Although Aristotle's theory does not match our current description of the nature of matter, it does introduce the idea of **density**. A denser substance has its mass – the amount of 'stuff' in it – in a smaller volume.

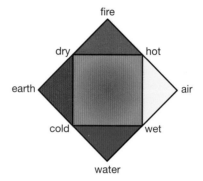

The Greek 'elements' had different properties: earth is dry and cold, water is cold and wet, air is wet and hot, and fire is hot and dry. As an example, wood contains earth and fire: when it is burnt, fire escapes and leaves earth-like ashes behind.

Density

We define the density of a substance as the mass of a unit volume of that substance. In equation form, this is:

$$density = \frac{mass}{volume}$$

$$\rho = \frac{m}{V}$$

Because mass **m** is measured in kilograms (kg) and volume **V** in cubic metres (m³), density ρ has the units of kilograms per cubic metre (kg/m³).

Heat and fire

The alchemists of the Middle Ages heated substances in furnaces to bring about chemical changes. They often confused heating, a physical process, and combustion, a chemical reaction. In the eighteenth century the French chemist Antoine Lavoisier carried out careful measurements. He showed that the total mass of reactants in a reaction was the same as the total mass of products.

However, because combustion causes heating, Lavoisier argued that something must change. He proposed that an invisible substance, which he called 'caloric', was transferred during combustion. Hot objects cooled down because they lost their caloric to the surroundings.

Worked example: Calculating the mass of a substance of known volume

Water has a density of 1000 kg/m³. What is the mass of water needed to fill a rectangular bath 175 cm long, 75 cm wide, and 50 cm deep?

Step 1: Write down what you know, and convert to standard units.

density ρ = 1000 kg/m³
length l = 175 cm = 1.75 m
width w = 75 cm = 0.75 m
depth d = 50 cm = 0.50 m

Step 2: Calculate the volume of the bath.

volume of a rectangular object = length x width x depth
volume = 1.75 m x 0.75 m x 0.50 m = 0.66 m³

Step 3: Write down the equation that links density, mass, and volume.

density = $\dfrac{mass}{volume}$ $\rho = \dfrac{m}{V}$

Step 4: Rearrange the equation to make the quantity needed (mass) the subject.

Multiply both sides by V.

$\rho = \dfrac{m}{V}$

$\rho \times V = \dfrac{m}{\cancel{V}} \times \cancel{V}$

$m = \rho V$

Step 5: Substitute the quantities into the equation and calculate the mass. Include the units in your answer.

m = 1000 kg/m³ x 0.66 m³ = 660 kg

Answer:

mass = 660 kg

Lavoisier was one of the first scientists to measure the amount of 'caloric' liberated in chemical reactions, using what he called a calorimeter. Calorimeters are still used to measure energy changes in chemical reactions.

Biochemists use calorimeters to measure the energy changes in reactions involving small molecules, such as drugs, or much larger molecules, such as proteins.

Synoptic link

You can learn more about the Thompson and Joule theory in P7.2 *What is heat?*

James Joule (1818–89) lived in Manchester and was a student of John Dalton, whose work you read about in P5.1B.

Developing the caloric theory

The caloric theory was initially supported by experiments. For example, when a hot object was placed in cold water, the temperature of the cold water rose as the hot object cooled: caloric was conserved.

At the end of the eighteenth century, Benjamin Thompson (later Count Rumford) observed cannons being made in Bavaria. Cannon-makers bored holes in solid brass cylinders. The drill got so hot it needed to be cooled with water. The old caloric theory explained this easily: as brass was cut out of the cannon, caloric escaped from the metal along with the metal fragments.

Thompson had special drills made that were extremely blunt. With these blunt drills he found he could heat up water as much as he liked without cutting out any metal. He concluded that the effect was due to the motion of the drill, not some mysterious substance coming out of the brass.

James Joule, an English brewer and keen scientist, made careful, repeated experiments to take this work further. He investigated the way in which electrical heating, or friction, could raise the temperature of water. He discovered that doing work on water by either method – electrical or mechanical – had the same effect. Raising the temperature of 1 kg of water by 1 °C always needed a transfer of 4100 J of energy, in modern units. This is very close to the accepted modern value, which is 4200 joules per kilogram per degree Celsius rise in temperature (written as 4200 J/kg °C).

Drilling cannons made the drill so hot it had to be cooled with water.

The fact that we name the unit of energy the **joule** (J) is not a coincidence. Joule's careful experiments did more than just show that the caloric theory was wrong: they established the law of conservation of energy that you met in P2.1C.

Questions

1 A volume of 3 m³ of air has a mass of 3.9 kg. Calculate the density of air.

2 The densest metal, osmium, has a density of 23 000 kg/m³. What is the volume of a piece of osmium of mass 55 kg?

3 Despite Joule's experimental results, many famous scientists, including Joule's friend Lord Kelvin, continued to think that the caloric theory was correct. Suggest reasons why they were not easy to convince.

B: Internal energy and specific heat capacity

You read in P6.1A that Joule did work on water to raise its temperature, using electrical heating or friction. When work is done on an object (it is heated), resulting in a rise in temperature, energy has been transferred to the object, increasing its thermal store. We say that its **internal energy** has increased. In a similar way, when an object cools down, energy is transferred from the object, and its internal energy decreases.

The change in temperature θ depends on the mass m of the object, the **specific heat capacity** c of the materials it is made of, and the energy transferred W. This relationship can be described by the equation:

change in internal energy (J) = mass (kg) × specific heat capacity (J/kg °C) × change in temperature (°C)

$$W = mc\theta$$

The specific heat capacity of a substance is the amount of energy you need to transfer to change the temperature of 1 kg of the substance by 1 °C. The specific heat capacity of water is about 4200 J/kg °C.

Internal energy changes produced by electrical working

When there is an electric current through a resistor, it gets hot. This effect is called Joule heating, after Joule who first described it. In calculations linking internal energy change and electrical working, you will need equations for power and energy that you met in P2.1B and P3.3:

$$power\ (W) = \frac{energy\ (J)}{time\ (s)} \quad and$$

$$power\ (W) = current\ (A) \times potential\ difference\ (V)$$

and for Joule heating of a resistor:

$$power\ (W) = [current\ (A)]^2 \times resistance\ (\Omega)$$

Writing the equations using symbols makes it easier to see the relationships between them:

$$P = \frac{W}{t}$$

$$P = IV$$

$$P = I^2R$$

Synoptic link

You can learn more about measuring energy changes in P8I *Measuring energy transfers.*

Find out about

- internal energy
- specific heat capacity

Key words

➤ internal energy
➤ specific heat capacity

Electrical heating raises the internal energy of the water. You need to supply 4200 J of energy to 1 kg of water to raise its temperature by just 1 °C.

Joule heating – the work done when an electric current passes through a wire raises its temperature.

Worked example: Relating electrical working to changes in temperature

A 2000 W electric kettle transfers 2000 J thermally into the water every second.
Calculate the time it will take to raise the temperature of 0.5 kg of water from 10 °C to 100 °C.

Step 1: Write down what you know, with the units.

power P = 2000 W = 2000 J/s
mass of water m = 0.5 kg
temperature change θ from 10 °C to 100 °C = 90 °C

Step 2: Write down the equation that links energy, mass, specific heat capacity, and temperature change.

change in internal energy $W = mc\theta$

Step 3: Substitute the quantities into the equation and calculate the increase in internal energy needed.

$W = 0.5 \text{ kg} \times 4200 \text{ J/kg °C} \times 90 \text{ °C}$
$W = 189\,000 \text{ J}$

Step 4: Write down the equation that links power P, energy W, and time t.

$$P = \frac{W}{t}$$

Step 5: Rearrange the equation to make time t the subject.

Multiply both sides by t.

Divide both sides by P.

$t \times P = \dfrac{W}{\cancel{t}} \times \cancel{t}$

$t \times P = W$

$\dfrac{t\cancel{P}}{\cancel{P}} = \dfrac{W}{P}$

$t = \dfrac{W}{P}$

Step 6: Substitute the quantities into the equation and calculate the time. Include the units in your answer.

$t = \dfrac{189\,0000 \text{ J}}{2000 \text{ W}} = 94.5 \text{ s}$

Answer:

time = 94.5 s (about one and a half minutes)

Friction between the match head and the matchbox raises the internal energy of the match head, until it is hot enough to ignite.

Internal energy changes produced by mechanical working

In P4.4A you saw that energy is transferred by mechanical work. The amount of work done is given by:

work (J) = force (N) × distance moved in the direction the force (m)

When work is done in lifting an object, it will gain gravitational potential energy **GPE**:

GPE (J) = mass (kg) × gravitational field strength (N/kg) × height (m)

and when the work done does not lift the object but accelerates it, the object gains kinetic energy:

kinetic energy (J) = ½ × mass (kg) × [(speed) (m/s)]²

Again, writing the equations using symbols makes it easier to see the relationships between them:

$$W = Fs \qquad GPE = mgh \qquad KE = \tfrac{1}{2}mv^2$$

Worked example: Relating mechanical working to changes in temperature

A lead bullet is fired from a rifle at a speed of 250 m/s. It strikes a steel plate, where it stops almost instantly. Assuming that all of the work done in decelerating the bullet raises its internal energy, calculate the temperature rise of the bullet after it has stopped.

(Mass of bullet = 6.5 g = 0.0065 kg; specific heat capacity of lead = 130 J/kg °C)

Step 1: Write down what you know, with the units. Convert to standard units.

speed of bullet v = 250 m/s
mass of bullet m = 6.5 g = 0.0065 kg
specific heat capacity of lead c = 130 J/kg °C

Step 2: Calculate the kinetic energy that the bullet loses when it stops.

$KE = \frac{1}{2}mv^2$
$KE = 0.5 \times 0.0065 \text{ kg} \times (250 \text{ m/s})^2$
$\quad = 0.5 \times 0.0065 \text{ kg} \times 62\,500 \text{ (m/s)}^2$
$\quad = 203 \text{ J}$

Step 3: Write down the equation that links energy W, mass m, and temperature rise θ.

$W = mc\theta$

Step 4: Rearrange the equation to make temperature rise θ the subject.

Divide both sides by m and c.

$\dfrac{W}{mc} = \dfrac{\cancel{m}c\theta}{\cancel{m}c}$

$\theta = \dfrac{W}{mc}$

Step 4: Substitute the quantities into the equation and calculate the temperature rise. Include the units in your answer.

$\theta = \dfrac{203 \text{ J}}{0.0065 \text{ kg} \times 130 \text{ J/kg °C}} = 240 \text{ °C}$

Answer:

temperature rise = 240 °C
so it would not be wise to pick it up with your fingers!

Questions

1 A block of copper has a mass of 2.4 kg. Calculate the increase in internal energy needed to raise the temperature of the block by 1 °C. (Specific heat capacity of copper = 390 J/kg °C)

2 The block of copper from question **1** is pushed a distance of 0.5 m across a rough, insulating surface by a constant force of 20 N. Assume that all of the energy transferred by this work increases the internal energy of the copper. Calculate the temperature rise of the copper block.

3 The same copper block is dropped from a tower 35 m tall onto a hard surface. Calculate the temperature rise of the copper block, assuming that all of the energy transferred in this process increases the internal energy of the copper.

C: Melting and evaporation

Find out about

- change of state
- specific latent heat

Key words

➤ change of state
➤ specific latent heat
➤ evaporation
➤ condensation

In making his measurements of caloric, Lavoisier used a calorimeter originally invented by Robert Bunsen. He knew that transferring the same amount of caloric to ice would always melt the same mass of ice. So Lavoisier used the amount of ice melted as a measure of the caloric (energy) transfer.

Changes of state

Lavoisier's idea relied on a scientific observation about **changes of state** – from solid to liquid, or from liquid to gas. In any change of state, the energy required to change the state of 1 kg of a material is constant. If you need to change the state of 2 kg of the substance, you need twice the energy.

The **specific latent heat** L of a substance is the amount of energy you need to transfer to change the state of 1 kg of the substance. This equation relates the energy W transferred to the mass m that changes state:

energy to cause a change of state (J) = mass (kg) × specific latent heat (J/kg)

$$W = mL$$

The word 'latent' means 'hidden'. When you heat a liquid or a solid, its temperature rises. But when you reach the melting point or boiling point of the substance, the temperature stops rising even though you continue to heat it. The energy you are supplying is 'hidden'.

The specific latent heat of fusion (melting) is the specific latent heat when a substance melts or solidifies. The specific latent heat of vaporisation is the specific latent heat when a substance **evaporates** or **condenses**.

Heating ice

The graph shows the temperature change in a sample of ice as energy is supplied at a uniform rate by an electrical heater. This assumes that no energy is lost to the surroundings.

While ice is melting, the temperature stays at 0 °C.

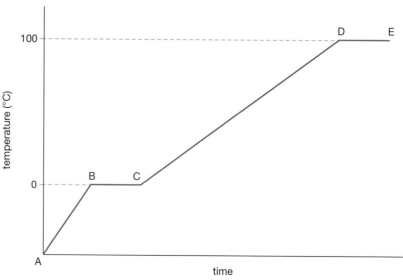

How the temperature changes as ice is heated.

- Between A and B, the electrical heater is doing work raising the internal energy of the ice at a uniform rate. The temperature is rising at a uniform rate.

- Between B and C, energy is being transferred to the ice, but it is not raising the temperature. Where is it going? This hidden (latent) energy is heating the ice, changing its state, transforming solid water into liquid water.

- At point C, all of the ice has melted, and the temperature rises at a uniform rate again. The specific heat capacity of water is nearly twice as large as the specific heat capacity of ice. The same amount of energy produces half the temperature rise in water as it did in ice, so the graph is not so steep.

- At point D, the water starts to boil. The energy transferred by the heater is changing the state of the water from liquid into gas.

Worked example: Calculations using latent heat

An electrical heater of power 60 W is placed into 200 g of water at 100 °C. Calculate the mass of water that evaporates in a time of 200 s.

(Specific latent heat of vaporisation of water = 2300 J/g)

Step 1: Write down what you know, with the units.

power of heater P = 60 W
time for heating t = 200 s
specific latent heat of vaporisation of water L = 2300 J/g

Step 2: Write down the equation that links power P, energy W, and time t. Rearrange the equation to make time t the subject, as you did in P6.1B.

$P = \dfrac{W}{t}$

$W = Pt$

Step 3: Calculate the energy supplied by the heater.

W = 60 J/s × 200 s = 12 000 J

Step 4: Write down the equation that links energy W, specific latent heat L, and mass m.

$W = mL$

Step 5: Rearrange the equation to make mass m the subject. Divide both sides by L.

$\dfrac{W}{L} = \dfrac{m\cancel{L}}{\cancel{L}}$

$m = \dfrac{W}{L}$

Step 6: Substitute the quantities into the equation and calculate the mass. Include the units in your answer.

$m = \dfrac{12\,000 \text{ J}}{2300 \text{ J/g}} = 5.2g$

Note that L is given in J/g, not J/kg, so the answer will be in g, not kg.

Answer:

mass = 5.2 g

Note that it takes a great deal of energy to evaporate water. This makes tumble dryers very expensive to run!

In the worked example, the specific latent heat was given in J/g. It is usually quoted in J/kg, which makes the numbers very large. For water, the specific latent heat of vaporisation = 2 300 000 J/kg. This large number is often written in standard form: 2.3×10^6 J/kg.

Change of state and change in properties

When an ice cube melts, it produces a pool of liquid water. The liquid is different from the solid: it is no longer hard and no longer has a fixed shape. It does have a fixed volume, and that volume is almost the same as the volume of the ice that melted. The change in density as water freezes or melts is small. Like a solid, a liquid is very, very hard to compress.

Water is an unusual liquid: its density decreases very slightly when it freezes. So ice is less dense than liquid water, and it floats. For most liquids, the density increases slightly when they freeze. For example, if you put a bottle of olive oil in the fridge, it will soon contain some solid olive oil at the bottom of the bottle.

When an ice cube melts, it produces almost the same volume of liquid water.

When a liquid evaporates, the change is much more dramatic. The density of the vapour is very, very much less than the density of the liquid. This is how a small amount of liquid is able to produce large billows of vapour.

The vapour from the cooling tower has a much lower density than the liquid water that produced it.

The table below shows the density of water in different states and at different temperatures.

Temperature (°C)	0	0	100	100
State of water	solid	liquid	liquid	vapour
Density (kg/m³)	920	1000	960	0.6

Water is about 1000 times more dense than steam. A scald from steam can be very painful, much more than you might expect from a small mass of vapour. This is because the specific latent heat of vaporisation of water is very large. When the steam meets your skin, it condenses and the internal energy it loses is transferred to your body.

Questions

1   A 2000 W electric kettle is accidentally left boiling with its lid off. In a time of 2 minutes, the mass of water in the kettle falls by 0.10 kg. Calculate the value of specific latent heat of vaporisation of water given by this data.

2   Archie drops 200 g of ice into 2.0 kg of water at 20 °C. He stirs the water until all the ice has melted. He measures the temperature of the 2.2 kg of water to be 11 °C.
   (Specific heat capacity of water = 4200 J/kg °C)
   a   Show that the internal energy of the 2.0 kg of warm water fell by about 76 000 J in cooling from 20 °C to 11 °C.
   b   Show that the internal energy of the 0.20 kg of melted ice increased by about 9000 J when its temperature increased from 0 °C to 11 °C.
   c   Use your answers to a and b to calculate the specific latent heat of melting of ice.

3   If you did real experiments like those in questions 1 and 2 in the kitchen, they would be likely to give a value of the specific latent heat of vaporisation that is too high, and a value of the specific latent heat of melting that is too low. Explain why this is.

P6.2 How does the particle model explain the effects of heating?

A: Solids, liquids, and gases

Find out about

- Dalton's atomic model
- the properties of solids, liquids, and gases and the particle model
- how temperature affects the behaviour of particles

Key word

➤ particle

Synoptic link

You can learn more about the particle model in C1.1B *What determines the state of a substance on Earth?*

The particle model

You read in P5.1B about John Dalton's work on what matter is made of. He wanted to explain the observation that gases always combine together in definite proportions. For example, 8 g of oxygen always react with 1 g of hydrogen to give 9 g of water.

Dalton's explanation used the Greek idea of **particles**, and he even used their word for them: atoms.

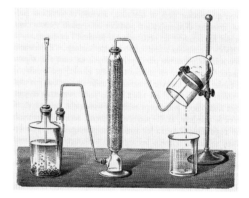

Nineteenth century apparatus to measure the amount of water produced when hydrogen burns in oxygen.

The particle model can explain observations not only in chemistry but in all the sciences, including some of the properties of solids, liquids, and gases.

Explaining the behaviour of solids, liquids, and gases

These pictures show a simplified view of particles in solids, liquids, and gases. The model shows the particles as simple spheres, but in fact they are atoms, molecules, or ions. This model is two-dimensional, while matter is three-dimensional. The 'flat' two-dimensional picture is easier to visualise and draw.

A solid copper sulfate crystal.

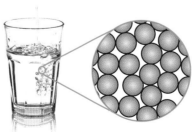

A glass of liquid water.

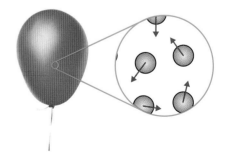

Gas in a balloon.

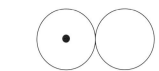

The particle model of matter

Greek and Roman ideas

The Greek philosopher Democritus, who lived around 400 BCE, suggested that everything was made of atoms. He thought it didn't seem 'right' that you could go on cutting matter more and more without coming to the smallest possible bit. He tried to relate the shape and size of the atoms to the properties of matter, for example, suggesting that atoms in iron are strong, with hooks that stick together.

Lucretius, a Roman poet and philosopher who lived in the first century BCE, had similar ideas. He used reasoning to argue that there must be a finite number of types of atom, but combined in different ways they can make a great variety of substances, just as with only 26 letters we have a whole language.

Democritus, Lucretius, and others are described as early 'atomists'. They began the process of building the particle model that we use today.

Dalton's atomic model

A scientific model needs to explain observations and to allow predictions. Dalton's atomic model did just that.

Here are his suggestions:

1 All matter consists of particles called atoms.

2 These atoms cannot be changed or destroyed.

3 All the atoms of an element are the same.

4 The atoms of different elements have different masses.

5 In a chemical reaction, atoms join together in simple ratios of mass, for example, 1 g of hydrogen with 8 grams of oxygen.

He published his ideas in a chemistry textbook. His chart showing the symbols for the elements is shown in P5.1B.

All five of the suggestions above were based on Dalton's scientific observations and measurements.

Unfortunately, he made one other suggestion, which was wrong:

6 When atoms join together, they do so in pairs: one atom of one element with one atom of another element.

Dalton did not have any evidence for this, and it took some years before chemists sorted it out: water is H_2O, not HO, as Dalton thought.

Dalton's symbol for the water molecule. He thought one hydrogen atom combined with one oxygen atom.

Before using the particle model to *explain* properties, you need to have a clear mental picture of how the model *describes* the arrangement of the particles.

Property of the material	Particle description
Solids have a fixed shape. If you support a solid from underneath, it will stay where it is and keep its shape.	The particles are arranged as close together as possible. Each particle is firmly fixed to its neighbours. There is nothing between the particles.
Liquids flow, but they have a fixed volume. To keep a liquid in place, it needs to be in a container with sides, such as a beaker.	The particles are close to each other, but they can move about. There is nothing between the particles.
Gases also flow, but they can escape from a beaker. They need to be trapped inside a container with a lid.	The particles are far apart from each other. They are all moving around at high speed. There is nothing between the particles. If you take the lid off the container, any particles moving upwards will fly out.

What holds the particles together in a solid and a liquid?

The particles in a solid are held in place by attractive forces between the particles called **bonds**. As you saw in P1.1B, you can picture these bonds as behaving like tiny springs, so the particles vibrate. These bonds are also present in a liquid. The bonds keep the particles close together in a liquid, but do not prevent them moving around. In a gas, there are no attractive forces between the particles – the bonds act only between particles that are close together.

The strength of the bonds between particles varies greatly from one substance to another. Diamond is very hard, and has particularly strong bonds between its particles. Bonds vary in strength even between similar chemical substances: sodium and iron are both metals, but iron is hard and strong, while sodium is soft and weak.

Changing state

When the temperature of a solid is increased, its particles gain kinetic energy: they move more. The increased kinetic energy makes each particle move further from its position. As it moves, the bonds attracting it to its neighbours pull it back, so it **vibrates** about its position.

stronger forces   weaker forces   no forces

The bonds between particles act only when the particles are close together.

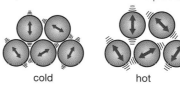

cold   hot

As the temperature rises, the particles in a solid vibrate more.

Key words

➤ bond
➤ vibration
➤ sublimation

If the temperature rises further, the particles have enough energy to move further from their neighbours. The particles move apart slightly, and the regular arrangement is lost. The solid melts into a liquid.

Further heating makes each particle move more and more vigorously. Some particles near the surface of the liquid, such as particle B in the diagram, gain enough energy to escape into the space above the liquid. The liquid is evaporating. Other particles, such as A, do not gain enough energy to escape the attractive forces of their neighbours.

As the temperature rises further and further, more and more surface particles can escape. Eventually, the boiling point is reached and all the particles escape to form a gas.

We normally think of carbon dioxide as a gas, but below −78.5 °C it is a solid. However, carbon dioxide does not melt – it changes directly from a solid to a gas. This change of state is called **sublimation**.

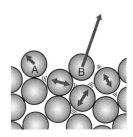

Some particles at the surface of a liquid can escape.

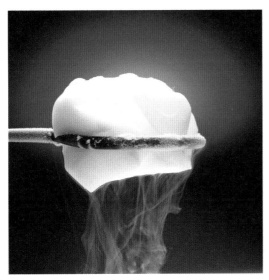

Solid carbon dioxide is known as dry ice. You can see the water vapour condensing where the cold carbon dioxide gas has sublimed from the solid carbon dioxide.

Whenever a substance changes state, it is still the same substance with the same number of identical particles. Its mass is conserved.

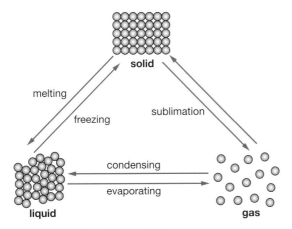

Changes of state are examples of physical changes.

Gas pressure

The particles in a gas are far apart. This explains why gases have very low density. It also explains why it is much easier to walk through air than through water. But can the particle model explain all the other properties of gases?

The particles in a gas move about rapidly. What happens when they meet the sides of their container, such as the balloon? The particles rebound, as shown here.

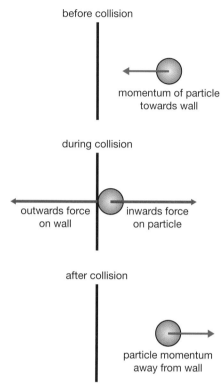

before collision

momentum of particle towards wall

during collision

outwards force on wall | inwards force on particle

after collision

particle momentum away from wall

When a particle in a gas hits the container wall, it rebounds.

On each rebound, the particle changes direction, so its momentum changes. This change of momentum is caused by the container wall exerting a force on the rebounding particle. The particle exerts a force of equal size and opposite direction on the container wall: the wall pushes the particle inwards, and the particle pushes the wall outwards.

In a real gas sample, there are many collisions like this. The total force on the container wall is the result of adding them all together.

Using the model to predict the behaviour of gases

The simple particle model can explain some observations about gases. If the temperature of a gas is raised, its pressure goes up. This is because the particles have more kinetic energy – they are moving faster – and so they have more momentum. The change in momentum when the particles hit the container wall is greater. They hit the wall more often, too, so there are more collisions and more forces on the walls.

If we put more gas particles into the container, more of them will hit the container wall each second, and this will increase the pressure. Pressure is defined as the force per unit area.

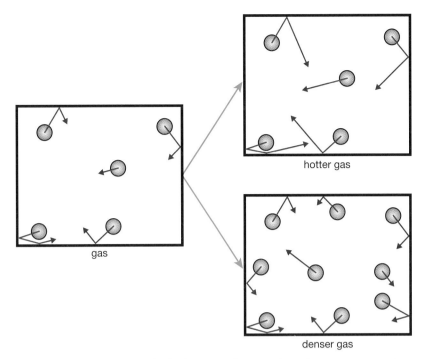

The particle model explains the behaviour of gases when the temperature rises and when the density is increased.

Worked example: Using the particle model to explain the behaviour of a gas

Explain what would happen to the pressure on the wall of a gas container when the gas particles are replaced by a gas with the same number of more massive particles travelling at the same speed.

Step 1: State what will happen to the momentum change as each particle bounces off the wall.

Each particle is more massive but has the same velocity. This means that it has greater momentum as it approaches the wall, and greater momentum in the opposite direction as it leaves the wall.

Step 2: State how the number of particles striking the wall will change.

The number of collisions with the wall in each second will not change, because the speed has not changed and the number of particles is the same.

Step 3: Explain how the force and pressure on the wall will change in terms of the momentum change each second.

Each collision will have a greater momentum change, and there will be the same number of collisions each second. The force (the total momentum change per second) on the wall will increase. The area of the wall is the same, so the pressure will increase.

Questions

1 Water is an unusual substance. When water freezes, it becomes less dense. Explain what must happen to the spacing of the particles as it freezes.

2 Dalton's suggestions 1 to 5 established the modern particle theory. Your studies of radioactivity in P5 show they are not always true. Explain the circumstances when suggestions 2, 3, and 4 are not true.

3 In a typical solid lattice, each particle is bonded to 12 neighbouring particles. When the solid melts, the particles move apart a little. In the liquid each particle has (on average) about 10.5 bonds to neighbouring particles. When the liquid evaporates, it turns into a gas, and the particles have no bonds to neighbouring particles. Explain why the latent heat of vaporisation is much greater than the latent heat of melting.

P6.3 How does the particle model relate to materials under stress?

A: Elastic materials

Find out about

- elastic and plastic materials
- stretching elastic and plastic materials
- Hooke's law and the spring constant
- energy stored in a stretched spring
- how inter-particle forces can explain elastic and plastic behaviour

Key words

➤ tension
➤ extension
➤ compression
➤ spring constant

In P4.1A, you saw how interaction pairs of forces act. As well as making things move, force interaction pairs can act on a solid material to change its shape. They can stretch, compress, or bend a material.

Stretching a resistance band.   Compressing a lime.   Bending a copper pipe.

To stretch the resistance band, the man is pulling each end outwards with the same force. This force is called the **tension** in the elastic. The band stretches – it increases in length when he pulls it. The amount it stretches is called the **extension**. The band will spring back to its original length when he stops pulling.

To squeeze the lime, the woman's hand exerts equal inward forces on each side, **compressing** the lime. The lime will stay squashed when she stops squeezing. It will not spring back.

To bend the pipe, the plumber has to apply a force to each end. The two forces are in opposite directions.

You need more than one force to change the shape of a material by stretching, compressing, or bending it.

Hooke's law

Thomas Hooke first investigated the stretching of springs in 1660. He found that the extension of a spring is directly proportional to the tension in the spring.

In the first photo on the page opposite, the red marker under the spring points at 26.1 cm. Kay adds a 50 g mass to the holder under the spring. It stretches the spring so that the red marker points at 27.6 cm. The extension is (27.6 − 26.1) cm = 1.5 cm.

A 50 g mass has a weight of 0.5 N. This 0.5 N force stretched the spring by 1.5 cm. If Kay doubled the force to 1 N, she would see double the extension (3.0 cm).

For this spring, a graph of force against extension gives a straight line through the origin. The tension force is directly proportional to extension.

The spring constant

Because the tension force F and the extension x are directly proportional, if you divide the force by the extension, you always get the same result for a particular spring. This constant k is called the **spring constant**.

$$\frac{\text{force (N)}}{\text{extension (m)}} = \text{spring constant (N/m)}$$

$$\frac{F}{x} = k \quad \text{and} \quad F = kx$$

This is the spring equation. The extension is measured in metres, and the units of the spring constant are N/m.

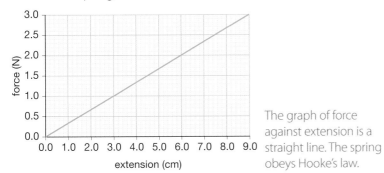

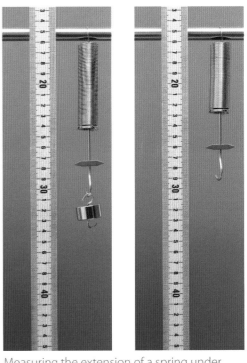

Measuring the extension of a spring under tension.

The graph of force against extension is a straight line. The spring obeys Hooke's law.

Worked example: Calculating and using the spring constant

Use the force–extension graph above to calculate the spring constant of the spring in N/m.

Step 1: Choose values of force and extension to read off the graph. Write the extension in metres.

force = 3.0 N

Always choose the largest convenient values to read off the graph.

extension = 9.0 cm = $\dfrac{9.0 \text{ cm}}{100 \text{ cm/m}}$ = 0.090 m

Step 2: Write down the spring equation.

spring constant = $\dfrac{\text{force}}{\text{extension}}$

Step 3: Substitute the quantities into the equation to find the spring constant.

$\dfrac{3.0 \text{ N}}{0.09 \text{ m}}$ = 33 N/m

spring constant = 33 N/m

Predict the extension of the spring under a tension force of 4 N.

Step 1: Write down the equation that links the spring constant, extension, and force.

force = spring constant × extension

$F = kx$

Step 2: Rearrange the equation to make the extension x the subject.

$\dfrac{F}{k} = \dfrac{kx}{k}$

Divide both sides by k

$x = \dfrac{F}{k}$

Step 3: Substitute in the value for k from above to find the extension with a force of 4 N. Include the units in your answer.

$x = \dfrac{4 \text{ N}}{33 \text{ N/m}}$ = 0.12 m

Answer:

extension = 0.12 m

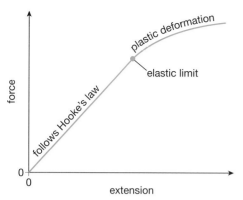
Stretching a real spring.

The graph for Kay's spring on the previous page extends only to a force of 3.0 N. The worked example assumes that the graph will continue to be a straight line for forces larger than 3.0 N. But if you exert too big a force on a spring, it is permanently stretched. It does not return to its original length when you remove the force. Hooke's law no longer applies.

Hooke's law applies to materials that are **elastic** – that return to their original shape when the force is removed, like the chest expander. In practice, it is likely that this spring will be permanently stretched by a force of 6 N. The spring passes its **elastic limit**. It then becomes **plastic** – the spring doesn't spring back to its original size and shape. The extension is no longer proportional to the tension force.

The energy stored in a stretched spring

A spring stores energy as it stretches. How can you find out how much energy it stores? The energy stored is the work done by the tension force in stretching the spring.

In P4.4A you saw that when a force moves, it does work. The work done (energy transferred) is given by:

work done (J) = force (N) × distance moved in the direction of the force (m)

$$W = Fs$$

This tells you the work done by a force that remains constant. But in stretching a spring, the force is not constant. It increases as the spring extends.

For a spring within its elastic limit, which obeys Hooke's law, the force and extension are proportional. We use the *average force* in the equation above. The graph shows that the average force is half the maximum force.

work done = average force × distance moved in the direction of the force

= ½ × (maximum force) × maximum extension

$$W = \tfrac{1}{2}Fs$$

The graph shows force against extension. The maximum extension is the base of the blue triangle, while the maximum force is the height of that triangle. The area of a triangle is ½ × base × height, so the work done is the area of the triangle between the graph and the extension axis.

Synoptic link

You can learn more about calculating the area under the line on a graph in P4.2B *Picturing motion*.

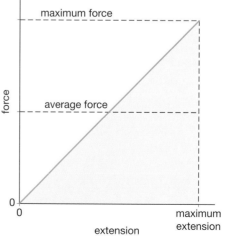

For a spring that obeys Hooke's law, the average force in stretching the spring is half the maximum force.

The work done can always be found from the area under the graph, even if the graph curves, like the graph for a real spring beyond its elastic limit.

work done (J) = force (N) × distance moved in the direction of the force (m)

$$W = F\,s$$

work done = average force × distance moved in the direction of the force

= ½ × (maximum force) × maximum extension

$$W = \tfrac{1}{2}\,F\,x$$

energy stored = ½ × spring constant × (maximum extension)^2

$$W = \tfrac{1}{2}\,kx^2$$

This equation does not apply to a curved graph for a spring stretched beyond its elastic limit. To find the energy stored in a spring that does not obey Hooke's law, you need to find the area under the curve on the force–extension graph.

Worked example: Calculating the energy stored in a stretched spring

Calculate the energy stored in a spring of spring constant 36 N/m when it is stretched from its original length of 11 cm to a length of 23 cm. The spring obeys Hooke's law.

Step 1: Write down what you know, with the units. Convert to standard units.

spring constant k = 36 N/m
length of spring l_1 = 11 cm = 0.11 m
length of stretched spring l_2 = 23 cm = 0.23 m

Step 2: Write down the equation for calculating the energy stored in a spring that obeys Hooke's law.

$W = \dfrac{1}{2}\,kx^2$

Step 3: Calculate the extension of the spring.

x = 0.23 m – 0.11 m = 0.12 m

Step 4: Substitute the quantities into the equation to calculate the energy stored in the spring.

W = 0.5 × 36 N/m × (0.12 m)^2
W = 0.5 × 36 N/m × 0.0144 m^2 = 0.26 J

Answer:

energy = 0.26 J (to 2 significant figures)

Key words

➤ elastic
➤ elastic limit
➤ plastic

Key words

➤ bond
➤ lattice

The particle model explains stretching and compressing

What makes a material behave in an elastic way or a plastic way?
The particle model helps explain this.

The particle model for elastic materials

You saw in P6.2 that there are forces known as **bonds** between the particles in a solid, holding the particles in place. A useful model treats these bonds as springs. The diagram shows part of a solid **lattice**. There are forces between neighbouring particles.

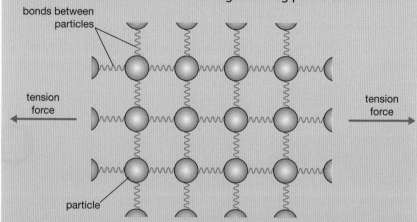

A model of forces in a solid lattice. Although the 'bonds' are coloured differently in this diagram, they are all identical.

If the solid is put into tension by the two equal forces shown, then all the green springs will stretch slightly. The solid will extend sideways until the green springs pull back inwards with the same force as the two tension forces pulling outwards. If the tension forces are increased, then each green spring will stretch more, in line with Hooke's law, and the whole solid will extend more. These tension forces do not affect the blue springs, so the thickness of the solid does not change.

If the forces push inwards, the solid will be compressed. Like the extension, the amount of compression will be directly proportional to the size of the pair of compressing forces.

There is a limit to how far the solid can be stretched and still return to its original size and shape: the elastic limit. Once this limit has been reached, further pulling does not just move particles further apart. It breaks the bonds and moves the particles out of their positions. This changes the structure of the solid, and it deforms plastically.

When copper wire is stretched it deforms before it breaks. The broken ends of the wire are curved inwards. The copper deformed plastically, just before the wire snapped.

This model is useful to explain the behaviour of solid materials whose particles can be treated as spheres packed neatly into a lattice.
The model works very well for metals. Polymer materials, such as rubber and plastics, are very different. In polymers, the particles are very long molecules made of thousands of particles joined together. A better model to explain their behaviour is a plate of spaghetti. The molecules slide over each other and the material stretches plastically.

Polymers do not obey Hooke's law. The force–extension graph for polymers such as rubber is not a straight line, even though rubber is an elastic material.

Stretching a polymer is like trying to pull a helping of spaghetti out of the dish. The long strands tangle up and slide over each other.

Questions

1 A shock-absorber spring in a car is squeezed by a pair of forces of 600 N as the car goes over a bump. The spring compresses by 5.0 cm. Calculate the spring constant in N/m.

2 A spring of spring constant 20 N/m is stretched by hanging a 2.5 N weight on it. Its original length was 8.5 cm. Calculate:
   a its extension
   b the length of the stretched spring.

3 Calculate the energy stored in the spring in the photo on page 203 when it is extended by 6.0 cm.

4 A student stretches an iron wire and a copper wire, making sure that neither wire passes its elastic limit. The wires are both the same thickness. She finds that the copper wire stretches more than the iron wire for the same force. Suggest an explanation for this in terms of the forces between the particles in the lattices of the two metals.

5 A rubber band is stretched and gives the force–extension graph shown here. Use the 'spaghetti model' to suggest why the graph starts with a small gradient, and then becomes steeper.

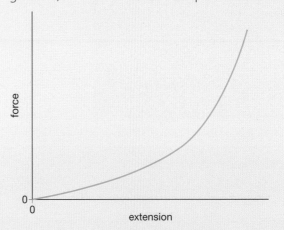

Force–extension graph for a rubber band.

Science explanations

P6 Matter – models and explanations

The scientific model of matter being made of atoms is now well established. We view atoms as consisting of a small, dense, positively charged nucleus surrounded by electrons in 'orbitals'. The particle model can be used to explain many properties of matter, and underpins explanations of the formation of the Universe including our Solar System.

You should know:

- how to measure and calculate the densities of substances in the solid and liquid states
- about specific heat capacity and specific latent heat, and be able to use these ideas to explain what happens to the temperature of a substance as it is heated and changes state
- how to describe and calculate the energy transfers associated with changes in a system when the temperature changes, due to mechanical, electrical, and thermal processes
- how the particle model describes and explains:
  - differences in densities of different substances
  - what happens when a substance is heated, including when there is a change of state
  - the relation between the temperature of a gas and its pressure and volume
  - **H** the difference between elastic and plastic deformation caused by stretching forces
- how to use the relationships between force, energy, and extension for an elastic object.

Ideas about Science

In addition to studying how matter behaves when you heat it or put it under stress, it is important to understand how scientists develop models and theories about the physical world.

You should be able to:

● describe and explain examples of scientific explanations that resulted from a leap of imagination from a creative thinker, and were modified when new evidence became available

● suggest how the particle model of matter can be used to explain phenomena, use the model to make predictions, and identify limitations of the model

● describe scientific discoveries that relied on careful observations, such as Joule's experiments to show the relationship between working and heating.

While ice is melting, the temperature stays at 0 °C.

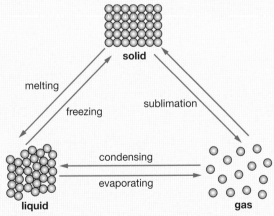

The particle model explains changes of state.

P6 Review questions

You will need the data in the table to answer some of the following questions.

Element	Atomic number	Density (kg/m³)	Hardness (MPa)	Melting point (°C)	Specific heat capacity (J/kg °C)
sodium	11	966	0.69	98	1200
iron	26	7873	490	1540	440
cobalt	27	8800	700	1495	410
nickel	28	8907	700	1455	430
copper	29	8933	874	1085	380
platinum	78	21 450	392	1769	130
gold	79	19 281	2450	1064	130
lead	82	11 343	38.3	327	130

Some properties of some of the elements. Hardness measures the pressure needed to make a dent in the element.

1 A 100 m copper cable has a cross-sectional area of 0.8 cm².

  a Calculate the volume and mass of the cable.

  b Use your answer to **a** to estimate the mass of a cable of the same dimensions made from gold.

2 Calculate how much energy would be needed to heat 50 g of gold from 20 °C up to its melting point. Give your answer in kJ, to 2 significant figures.

3 An electric furnace with a power rating of 10 kW is used to melt 20 kg of iron. Calculate how long it would take to heat the iron from 20 °C to its melting point, and then to melt it. Give your answer to the nearest minute. (Specific latent heat of fusion of iron = 272 kJ/kg)

4 A car has two brakes on each of its four wheels. Assume each brake has the equivalent of 0.5 kg of iron.

  a Calculate the temperature rise in the brakes when a 1500 kg car is brought to a halt from a speed of 20 m/s.

  b Explain what additional assumption you have to make to do this calculation.

5 Two students are looking for patterns in the data in the table, and explanations for those patterns.

These are some of their comments:

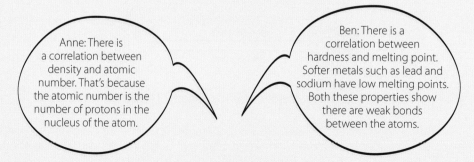

Anne: There is a correlation between density and atomic number. That's because the atomic number is the number of protons in the nucleus of the atom.

Ben: There is a correlation between hardness and melting point. Softer metals such as lead and sodium have low melting points. Both these properties show there are weak bonds between the atoms.

Discuss whether you agree with each of the students, using data in the table and your knowledge of the particle model to support your answers.

6 Deepa blows up a party balloon and ties it. She puts the balloon on a hot radiator. After a short time it bursts. Use the particle model for gases to explain why it bursts.

7 In an experiment to stretch a rubber band, a student records the extension of the band as weights are added. He plots this graph.

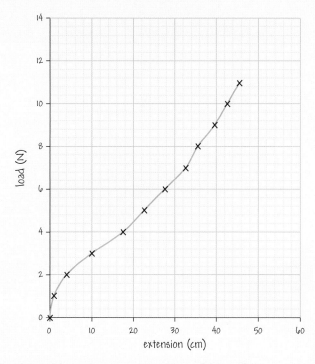

a What load would produce an extension of 20 cm?

b Suggest what the extension would be for a load of 12 N.

c Explain why it would not be sensible to predict the extension for a load of 20 N.

d Use the graph to calculate the energy stored in the rubber band when the extension is 30 cm.

e Explain why you should not use the equation:
energy stored = ½ × force × extension
to find the energy stored by this rubber band. Use a calculation in your answer.

P7 Ideas about Science

Why study Ideas about Science?

In everyday life, both in and out of school, you will come across scientific ideas in many different situations. In order to make sense of these ideas, you need to understand how science explanations are developed, the kinds of evidence and reasoning behind them, their strengths and limitations, and how far we can rely on them.

You also need to think about the impacts of science and technology on society and how people respond to the new ideas, inventions, and processes that science makes possible.

What you already know

- Science explanations are based on evidence, and as new evidence is gathered, explanations may change.

- How to plan and carry out scientific enquiries, choosing the most appropriate techniques and equipment.

- How to collect and analyse data and draw conclusions.

Case studies

In this chapter you will explore some of the Ideas about Science that you have studied across the course in different contexts.

P7.1 How can solar energy make a difference?
Find out about how a Nobel Prize-winning discovery is making a difference to the lives of many families in Africa, and how solar energy can help the UK reduce its dependence on fossil fuels.

P7.2 What is heat?
Find out how careful experimentation led to Victorian scientists having a better understanding of energy.

Find out about

- examples of applications of science that have made a positive difference to people's lives
- how an application of science can provide a sustainable solution to improve people's lives

Key word

➤ sustainable

Synoptic link

You can learn more about air pollution in C1.1D *How do human activities affect the atmosphere?*

Many children across Africa do their homework using a smoky kerosene lamp.

Solar lamps enable children to study for an extra hour each night.

In 2014 the Nobel Prize in Physics was awarded to three scientists, based in Japan and the US, for the invention of blue light-emitting diodes (LEDs). Why was this invention so important?

Nobel Prizes are awarded by the Royal Swedish Academy of Sciences. This is what they said:

'This year's Nobel Laureates are rewarded for having invented a new energy-efficient and environment-friendly light source – the blue light-emitting diode (LED). In the spirit of Alfred Nobel, the Prize rewards an invention of greatest benefit to mankind; using blue LEDs, white light can be created in a new way.'

Why do LED lights make a difference?

Blue LEDs allowed new white LED lamps to be developed. Before this they were only red or green. While this work was ongoing, scientists were also improving the efficiency of photovoltaic solar panels. The combination of bright LED lamps and small photovoltaic panels provides light without mains electricity or disposable batteries.

In Africa over 80% of the people living outside towns and cities don't have mains electricity. People rely on small kerosene lamps or candles for light. Kerosene is a product from crude oil that burns with a smoky flame.

Loise Njogu and her two children live in Narok, Kenya. Loise used to use kerosene to light her home, but the flame can be dangerous, especially with children around. Loise had an opportunity to buy a solar lamp. It has made a big difference to the life of the family.

Before, they did not have enough kerosene for the children to work after dark. Using the solar lamp, the children now have more time to do their homework. Loise is saving $14.50 a month that she used to spend on kerosene, so there is now more money to spend on other things. She says, 'At least the kids study well and I can do my chores better. You don't get chest problems like before.'

It is the same in other parts of Africa where people can buy solar lamps.

- Families save the money they would have spent on kerosene – about 10% of the family income is often spent on kerosene.
- Children are able to study for longer in the evening, so they can make the most of their education and have a brighter future.
- Many report that the improved air quality inside the home has led to fewer coughs and eye problems.

Using solar lamps is much more **sustainable**.

- Smaller amounts of fossil fuels are burned, emitting less CO_2.
- Fewer particulates are released into the atmosphere. As well as causing health problems, black carbon particulates absorb solar radiation and contribute to global warming.

Not only in Africa

If you have travelled on a motorway or main railway line in the UK recently, you may have noticed that solar power is making a difference in the UK too. More and more people are installing solar panels on the roof of their homes, and farmers are turning some of their fields over to 'solar farms'.

Installing solar panels on the house roof brings benefits to the householder and also to the wider community. The householder reduces their electricity bill – and may even be paid for any energy they feed back into the National Grid. And everyone benefits because less electricity needs to be generated at the power station. In Sheffield, solar panels on houses generate enough electricity to meet up to a third of the residents' needs (around 1410 kWh). In Oxfordshire, a solar farm with 3000 solar panels supplies electricity to a local business park. It has a capacity of 0.7 MW and can generate up to 682 MWh.

Food or electricity?

Some people object to seeing fields of solar panels. Others argue that farmland should be used to produce food and not solar energy. However, some farmers choose to do both. An energy company pays the farmer for the use of the land. There may not be enough space to grow and harvest crops, but sheep or poultry can be kept in the fields. Alternatively, the field could be seeded with wild flowers to increase the **biodiversity**.

Who should decide?

Installing solar panels on the roofs of suitable offices and factories would greatly increase the generation of electricity from renewable sources.

Putting solar tiles on south-facing roofs could be included in building regulations for new houses.

But both these initiatives would be expensive. Should the Government bring in laws to make them happen? Should it be left to individuals to choose?

Who should decide about how we generate electricity in the UK?

This house has solar panels on the roof to generate electricity for the household.

Synoptic link

You can learn more about how electricity is generated in the UK in P2.2B *What happens in a power station?*

Key word

➤ biodiversity

Some farmers use their land for grazing as well as solar panels.

Questions

1 Explain why the invention of the blue LED was described as 'an invention of greatest benefit to mankind'.

2 Suggest what the author means by saying that children who are able to study longer in the evenings will have a 'brighter future'.

3 Use the example of solar lights in Africa to explain the idea of sustainability.

4 What would a home owner need to take into account before deciding to spend money on solar panels?

5 What factors might a farmer take into account when deciding whether to use some of their land to generate solar power?

P7.2 What is heat?

Find out about

- how Joule measured the 'mechanical equivalent of heat'
- evidence for conservation of energy

Key word

➤ mechanical equivalent of heat

Toolmakers plunge hot metals into cold water to cool the metal rapidly, a process called quenching.

In P6.1 you read a little about James Joule and Benjamin Thompson (also known as Count Rumford). They were among the scientists who established that doing the same amount of work on a material produced the same temperature change no matter which method you used to do the work. This section tells more of the story.

Caloric

Up until the middle of the nineteenth century, it was commonly believed that heat was a material substance, a fluid named caloric. Hot objects contained lots of caloric, and cold objects contained less. There was plenty of experimental evidence to support this theory:

- Caloric was conserved. When a lump of hot iron was placed in water, the caloric flowed from the hot iron (which cooled) to the water (which got warmer).

- Most materials expand on heating. The caloric pushed the atoms further apart.

- Specific heat was a measure of the space between the atoms. Water, with a high specific heat capacity, had lots of space between the atoms; lead, with a low specific heat capacity, must have much less.

There was discussion about the weight of caloric. Rumford showed that there was no weight change when ice melted into water. This did not disprove the existence of caloric, but simply implied that it must be weightless.

It was more difficult to use the caloric theory to explain heating by friction. Where did the caloric come from when two things rubbed together became warmer? Humphry Davy showed that when two pieces of ice were rubbed together in a vacuum, they began to melt. Davy concluded: "The immediate cause of the phenomenon of heat is motion."

Mechanical equivalent of heat

Benjamin Thompson was made Count Rumford by the Bavarian Government for his work in reorganising the army. It was while watching cannons being made that he became intrigued by the amount of heat generated as the metal was worked. Many people knew that working metal made it hot, but nobody had tried to find out why.

> *The more I meditated on these phenomena, the more they appeared to me to be curious and interesting. A thorough investigation of them seemed even to bid fair to give a farther insight into the hidden nature of heat; . . . a subject on which the opinions of philosophers have, in all ages, been much divided.*

Rumford was the first person to look for a relationship between the mechanical work done against friction and an increase in temperature. His experiment showed that boring a cannon continued to produce heat – the material did not run out of caloric. In 1798 he reported the results of his experiments:

> Total quantity of ice-cold water which, with the heat actually generated by friction, and accumulated in 2 hours and 30 minutes, might have been heated 180 degrees, or made to boil = 26.58 pounds.
>
> From 'An Inquiry concerning the Source of the Heat which is Excited by Friction.' Benjamin Count of Rumford. *Philosophical Transactions of the Royal Society of London* Vol. 88 (1798), pp.80–102.

Joule calculated that in Rumford's experiment, 1034 foot-pounds of work would raise the temperature of 1 pound of water by 1 degree Fahrenheit. In SI units the experiment showed that about 6000 J of energy was equivalent to 1 Calorie, the unit used to measure heat. One Calorie was defined as the heat needed to raise the temperature of 1 kg of water from 0 °C to 1 °C. Although it is not an SI unit, it is still used as a unit for measuring the energy value of foods, where it is given the abbreviation kcal.

At the time when Joule was working in England, Julius von Mayer was thinking about the same issues in Germany. He found that agitating water raised its temperature. Mayer was the first to use the term **mechanical equivalent of heat** to describe the equivalence of mechanical work and heat.

Joule's interest in heat began when he was experimenting with the new 'electromagnetic engines' that could be used as generators or motors. In 1843 he reported to the Royal Society on his experiments, comparing:

● the heating effect of an electric current from a chemical cell

● the heating effect of an electric current from a generator driven by a falling weight

● the work done when an electric motor was used to lift a load.

Joule went on to design experiments to find a consistent value for the 'conversion factor' between mechanical work and heat. In his most important experiment, falling weights turned paddle-wheels that stirred water. He calculated the work done by the weights as they fell and measured the temperature rise of the water.

Careful experimentation

It is very difficult to measure energy exactly in heating experiments, because some energy always dissipates to the surroundings, unless everything is at room temperature. In accounting for all the energy, the experimenter needs to know the specific heat capacity of every part of the system, as well as the material they are measuring in the experiment. Joule was a great experimental scientist because he tried to think of everything that might affect the outcome.

In his report to the Royal Society in 1850 Joule described in great detail how he controlled for all the factors he could think of.

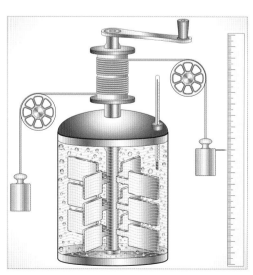

Joule's apparatus. The falling weights stirred the water, and this motion raised the temperature of the water.

Changing minds

In the following years many other scientists also carried out experiments. They were all trying to find out whether a given amount of mechanical (or electrical) working always produced the same amount of heat. Some of these results are shown in the table below. No matter how they carried out the experiments, the exchange rate between work and heat was always in the range 3.9–4.7 kJ for every Calorie. (Of course, nineteenth-century scientists did not use the joule. In England, mechanical work was measured in foot-pounds, where 1 foot-pound = 1.4 J.)

Date	Experimenter	Method	Result: the value of 1 Calorie in kJ
1798	Thompson	tool driven by horses drilled a brass cannon; the energy produced was used to heat water	about 6
1842	Mayer	compressing gases and measuring the temperature change	3.5
1843	Joule	several experiments in which an electric generator was driven by falling weights; the electric current produced was used to heat water	4.76 5.38 5.60 4.90
1843	Joule	electric current from a chemical cell: • drove a motor to lift weights • passed through a coil and heated water	5.51 3.15
1845	Joule	first paddle-wheel experiment	4.80
1847	Joule	improved paddle-wheel experiment: • churning water • churning whale oil (using the known specific heat capacity for whale oil) • churning mercury (using the known specific heat capacity for mercury)	4.21 4.22 4.24
1848	Joule	paddle-wheel with water, taking greater care	4.15
1850	Joule	friction of iron plates rubbed together	4.21
1857–1859	various experimenters	a variety of indirect electrical methods used; however, electrical units were not yet standardised	values in the range 3.9–4.7
1850–1875	various experimenters	a variety of mechanical working methods, including boring metals, crushing lead, measuring the output of a steam engine, friction of metals, and expansion and contraction of metals	values in the range 4.05–4.35
1867	Joule	heating by a known electric current through a known resistance	4.22
1878	Joule	improved paddle-wheel experiment (weighted average of 34 experiments, with corrections)	4.172
1879	Rowland	paddle-wheel driven by a steam engine	4.179

Results of some of the experiments carried out to measure a 'mechanical equivalent of heat', converted to SI units.

By 1878, the conversion factor had been calculated to a precision of ±0.001 kJ. At this point other factors became significant, such as the precision with which the acceleration due to gravity could be measured. This conversion factor, 4.17 kJ, is the energy needed to heat 1 kg of water by 1 °C; that is, the specific heat capacity of water.

In 1950, the International Committee for Weights and Measures in Paris accepted W. J. de Haas's recommended value of 4.1855 kJ/kg °C for the specific heat capacity of water at 15 °C. Joule and other scientists, working with nineteenth-century apparatus, had achieved values very close to the value used today.

Conservation of energy

By 1879 there was general agreement that no matter which path was chosen, heat, mechanical work, electrical work, and chemical energy were all equivalent, provided everything was accounted for. The fluid caloric was no longer accepted as a scientific explanation of changes that took place during heating. The principle of **conservation of energy** was agreed.

> ### Synoptic link
>
> You can learn more about specific heat capacity in P6.1B *Internal energy and specific heat capacity.*

> ### Key word
>
> ➤ conservation of energy

Questions

1 There was experimental evidence to support the caloric theory. Identify three *observations* about heating materials that can be explained by the caloric theory. For each observation describe the caloric *explanation*.

2 One of the aims of science is to develop good explanations of natural phenomena. Which scientist in this story set out to explain an everyday observation? Justify your answer.

3 Look at the table of results. What information from that table would give other scientists confidence that there is a constant link between mechanical work and heat?

4 In a version of Joule's paddle-wheel experiment, a mass of metal totalling 26.3 kg fell through a height of 1.6 m, and turned paddles immersed in 6.3 kg of water in a calorimeter. This was done 20 times, and the temperature of the water and calorimeter rose a total of 0.31 °C. Calculate the value for the specific heat capacity of water given by this data.

5 The table of results shows that Joule repeated and improved his paddle-wheel experiment to account for a number of factors. Look at the diagram of Joule's apparatus and suggest two factors that he would have needed to consider to make sure his results were as accurate as possible.

6 The title of this topic is 'What is heat?'. At the beginning of the nineteenth century most scientists thought that the answer to the question was the weightless fluid, caloric. By the end of the century most had changed their minds.
   a Suggest why many scientists did not change their ideas when Joule presented his results to the Royal Society in 1850.
   b What do you think most scientists would have answered to the question 'What is heat?' by the end of the nineteenth century?

Ideas about Science

Learning about the Ideas about Science in this course will help you understand how scientific knowledge is obtained, how to respond to science stories and issues in the wider world, and the impacts of scientific knowledge on society.

IaS1: What needs to be considered when investigating a phenomenon scientifically?

The aim of science is to develop good explanations for natural phenomena. There is no single 'scientific method' that leads to explanations, but scientists do have characteristic ways of working. In particular, scientific explanations are based on a cycle of collecting and analysing data.

Usually, developing an explanation begins with proposing a hypothesis. A hypothesis is a tentative explanation for an observed phenomenon ('this happens because…').

The hypothesis is used to make a prediction about how, in a particular experimental context, a change in a factor will affect the outcome. A prediction can be presented in a variety of ways, for example, in words or as a sketch graph.

In order to test a prediction and the hypothesis upon which it is based, it is necessary to plan an experiment that enables data to be collected in a safe, accurate, and repeatable way.

In a given context you should be able to:

- use your scientific knowledge and understanding to develop and justify a hypothesis and prediction

- suggest appropriate apparatus, materials, and techniques, justifying the choice with reference to the precision, accuracy, and validity of the data that will be collected

- explain the importance of accuracy and precision when determining scientific quantities

- use scientific quantities (such as mass, volume, and temperature), and know how they are measured

- identify factors that need to be controlled, and how they could be controlled

- suggest an appropriate sample size and/or range of values to be measured, and justify the suggestion

- plan experiments and describe procedures to make observations, collect data, and test a prediction or hypothesis

- identify hazards associated with the data collection and suggest ways of minimising the risk.

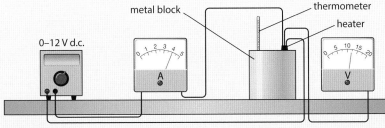

This apparatus could be used to measure the effectiveness of different insulation materials. Can you write a testable hypothesis for this investigation? Which factor would you change during the investigation, and which ones would you need to control?

IaS2: What processes are needed to draw conclusions from data?

The cycle of collecting, presenting and analysing data usually involves translating data from one form to another, mathematical processing, graphical display, and analysis; only then can we begin to draw conclusions.

A set of repeat measurements can be processed to calculate a range within which the true value probably lies and to give a best estimate of the value (mean).

Displaying data graphically can help to show trends or patterns, and to assess the spread of repeated measurements.

Mathematical comparisons between results and statistical methods can help with further analysis.

When working with data you should be able to:

- produce appropriate tables, graphs, and charts to display the data
- use the appropriate units and be able to convert between units
- use prefixes (from tera to nano) and powers of ten to show orders of magnitude
- use an appropriate number of significant figures.

When displaying data graphically you should be able to:

- select an appropriate graphical form, using appropriate axes and scales
- plot data points correctly, drawing an appropriate line of best fit and indicating uncertainty (e.g., range bars).

When analysing data you should be able to:

- identify patterns or trends
- use statistics (range and mean)
- obtain values from a line on a graph (including gradient, interpolation, and extrapolation).

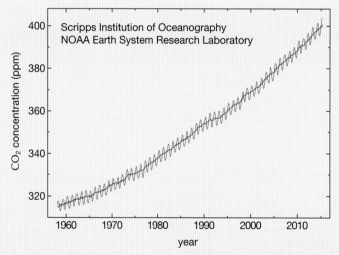

This graph displays data on the concentration of carbon dioxide in the atmosphere in Hawaii since 1958. What patterns can you see in the data? What is the overall trend?

Data can never be relied on completely because observations may be incorrect and all measurements are subject to uncertainty, arising from the limitations of the measuring equipment and the person using it.

Experiments and data obtained must be evaluated before we can make conclusions based on the results. There could be many reasons why the quality (accuracy, precision, repeatability, and reproducibility) of the data could be questioned and a number of ways in which they could be improved. A result that appears to be an outlier should be treated as data, unless there is a reason to reject it (e.g., measurement or recording error).

In a given context you should be able to:

- discuss the accuracy, precision, repeatability, and reproducibility of a set of data
- identify random and systematic errors that are sources of uncertainty in measurements
- explain the decision to discard or retain an outlier
- suggest improvements to an experiment, and explain why they would increase the quality of the data collected
- suggest further investigations that could be done.

A prediction is based on a tentative explanation (a hypothesis). When collected data agree with the prediction, it increases our confidence that the explanation is correct. But it does not *prove* that the explanation is correct. Disagreement between the data and the prediction indicates that one or other is wrong, and decreases our confidence in the explanation.

In a given context you should be able to:

- use observations and data to make a conclusion
- explain how much the data increases or decreases confidence in a prediction or hypothesis.

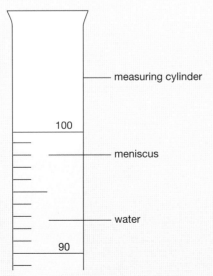

The volume of a liquid can be measured using a measuring cylinder. But there will be uncertainty in the measurement. Can you suggest a source of random error, a source of systematic error, and a mistake that could be made when taking this kind of measurement?

IaS3: How are scientific explanations developed?

Scientists often look for patterns in data to identify correlations that can suggest cause-and-effect links. They then try to explain these links.

The first step is to identify a correlation between a factor and an outcome. The factor may be the cause, or one of the causes, of the outcome. In many situations, a factor may not always lead to the outcome, but increases the chance (or the risk) of it happening. In order to claim that the factor causes the outcome we need to identify a process or mechanism that might account for how it does this.

You should be able to use ideas about correlation and cause to:

● identify a correlation in data presented as text, in a table, or as a graph

● distinguish between a correlation and a cause-and-effect link

● suggest factors that might increase the chance of a particular outcome in a given situation, but do not always lead to it

● explain why individual cases do not provide convincing evidence for or against a correlation

● explain why you would accept or reject a claim that a factor is a cause of an outcome, based on the presence or absence of a causal mechanism.

Scientific explanations and theories do not 'emerge' automatically from data, and are separate from the data. Proposing an explanation involves creative thinking. Collecting sufficient data from which to develop an explanation often relies on technological developments that enable new observations to be made.

As more evidence becomes available, a hypothesis may be modified and may eventually become an accepted explanation or theory.

A scientific theory is a general explanation that applies to a large number of situations or examples (perhaps to all possible ones), which has been tested and used successfully, and is widely accepted by scientists. A scientific explanation of a specific event or phenomenon is often based on applying a scientific theory to the situation in question.

You should be able to:

● describe and explain examples of scientific explanations that have developed over time, and how they were modified when new evidence became available.

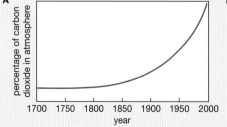
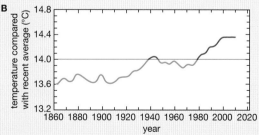

The graphs show how global temperatures and carbon dioxide levels have changed. Can you describe the correlation shown by this pair of graphs?

Findings reported by an individual scientist or group are carefully checked by the scientific community before being accepted as scientific knowledge. Scientists are usually sceptical about claims based on results that cannot be reproduced by anyone else, and about unexpected findings until they have been repeated (by themselves) or reproduced (by someone else).

Two (or more) scientists may legitimately draw different conclusions about the same data. A scientist's personal background, experience, or interests may influence their judgements.

An accepted scientific explanation is rarely abandoned just because new data disagrees with it. It usually survives until a better explanation is available.

You should be able to:

● describe the 'peer review' process, in which new scientific claims are evaluated by other scientists.

Models are used in science to help explain ideas and to test explanations. A model identifies features of a system and rules by which the features interact. It can be used to predict possible outcomes. Representational models use physical analogies or spatial representations to help visualise scientific explanations and mechanisms. Descriptive models are used to explain phenomena. Mathematical models use patterns in data of past events, along with known scientific relationships, to predict behaviour; often the calculations are complex and can be done more quickly by computer.

Models can be used to investigate phenomena quickly and without ethical and practical limitations, but their usefulness is limited by how accurately the model represents the real world.

For a variety of given models (including representational, descriptive, mathematical, computational, and spatial models) you should be able to:

● use the model to explain a scientific idea, solve a problem, or make a prediction

● identify limitations of the model.

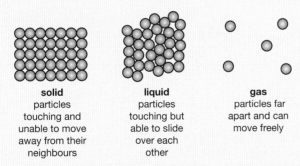

solid
particles touching and unable to move away from their neighbours

liquid
particles touching but able to slide over each other

gas
particles far apart and can move freely

The diagram represents the particle model of matter. Can you use it to explain changes of state? What are the limitations of the representation?

IaS4: How do science and technology impact on society?

Science and technology provide people with many things that they value, and that enhance their quality of life. However, some applications of science can have unintended and undesirable impacts on the quality of life or the environment. Scientists can devise ways of reducing these impacts and of using natural resources in a sustainable way.

You should be able to:

● describe and explain examples of applications of science that have made significant positive differences to people's lives.

Everything we do carries a certain risk of accident or harm. New technologies and processes can introduce new risks. The size of a risk can be assessed by estimating its chance of occurring in a large sample, over a given period of time.

To make a decision about a course of action, we need to take account of both the risks and benefits to the different individuals or groups involved. People are generally more willing to accept the risk associated with something they choose to do than something that is imposed, and to accept risks that have short-lived effects rather than long-lasting ones. People's perception of the size of a particular risk may be different from the statistically estimated risk. People tend to overestimate the risk of unfamiliar things (such as flying as compared with cycling), and of things whose effect is invisible or long-term (such as ionising radiation).

Electric motors exist in all sizes, from the very small to very large. Can you describe and explain examples of how electric motors make a positive difference to people's lives?

You should be able to:

● identify examples of risks that have arisen from a new scientific or technological advance

● for a given situation:

  ■ identify risks and benefits to the different individuals and groups involved

  ■ discuss a course of action, taking account of who benefits and who takes the risks

  ■ suggest reasons for people's willingness to accept the risk

  H ■ distinguish between perceived and calculated risk.

Some forms of scientific research, and some applications of scientific knowledge, have ethical implications. In discussions of ethical issues, a common argument is that the right decision is the one that leads to the best outcome for the greatest number of people.

Where an ethical issue is involved you should be able to:

● suggest reasons why different decisions on the same issue might be appropriate in view of differences in personal, social, economic, or environmental context.

● make a decision and justify it by evaluating the evidence and arguments

● distinguish questions that could be answered using a scientific approach, from those that could not

● state clearly what this issue is and summarise different views that may be held.

Scientists must communicate their work to a range of audiences, including the public, other scientists, and politicians, in ways that can be understood. This enables decision-making based on information about risks, benefits, costs, and ethical issues.

You should be able to:

● explain why scientists should communicate their work to a range of audiences.

P8 Practical techniques

Why study practical techniques?

Practical work is an essential part of science. It helps us investigate what happens in the world around us. It also helps us explain how and why these things happen.

The aim of science is to develop good explanations for observations in the natural world. Scientific explanations are based on data, so scientists collect data to make sense of their observations.

Practising practical techniques helps us to collect data in a safe, ethical, and repeatable way, and to improve the accuracy of the data we collect. It is important that different people use the same techniques and standard procedures to collect data. This helps them compare their data more easily.

Practical work not only helps us to develop explanations, but also to test explanations proposed by other people. Understanding some of the ways scientists collect data helps us to make informed decisions about scientific issues in the news and in our own lives.

Practical techniques

- Using appropriate apparatus to make and record a range of measurements accurately, including length, mass, time, volume, and temperature.
- Using measurements to determine the density of solids and liquids.
- Using appropriate apparatus to measure and observe the effects of forces, including the extension of springs.
- Using appropriate apparatus and techniques for measuring motion, including determination of speed, and of rate of change of speed (acceleration and deceleration).
- Making observations of waves in fluids and solids to identify the suitability of apparatus to measure speed, frequency, and wavelength.
- Safely using appropriate apparatus in a range of contexts to measure energy changes/transfers and associated values, such as work done.
- Using appropriate apparatus to measure current, potential difference (voltage), and resistance.
- Using appropriate apparatus to explore the characteristics of a variety of circuit elements.
- Using circuit diagrams to construct and check series and parallel circuits, including a variety of common circuit elements.

A: Measuring length, temperature, and volume

Find out about

- using appropriate apparatus to accurately measure and record length, temperature, and volume of liquids and gases

Apparatus and materials

- ➤ ruler
- ➤ thermometer
- ➤ measuring cylinder
- ➤ syringe
- ➤ pipette
- ➤ analogue meter

Many measuring instruments have a linear scale. This is a series of equally spaced lines, or **graduations**. You use the scale to read off a value.

You may have to use a linear scale on:

- a ruler (to measure length)
- a thermometer (to measure temperature)
- a measuring cylinder, syringe, or pipette (to measure the volume of a liquid or gas)
- an analogue meter.

When a measurement falls between two graduations, it has to be estimated. This means there will be **uncertainty** in the measurement.

Procedure

1 Look at the scale you are reading. Usually, not all of the graduations will be marked with a number. Decide what the distance between two graduations represents.

2 If the reading is between two graduations, decide which graduation it is closest to. Record this as the measurement.

3 Record the uncertainty of the measurement as ± half the smallest graduation.

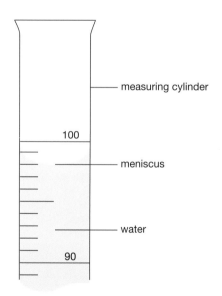

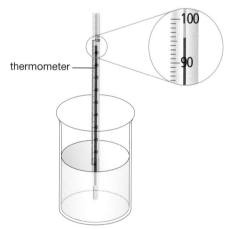

Liquid in a measuring cylinder has a curved top surface. This is called the **meniscus**. The volume is read from the bottom of the meniscus. You should always make the reading at eye level. The volume of water in the diagram is 98 ± 0.5 cm³.

A thermometer has a linear scale. The coloured liquid inside the thermometer expands as the temperature goes up, and rises up the narrow glass tube. Here, the reading is between 95 °C and 96 °C, but is closest to 96 °C. We would record the measurement as 96 °C ± 0.5 °C.

Key words

- ➤ graduation
- ➤ uncertainty
- ➤ meniscus

B: Measuring mass

Mass is measured using a balance. Choose a balance with a level of accuracy fit for the purpose of the task – to how many significant figures do you need to measure the mass?

If a very sensitive balance is used, it is necessary to shield the balance from drafts to get an accurate measurement.

Find out about

● using appropriate apparatus to accurately measure and record mass

Apparatus and materials

➤ balance
➤ weighing vessel

Procedures

Weighing direct

1   Check that the balance is clean and reading zero.

2   Place a suitable empty weighing vessel on the balance platform. Set the display to zero. (This is known as taring the balance.)

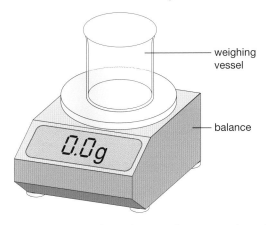

weighing vessel

balance

3   Place the sample in the weighing vessel on the balance platform.

4   The reading on the balance is the mass of the sample.

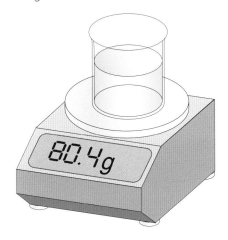

Weighing by difference

1   Check that the balance is clean and reading zero.

2   Place the sample in a suitable clean, dry weighing vessel on the balance platform. Record the mass.

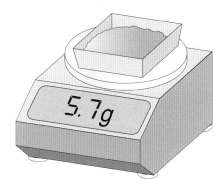

3   Transfer the sample to another container. Weigh the weighing vessel and record its mass.

4   Calculate the mass of the sample from the difference between the two measurements.

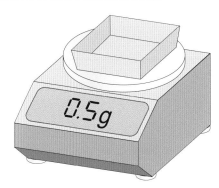

C: Measuring time

Find out about

- using appropriate apparatus to make and record measurements accurately, including time

Apparatus and materials

➤ timer (such as a stopwatch or stop clock)

Time is measured using a timer such as a stopwatch or stop clock. The timer may be part of a computer datalogging system.

You may wish to measure, for example, how long it takes for:

- a wave to cross a tank of water
- a trolley to roll down a slope
- an echo of sound to return from a distant building
- a person to react to a stimulus.

Procedure

A stopwatch showing a time of 42 s. This is an example of a digital meter.

A stop clock showing a time of 42 s. This is an example of an analogue meter.

1 At the starting point, start the timer (or if the timer is already running, make a note of the start time).

2 At the end point, stop the timer (or if the timer needs to keep running, make a note of the end time).

3 If the start time was not zero, subtract the start time from the end time.

Uncertainty

A digital stopwatch may show the time to tenths (0.1) or hundredths (0.01) of a second. However, when using a stopwatch, human reaction time can be up to 0.5 s. Therefore, you may need to record your measurement of the time with an uncertainty of ±0.5 s.

Minutes and seconds

Remember that 1 minute is divided into 60 seconds. This means that 1 minute 50 seconds is *not* the same as 1.50 minutes. (1.50 minutes is one-and-a-half minutes, which is 1 minute 30 seconds.)

Measuring reaction time

It takes time for the human body to react to seeing an event. This time is called the **reaction time**. You will need to work with a partner to measure each other's reaction times. This method uses the fact that a metre rule falls with a known acceleration (**g**, the acceleration due to gravity).

The time **t** in seconds taken for the rule to fall a distance d in metres can be calculated from the equation:

$$t = \sqrt{\frac{2d}{g}}$$

Procedure

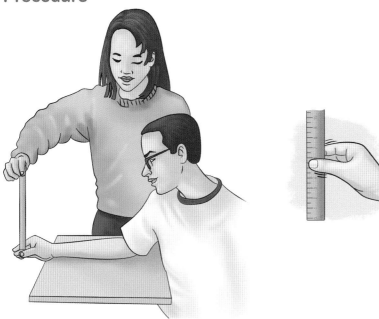

Joe's reaction time is the time it takes for him to catch the rule after Maya drops it. They can calculate this from the length of rule below his thumb and finger.

1. The person to be tested (the subject) sits with their arm resting on the table with their hand beyond the table. The assessor holds the rule vertically just above the subject's open thumb and forefinger.

2. When the subject is ready, the assessor releases the rule, without warning.

3. As soon as the subject sees the rule fall, they close their hand to catch it.

4. Record the distance, in metres, the rule fell before it was caught.

5. Use the equation to calculate the reaction time.

Apparatus and materials

➤ metre rule

Key words

➤ reaction time

Synoptic link

You can learn more about reaction times in P4.3E *Travelling safely*.

D: Measuring the density of solids and liquids

Find out about

- using appropriate apparatus to make and record measurements accurately to determine the density of solids and liquids

Apparatus and materials

➤ balance
➤ displacement can
➤ measuring cylinder
➤ object being measured

Synoptic link

You can learn more about calculating density in P6.1A *Early ideas about matter and energy.*

A dense material has a lot of mass packed into a small volume. If you measure the mass and volume of an object, you can then calculate the density of the material it is made of:

$$density = \frac{mass}{volume}$$

Units for density are kg/m^3 or g/cm^3.

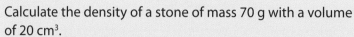

Worked example: Calculating density

Calculate the density of a stone of mass 70 g with a volume of 20 cm^3.

Step 1: Write down what you know, with the units.

mass = 70 g   volume = 20 cm^3

Step 2: Write down the equation you will use.

$$density = \frac{mass}{volume}$$

Step 3: Substitute in the quantities and calculate the density.

$$density = \frac{70\ g}{20\ cm^3}$$

Answer: density = 3.5 g/cm^3

Procedure

1 Use a balance to weigh the object. Record its mass.

2 Find the volume of the object.

   a If the object has a regular shape, such as a rectangular block, you can calculate its volume.

   volume of a rectangular block = length × breadth × height

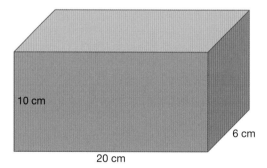

The volume of this block is 20 cm × 6 cm × 10 cm = 1200 cm^3.

b An object may have an irregular shape. To find its volume, it is easiest to measure the volume of water it displaces:

- Fill the displacement can with water just to the level of the spout.
- Immerse the object and collect the water it displaces. Measure and record the volume of water displaced.

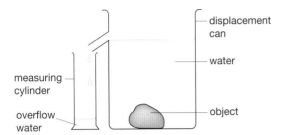

To measure the volume of an irregularly shaped solid, use a displacement can.

c For a liquid, measure the mass of a known volume of the liquid.

- Weigh the cylinder.
- Put in a measured volume of liquid and weigh again.

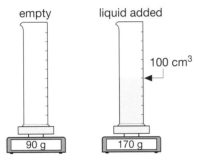

To find the density of a liquid, weigh an empty measuring cylinder, then add a known volume of the liquid and weigh again.

3 Calculate the density of the material.

E: Measuring the effect of a force on a spring

Find out about

● using appropriate apparatus to measure and observe the effects of forces, including the extension of springs

Apparatus and materials

➤ clamps
➤ clamp stand
➤ metre rule
➤ metal slabs
➤ slotted masses and holder
➤ spring
➤ set square
➤ eye protection

Wear eye protection in case the spring breaks.

CHECK SAFETY
Never work
unsupervised

Synoptic link

You can learn more about the effect of forces on materials, including springs, in P6.3A *Elastic materials*.

You can load a spring with masses and measure its change in length with a ruler. The force applied is the weight of the load. A load of 100 g provides a force of 1.0 N.

You can use a similar procedure to investigate the extension of other materials under load.

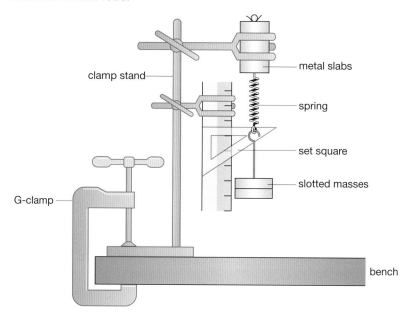

Procedure

1 Clamp the clamp stand to the bench. This stops it falling over.

2 Tightly clamp the loop at one end of the spring between the metal slabs.

3 Clamp the metre rule vertically, close to the spring, but not touching.

4 Use the set square to record the position of the bottom of the spring on the metre rule.

5 Suspend the first slotted mass from the spring. Record the new position of the bottom of the spring.

6 Add further slotted masses, recording the load and the position of the spring each time.

7 Plot a graph to show how the length of the spring changes as the load increases.

F: Measuring speed

The average speed of a moving object is calculated using the equation:
$$\text{speed} = \frac{\text{distance travelled}}{\text{time taken}}$$

Procedure

To determine the speed of a moving object, you need to measure the time the object takes to travel a measured distance. The shorter the time period over which the speed is measured, the closer the average speed is to an instantaneous speed.

Example 1: using a metre rule and stopwatch to determine average speed

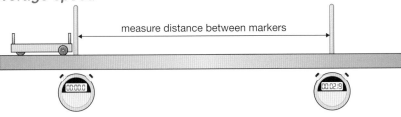

measure distance between markers

The trolley travels 2.50 m in 2.19 s. The average speed is 1.1 m/s (to 2 significant figures).

1 Measure the distance between two markers in metres.
2 Start the stopwatch as the moving object passes the first mark.
3 Stop the stopwatch as the moving object passes the second mark.
4 Use the equation to calculate the average speed of the trolley.

Example 2: using a datalogger to determine instantaneous speed

For short time intervals, a datalogger is more accurate than a hand-held stopwatch. The **interface** measures the time it takes for a trolley to pass through a light gate. The instantaneous speed can be calculated.

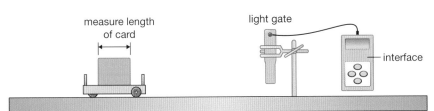

measure length of card

light gate

interface

The card passes though the light gate as the trolley travels along the bench. A sensor in the light gate sends a signal to the interface to start and stop the timer.

1 Measure the length of the card in metres.
2 Set the datalogger to measure the time it takes for the card to pass through the light gate.
3 Use the equation to calculate the speed of the trolley. Some dataloggers will let you input the card length into the interface, which then automatically calculates the speed.

Find out about

● using appropriate apparatus and techniques for measuring motion, including determination of speed

Apparatus and materials

➤ stopwatch
➤ metre rule or tape measure
➤ dynamics trolley
➤ card
➤ two clamp stands
➤ clamps
➤ datalogger with light gates

Protect the bench, and your feet and hands from falling trolleys.

CHECK SAFETY
Never work unsupervised

Synoptic link

You can learn more about calculating speed in P4.2A *Describing motion*.

Key word

➤ interface

G: Measuring acceleration

Find out about

● using appropriate apparatus and techniques for measuring motion, including determination of rate of change of speed (acceleration and deceleration)

Apparatus and materials

➤ metre rule
➤ dynamics trolley
➤ card
➤ two clamp stands
➤ clamps
➤ ramp
➤ wooden blocks
➤ datalogger with light gates

Protect the bench, and your feet and hands from falling trolleys.

CHECK SAFETY
Never work
unsupervised

Synoptic link

You can learn for more about calculating acceleration in P4.2A *Describing motion*.

Acceleration is the rate of change of velocity. It can be calculated using the equation:

$$\text{acceleration} = \frac{\text{change in velocity}}{\text{time taken}}$$

In a situation where the object is moving in a straight line, we can measure the rate of change of speed rather than velocity.

Procedure

Dataloggers use a variety of ways to determine acceleration. Here we describe how you could use a simple datalogger that measures only time intervals.

Measuring the acceleration of a trolley down a slope

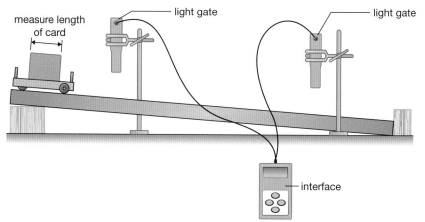

The card passes though each light gate as the trolley accelerates down the slope. The sensors in the light gates send signals to the interface to start and stop the timer.

1　Set the datalogger to measure the time it takes for the card to pass through each light gate, and the time to travel from one light gate to the next.

2　Measure the length of the card.

3　Set the trolley to run down the slope with the card passing through the light gates.

4　Record the times.

5　Use the times to calculate:

● the speed of the trolley through each gate

● the change in speed

● the acceleration of the trolley.

H: Observing waves on water

Making measurements of waves on water can be quite challenging. One arrangement you can use is a ripple tank.

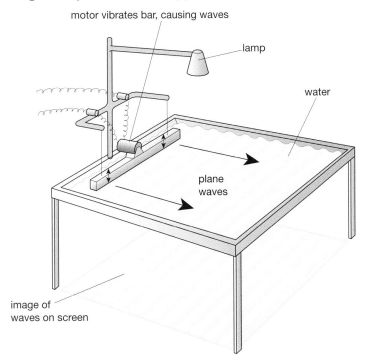

motor vibrates bar, causing waves

lamp

water

plane waves

image of waves on screen

A ripple tank is a shallow tank of water with a transparent bottom. Waves are generated using a motor attached to a narrow bar. A light placed above the tank will cast shadows of the waves on the floor.

Procedure

1   To determine the speed of waves on the water:

   ● Place two markers in the tank and measure their separation.

   ● Nudge the wooden bar to generate a single wave that travels across the tank.

   ● Measure the time taken for the wave to travel from one marker to the next.

   ● Calculate the wave speed using the equation:

$$\text{speed} = \frac{\text{distance travelled}}{\text{time taken}}$$

2   To determine the wavelength of waves on the water:

   ● Place two markers in the tank and measure their separation.

   ● Switch on the motor so that a continuous stream of waves moves across the tank.

   ● Count the number of whole waves between the markers.

   ● Calculate the wavelength by dividing the separation of the markers by the number of waves.

3   To determine the frequency of the waves in **2**, use the equation:

$$\text{frequency} = \frac{\text{wave speed}}{\text{wavelength}}$$

Find out about

● making observations of waves in fluids and solids to identify the suitability of apparatus to measure speed, frequency, and wavelength

Apparatus and materials

➤ ripple tank
➤ stopwatch
➤ ruler

Keep mains electrical equipment away from water. Clean up any spills.

CHECK SAFETY
Never work unsupervised

Synoptic link

You can learn more about properties of waves in P1.3A *What is a wave?*

I: Measuring energy transfers

Find out about

- safely using appropriate apparatus in a range of contexts to measure energy changes/transfers and associated values, such as work done

CHECK SAFETY
Never work
unsupervised

Apparatus and materials

➤ electric motor
➤ low-voltage power supply
➤ connecting leads
➤ ammeter
➤ voltmeter
➤ stopwatch
➤ metre rule
➤ load and string
➤ G-clamp (to fix motor to bench)

Synoptic link

You can learn more about calculating energy transfers in P3.3 *What determines the rate of energy transfer in a circuit?*, P4.4A *Work done*, and P6.1B *Internal energy and specific heat capacity.*

You can calculate the energy transferred from an electric power supply using the equation:

energy transferred = power × time = current × potential difference × time

You can calculate the energy transferred when mechanical work is done using the equation:

energy transferred = work done = force × distance

Energy transferred may give rise to a change in temperature. You can calculate the energy transferred to a thermal store using the equation:

energy transferred = mass × specific heat capacity × temperature rise

Whenever energy is transferred, some energy is dissipated to the surroundings. By calculating the energy input to a system, and the energy stored at the end, you can find how much the energy was dissipated.

Procedure

In each case you can determine the energy input by measuring the quantities given in the equations.

Example 1: using an electric motor to raise a load

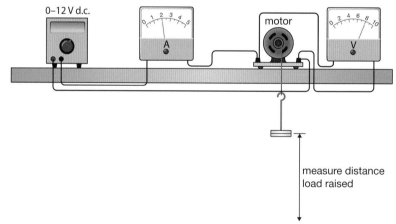

measure distance
load raised

An electric motor is used to lift a known load through a measured distance.

1 Connect up the motor and ammeter in series with the power supply.

2 Connect the voltmeter in parallel with the motor.

3 Switch on the power supply and find the setting that allows a suitable load to be lifted steadily.

4 Reset the load to the extent of the string. The load should not be touching the floor at the start.

5 Measure the time it takes to lift the load a measured distance. Record the current and potential difference while the motor is working.

6 Use the equations above to calculate:
   - the electrical work done by the power supply
   - the mechanical work done to lift the load (remember the force to lift the load is its weight in newtons)
   - the energy dissipated to the surroundings during the process.

Example 2: using an electric heater to heat a metal block

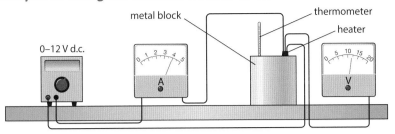

A metal block is heated using a small electric heater. The block may be wrapped in an insulating material to reduce energy being transferred to the surroundings. The change in temperature is recorded.

1 Connect up the heater and ammeter in series with the power supply.

2 Connect the voltmeter in parallel with the heater.

3 Record the starting temperature of the metal block.

4 Switch on the heater for 10 minutes.

5 Continue to observe the temperature after the heater is switched off. Record the highest temperature reached.

6 Use the equations on the previous page to calculate:

- the electrical work done by the power supply

- the thermal energy transferred to the metal block

- the specific heat capacity of the metal.

Example 3: using mechanical work to heat lead

1 Weigh about 500 g of lead shot into a plastic cup. Use a thermometer to record its temperature.

2 Place an end cap on one end of the cardboard tube and put the shot into the tube. Seal the open end of the tube.

3 Turn the tube over 40 times so that the shot falls the length of the tube 40 times.

4 Pour the shot into the plastic cup and record its temperature.

5 Use the equations on the previous page to calculate:

- the work done in raising the lead shot the length of the tube before each fall

- the thermal energy transferred to the lead during the process

- the energy dissipated to the surroundings during the process.

Apparatus and materials

➤ low-voltage power supply
➤ connecting leads
➤ heater
➤ ammeter
➤ voltmeter
➤ stopwatch
➤ thermometer
➤ metal block

Apparatus and materials

➤ top-pan balance
➤ cardboard tube 50–100 cm long with end caps
➤ lead shot
➤ thermometer
➤ metre rule
➤ plastic cup

Wear gloves if handling the lead shot.

J: Measuring current, potential difference, and resistance

Find out about

- using appropriate apparatus to measure current, potential difference (voltage), and resistance

Apparatus and materials

➤ low-voltage power supply
➤ multimeter
➤ connecting leads

CHECK SAFETY
Never work
unsupervised

Using a multimeter

A digital multimeter multimeter can be set to measure current, voltage, or resistance.

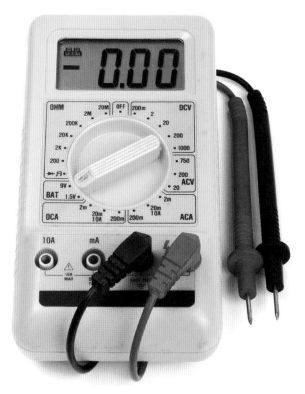

A multimeter can measure current, voltage, or resistance.

Measuring the potential difference across a resistor in a circuit

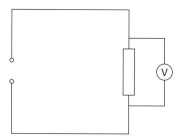

To measure the potential difference across a component, connect the voltmeter in parallel with the component.

1 Turn the multimeter dial to the 'V = 20' setting. The display should read 0.00.

2 Use a lead to connect the terminal labelled 'COM' to the side of the resistor connected to the negative terminal on the power supply.

3 Use a second lead to connect the other side of the resistor to the terminal labelled 'VΩmA'.

4 Record the reading on the meter in volts.

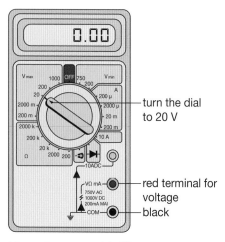

turn the dial
to 20 V

red terminal for
voltage

black

Measuring potential difference.

Measuring the current through a resistor in a circuit

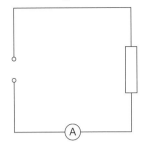

To measure the current through a component, connect the ammeter in series with the component.

1   Turn the multimeter dial to the 'A = 200 mA' setting: always start at the highest reading. The display should read 0.00.

2   Make a break in the circuit where you need to measure the current.

3   Use a lead to connect the terminal labelled 'COM' to the negative terminal on the power supply.

4   Use a second lead to connect the terminal labelled 'VΩmA' to the positive terminal on the power supply.

5   The display will show the current in milliamps (mA). Record the current in mA.

6   To convert from milliamps to amps, divide by 1000.

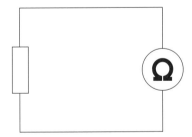

start at the highest mA reading

'VΩmA' terminal connects to + terminal on power supply

'COM' terminal connects to – terminal on power supply

Measuring current.

Measuring resistance directly

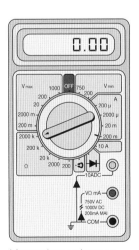

You can use the multimeter to measure the resistance of a component.

1   Turn the dial to the '2000k' setting. The display will go blank or read 'ERR' (error).

2   Plug leads into the 'COM' and 'VΩmA' terminals.

3   Touch the ends of the leads together. If all is well, the meter should read 0. (It is reading the resistance of the connecting leads, which is almost zero.)

4   Connect the ends of the leads to either end of the component you are testing.

5   Turn the dial through the Ω ranges until a reading is displayed. The setting of the switch shows the maximum resistance that can be displayed.

6   Record the reading on the display.

Measuring resistance.

K: Exploring the characteristics of circuit elements

Find out about

● using appropriate apparatus to explore the characteristics of a variety of circuit elements

Apparatus and materials

➤ low-voltage, variable power supply
➤ connecting leads
➤ ammeter
➤ voltmeter
➤ components e.g. lamp, thermistor, LDR, diode

CHECK SAFETY
Never work
unsupervised

Synoptic link

You can learn more about using components in circuits in P3.2C *Variable resistors, diodes, and sensors.*

When you connect electrical components in circuits, it is important to know how they will affect the current in the circuit when the potential difference across them changes. Many components do not obey Ohm's law (see P3.1B). A current–voltage graph is a useful way of displaying that information.

Procedure

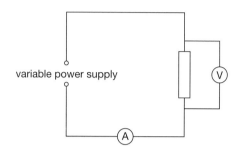

variable power supply

1 Connect the component you are investigating in series with the ammeter and power supply.

2 Connect the voltmeter across the component.

3 Set the power supply to its lowest output and switch on.

4 Increase the output from the power supply in steps. Record the potential difference across the component and the current in the circuit each time. Do not increase the potential difference beyond the tolerance of the component.

5 Turn the potential difference back to the minimum. Reverse the connections to the power supply so that the potential difference across the component is in the opposite direction. You may need to reverse the connections to the voltmeter and ammeter.

6 Repeat step **4**, remembering to record the current and potential difference as negative if you reversed the meters.

7 Plot a graph to show how the current in the circuit changes as the potential difference across the component changes.

L: Constructing and troubleshooting circuits

Connecting a branching electric circuit like this one can be confusing. It helps if you follow the same procedure each time.

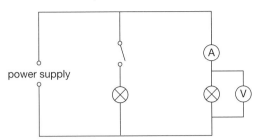

Find out about

- using circuit diagrams to construct and check series and parallel circuits, including a variety of common circuit elements

Apparatus and materials

- ➤ low-voltage power supply
- ➤ connecting leads
- ➤ voltmeter
- ➤ ammeter
- ➤ lamps

CHECK SAFETY
Never work
unsupervised

Procedure

1   First connect together the series loop that includes the power supply.
    Lay the components out in the same positions as in the diagram.
    Then connect them with leads.

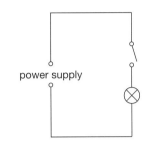

2   Add the second, parallel loop of the circuit.

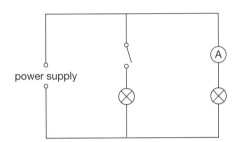

3   Finally connect the voltmeter in parallel with the component across which you will measure the potential difference.

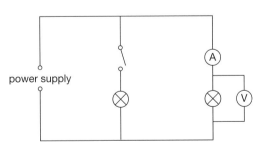

Troubleshooting

How do you find the problem when your circuit doesn't do what you expected?

Common problems and possible solutions

- Poor connections between connecting leads and components – push the plugs firmly into the terminals.

- Components connected the wrong way round – if you're using batteries, check they are all pointing in the same direction; check the direction of diodes.

- Component is broken – check the filaments in any lamps are intact; replace a component with a new one.

M: Uncertainty in measurements

Key words

➤ variation
➤ true value
➤ uncertainty
➤ random error
➤ systematic error
➤ outlier
➤ accuracy
➤ precision

If you measured the pulse rate of 20 people, you wouldn't get the same value for everybody. There would be **variation** in the data – in other words, there would be a range of measured values. This is because there is variation in the population. Everybody is different, and there are factors (such as diet, exercise, and stress) that cause the pulse rate to be different in each person.

If each of the 20 people measured the length of the same piece of paper, you might expect them all to come up with the same length. But you could still see variation in the data. This is due to the measurements themselves. Measured values are usually different to the **true value**, and each time a measurement is taken we can't be certain how close it is to the true value. So it is useful to give an indication of **uncertainty** when recording a measurement.

For example, you could record the volume of a liquid as 15.30 ± 0.05 cm³. From this we can see that:

- the measured value (which could be the mean of several measurements) is 15.30 cm³
- there is uncertainty in the measurement
- the person who took the measurement is confident that the true value is between 15.25 cm³ and 15.35 cm³.

Sources of uncertainty

There are two general sources of uncertainty in measurements: systematic errors and random errors.

Random error causes repeated measurements to give different values. This can happen, for example, when making judgements about the colour change at an end point or when estimating the reading from a thermometer.

A random error is not a mistake made by the person taking the measurement. A random error is a source of variation in measurements that cannot be eliminated, although there are often things we can do to reduce the amount of variation it causes.

Systematic error causes all repeated measurements to be the same amount higher or lower than the true value. This can happen when using an incorrectly calibrated measuring instrument or when taking measurements at a consistent, but wrong, temperature.

An example of how random and systematic errors can occur

The two different types of error are illustrated in the following example. The flask shown in the margin is used to measure out 25 cm³ of a solution.

For the flask in the diagram, the manufacturer states that the line indicates a measured volume of 25.00 ± 0.06 cm³. So even if the measured volume of liquid is exactly aligned with the marked line each time, the volume could be consistently larger or smaller than 25.00 cm³ (by up to 0.06 cm³). This is systematic error.

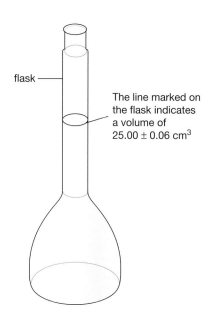

flask

The line marked on the flask indicates a volume of 25.00 ± 0.06 cm³

This flask is used to measure a particular volume of liquid.

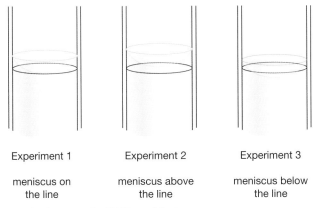

Experiment 1	Experiment 2	Experiment 3
meniscus on the line	meniscus above the line	meniscus below the line

Random errors in the use of a 25.00 cm³ flask.

It is difficult to fill a flask with liquid so that the bottom of the meniscus is aligned exactly with the marked line. In experiments 2 and 3 in the diagram above, the meniscus is not aligned exactly – so the measured amounts are not 25.00 cm³. This is an example of random error. We could reduce the size of the error by aligning the meniscus as closely as possible to the line each time, but it would be very difficult to completely eliminate this source of error.

The difference between 'error' and 'mistake'

Random and systematic errors are not mistakes. Mistakes are failures by the person taking the measurement, such as taking readings from a sensitive balance in a draught. Mistakes of this kind lead to **outliers** in results, and should be avoided by people doing practical work. If it is known that a mistake was made when taking or recording a measurement, the measurement should be taken again.

Accuracy and precision

An analysis or test is often repeated to give a number of measured values, which are then averaged to produce the result.

- **Accuracy** describes how close a result is to the true or 'actual' value.
- **Precision** is a measure of the spread of measured values. A big spread indicates a greater uncertainty than a small spread.

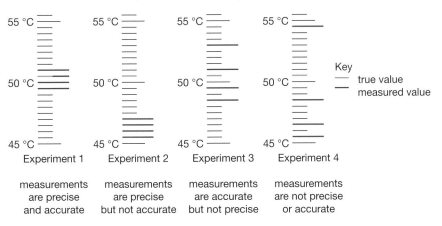

				Key
				— true value
				— measured value
Experiment 1	Experiment 2	Experiment 3	Experiment 4	
measurements are precise and accurate	measurements are precise but not accurate	measurements are accurate but not precise	measurements are not precise or accurate	

Maths skills

The aim of science is to develop good explanations for observations of the natural world. Scientific explanations are based on data. Making sense of the data requires mathematical skills, including making calculations, and presenting and reading graphs and charts. This section of the book will support you in making sense of your own data from experiments and also the data presented by others.

Throughout the book are worked examples to remind you how to apply your mathematical skills in science contexts.

Numbers and units

At the heart of most scientific enquiries are measurements. Measurements are stated as a number and unit. When doing calculations it is important to be consistent in the units you use.

In science we use the SI system of measurements: the base units of kilogram (kg), metre (m), second (s), ampere (A), kelvin (K), and mole (mol) together with derived units including metre per second (m/s), newton (N), metre cubed (m^3), and degrees Celsius (°C).

These are the units you will use in your Physics studies:

Quantity	Unit
mass	kilogram (kg)
length	metre (m)
time	second (s)
area	metre squared (m^2)
volume	metre cubed (m^3), decimetre cubed (dm^3)
energy	joule (J), kilowatt-hour (kWh)
temperature	degrees Celsius (°C), kelvin (K)
acceleration	metres per second per second (m/s^2)
density	kilogram per metre cubed (kg/m^3)
electric charge	coulomb (C)
electric current	ampere (amp, A)
electric potential difference	volt (V)
electric resistance	ohm (Ω)
force	newton (N)
frequency	hertz (Hz)
gravitational field strength	newton per kilogram (N/kg)
magnetic flux density (magnetic field strength)	tesla (T)
momentum	kilogram-metre per second (kg m/s)
power	watt (W)
pressure	pascal (Pa)
radioactivity	becquerel (Bq)
specific heat capacity	joule per kilogram degree Celsius (J/kg °C)
specific latent heat	joule per kilogram (J/kg)
speed, velocity	metre per second (m/s)

Standard form

Sometimes the numbers used in scientific measurements and calculations are very large or very small. For example, the distance from the Earth to the Sun is 146 900 000 000 m.

This is difficult to read and it can be easy to 'lose' one of the zeroes in a calculation. It is more convenient to express the number in **standard form**.

A number written in standard form has two parts:

The power of 10 may be positive or negative.

> a decimal number more than one, less than ten

> the multiplier (10 raised to the power needed to give the correct value of the number)

$$1.469 \times 10^{11}$$

Worked example: Converting large and small numbers to standard form

1 *It is estimated that there are 8 700 000 species on Earth. Write this number in standard form.*

Step 1: Find the decimal number that is more than one and less than 10.

8.7

Step 2: Find how many times you need to *multiply* 8.7 by 10 to get 8 700 000

$8\,700\,000 = 8.7 \times 10 \times 10 \times 10 \times 10 \times 10 \times 10$

> Multiply by 10 six times, which is the same as multiplying by 10^6.

Answer:

$8\,700\,000 = 8.7 \times 10^6$

2 *The diameter of a white blood cell is about 0.000012 m. Write this quantity in standard form.*

Step 1: Find the decimal number that is more than one and less than 10.

1.2

Step 2: Find how many times you need to *divide* 1.2 by 10 to get 0.000012.

Remember, dividing by 10 is the same as multiplying by $\frac{1}{10}$

$0.000\,012 = 1.2 \times \frac{1}{10} \times \frac{1}{10} \times \frac{1}{10} \times \frac{1}{10} \times \frac{1}{10}$

$= 1.2 \times \frac{1}{10^5}$

$= 1.2 \times 10^{-5}$

> Divide by 10 five times, which is the same as multiplying by 10^{-5}.

> The negative power shows the number is *less* than 1.

Answer:

$0.000\,012 \text{ m} = 1.2 \times 10^{-5} \text{ m}$

You should make sure you know how to work with numbers in standard form on your calculator. Different calculators have different labels on the button, for example:

EE   or   EXP   or $\times 10^x$

Prefixes for units

Sometimes prefixes for units are used instead of writing the quantity in standard form. For example, the diameter of a white blood cell is 1.2×10^{-5} m, which is 12 μm.

The table shows the prefixes that are used with scientific quantities.

nano	micro	milli	centi	deci	kilo	mega	giga	tera
n	μ	m	c	d	k	M	G	T
0.000 000 001	0.000 001	0.001	0.01	0.1	1000	1 000 000	1 000 000 000	1 000 000 000 000
$\times 10^{-9}$	$\times 10^{-6}$	$\times 10^{-3}$	$\times 10^{-2}$	$\times 10^{-1}$	$\times 10^{3}$	$\times 10^{6}$	$\times 10^{9}$	$\times 10^{12}$

Order of magnitude

Rounding a number to the nearest **order of magnitude** means rounding the number to the nearest power of 10.

Worked example: Order of magnitude

The radius of a carbon atom is measured to be about 0.07 nm.
What is this in metres to the nearest order of magnitude?

Step 1: Write down the length in metres.

0.07 nm $= 0.07 \times 10^{-9}$ m $= 7 \times 10^{-11}$ m

> 7 is closer to 10 than to 1

Step 2: Write down the value to the nearest power of 10

7×10^{-11} m $\approx 10 \times 10^{-11}$ m

10×10^{-11} m $= 1 \times 10^{-10} = 10^{-10}$

Answer:

7×10^{-11} m $\approx 10^{-10}$ m (to nearest order of magnitude)

Sometimes when two measurements are compared we simply want to know if they are in the same order of magnitude. If two numbers differ by an order of magnitude, then one number is about 10 times bigger than the other.

Worked example: Comparing orders of magnitude

The radius of a hydrogen atom is measured to be about 0.025 nm. The radius of a lead atom is measured to be about 0.18 nm. Compare the size of hydrogen atoms and lead atoms, and decide if their sizes are the same order of magnitude.

Step 1: Write down what you know, ensuring both measurements are in the same units.

hydrogen: 0.025 nm
lead: 0.18 nm

Step 2: Divide the larger number by the smaller number.

$\dfrac{\text{larger value}}{\text{smaller value}} = \dfrac{0.18 \text{ nm}}{0.025 \text{ nm}} = 7.2$

Answer:

Lead atom is 7.2 times larger, which is less than 10 times larger – this means they are the same order of magnitude.

Significant figures

Data from measurements in scientific experiments should show the **precision** of the measurement. The number of **significant figures** shows the precision that can be claimed for a piece of data.

The first significant figure in a number tells you the approximate size of the number. The first significant figure in a number is the first non-zero digit from the left.

For example, in the number 5437 the first significant figure is the 5, this tells you that the value is more than 5000 and less than 6000. You can round the number to any number of significant figures. So this number is 5000 (to 1 significant figure), 5400 (to 2 significant figures), or 5440 (to 3 significant figures).

The same principle applies to numbers less than one. In the number 0.0342 the first significant figure is 3, so we know the number is between three-hundredths and four-hundredths. The value is 0.03 (to 1 significant figure) or 0.034 (to 2 significant figures).

You may see significant figures abbreviated to 'sig. fig.' or 'S.F.'

Significant figures are a more useful way of expressing precision than decimal places. For example, a length measured with a metre ruler is made to the nearest millimetre (thousandth of a metre). The length of an A4 sheet of paper can be written as 297 mm, 29.7 cm, 0.297 m, and 2.97×10^{-1} m. All of those measurements are given to the same number of significant figures, even if the number of decimal places is different.

A calculated value should be given to the same number of significant figures as the least precise measurement in the data.

Worked example: Significant figures

Calculate the area of a rectangle with sides 26 mm and 13 mm.
Give your answer to 2 significant figures.

Step 1: Write down what you know.

length = 26 mm
breadth = 13 mm

Step 2: Write down the equation you will use.

area of rectangle = length × breadth

Step 3: Substitute in the numbers and calculate the area.

area = 26 mm × 13 mm
= 338 mm²

Step 4: Start at the first non-zero digit and count 2 significant figures.

338 mm²

Step 5: Apply the 5 or more rounding rule to the next digit.

area = 340 mm²

Answer:

area = 340 mm² (2 significant figures)

Making sense of data

Once data has been collected from an experiment it can be processed to show any patterns. This processing often means doing calculations and plotting graphs.

Using percentages

Percentages appear everywhere, for example, in interest rates on loans, discounts in the sales, and, of course, in science. Percentage is a way of describing a fraction of something. 'Per cent' (symbol %) means 'per hundred'. If 20 people out of a group of 100 people are left-handed, then we could say that 20% are left handed – and therefore that 80% are right-handed or ambidextrous.

If one quarter of a population have blonde hair we could say that 25 out of every 100 people have blonde hair – that is 25% have blonde hair.

Percentages can be used to make comparisons between sets of data, to calculate efficiency, or to calculate the yield of a process.

Worked example: Calculating percentages

A student carries out an experiment to find the best way to germinate seeds. One seed tray has 80 seeds and 60 of them germinate to produce plants. A second tray has 90 seeds and 70 of them germinate. Which tray gives the better yield of plants?

Step 1: Write down what you know.

Tray 1:	Tray 2:
number of seeds = 80	number of seeds = 90
number of plants = 60	number of plants = 70

> Tray 2 produced more plants, but there were more seeds so percentage yields make it easier to compare.

Step 2: Write down an equation to work out the percentage yield.

$$\text{yield} = \frac{\text{number of plants}}{\text{number of seeds}} \times 100\%$$

Step 3: Substitute in the values to calculate the percentage yield.

$$\text{yield 1} = \frac{60}{80} \times 100\% \qquad \text{yield 2} = \frac{70}{90} \times 100\%$$
$$= 0.75 \times 100\% \qquad\qquad = 0.78 \times 100\%$$
$$= 75\% \qquad\qquad\qquad = 78\%$$

Answer: Tray 2 had a slightly better yield (78%) than tray 1 (75%).

Finding the best estimate

The **range** of a data set describes the spread of data. For example, in a class of students the heights of the students may have a range from 160 cm to 185 cm.

The **average** of a data set is the single number that best represents the data set. There are different ways of representing that average.

The most commonly used average is the **mean value**. The mean value is found by adding up a set of measurements and then dividing by the number of measurements.

$$\text{mean} = \frac{\text{sum of all the measurements}}{\text{number of measurements}}$$

Worked example: Finding the mean

A group of students measure their heights. The measurements are: 160 cm, 165 cm, 167 cm, 168 cm, and 185 cm. Calculate the mean height.

Step 1: Write down what you know.

heights: 160 cm, 165 cm, 167 cm, 168 cm, and 185 cm

number of students: 5

Step 2: Write down an equation to work out the mean height.

$$\text{mean} = \frac{\text{sum of all the measurements}}{\text{number of measurements}}$$

Step 3: Substitute in the values to calculate the percentage yield.

$$\text{mean} = \frac{160\ cm + 165\ cm + 167\ cm + 168\ cm + 185\ cm}{5}$$

$$= \frac{845\ cm}{5}$$

$$= 169\ cm$$

Answer:

mean height = 169 cm

Sometimes the mean is not a good representation of the data. In the example of the group of students above, only one of the students is taller than the mean value. The 185 cm measurement has distorted the calculation because it is so much larger than the others.

A better representative value is sometimes the **median**: the middle value. In this data set, the median is 167 cm.

In a large data set with many values, the **mode** might be the best representative value – that is the value that occurs most often.

Whether you choose the mean, the median or the mode, it is always good to also give the range over which the data was spread.

Making sense of graphs

Scientists use graphs and charts to present data clearly and to look for patterns in the data. You will need to plot graphs or draw charts to present data, and then describe the patterns or trends and suggest explanations for them. Examination questions may also give you a graph and ask you to describe and explain it.

Reading the axes

Look at the two charts in the margin, which both provide data about daily energy use in several countries.

On the first chart the value for China is greater than for the US. But on the second chart the value for the US is much greater than for China. Why are the charts so different if they both represent information about energy use?

Look at the labels on the axes. One shows the *energy use per person per day*, the other shows the *energy use per day by the whole country*.

The first graph shows that China uses a similar amount of energy to the US. But the population of China is much greater so the energy use per person is much less.

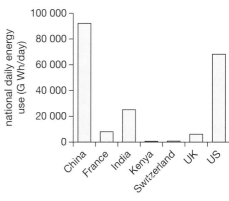

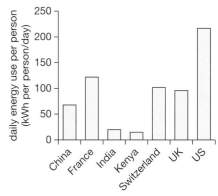

Graphs to show daily energy use in a range of countries, total and per person.

First rule of reading graphs: Read the axes and check the units.

Describing the relationship between variables

The pattern of points plotted on a graph shows whether two factors are related.

Look at the graph of how the mass of a baby changes in the first 12 weeks after birth.

The two variables are age and mass. The graph tells a story about the relationship between these two variables – the baby gets a little lighter in the first two weeks and then heavier. But we can describe the pattern in more detail than that. Between three weeks and nine weeks her mass increases steadily, then increases less quickly up to 12 weeks. The slope of the graph – the **gradient** – is constant between three weeks and nine weeks.

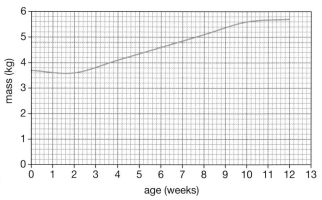

Graph showing how the mass of a baby changes in the first 12 weeks after birth.

Calculating the gradient of a graph

Many graphs show how a quantity changes with time – it might be the size of a population, the height of a plant, the concentration of a substance, or the speed of a moving object. Time is plotted on the *x*-axis and the changing quantity being measured is plotted on the *y*-axis. The gradient of such graphs describes the **rate** of change of the quantity with time.

$$\text{rate of change of quantity} = \frac{\text{change in quantity (}y\text{-axis)}}{\text{time taken to change (}x\text{-axis)}}$$

Worked example: Finding the gradient of a straight-line graph

The graph shows how a baby's mass changed in the weeks after she was born. Use the graph to work out the average rate at which her mass increased between three weeks and nine weeks.

Step 1: Use crosses (X) to mark on the line the points the question is asking about.

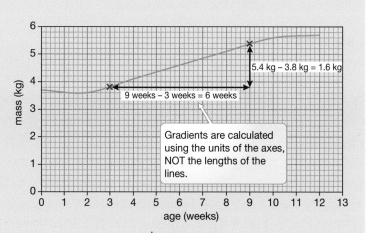

5.4 kg – 3.8 kg = 1.6 kg

9 weeks – 3 weeks = 6 weeks

Gradients are calculated using the units of the axes, NOT the lengths of the lines.

Step 2: Write down the equation to calculate the average rate.

$$\text{rate of change of mass} = \frac{\text{change in mass}}{\text{time taken for change}}$$

Step 3: Substitute in the values from the graph, including the units.

$$\text{rate of change of mass} = \frac{1.6 \text{ kg}}{6 \text{ weeks}} = 0.27 \text{ kg/week}$$

Answer: average rate of growth = 0.27 kg/week

Sometimes the graph is a curve – the gradient is changing. To calculate the gradient at a point on the curve, you need to find the gradient of the tangent to the curve at that point.

Worked example: Finding the gradient of the tangent to a curve

The graph shows how the population of Africa changed between 1950 and 2015. Use the graph to work out the rate at which the population was growing in 1990.

Step 1: Use crosses (X) to mark on the line the point the question is asking about.

Step 2: Draw a tangent to the line at that point. The tangent just touches the curve and has the same gradient as the curve at that point.

Step 3: Make the tangent the hypotenuse of a right angle triangle large enough for you to calculate the gradient of the line.

Choose the length of the base of the triangle to give an exact quantity; this will improve the accuracy of your calculation.

Step 4: Write down the equation to calculate the rate.

Step 5: Substitute in the values from the graph, including the units.

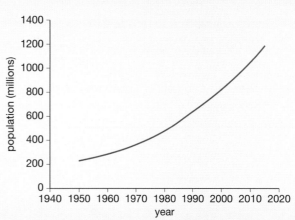

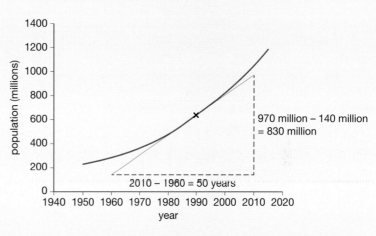

970 million – 140 million = 830 million

2010 – 1960 = 50 years

Graph to show the population of Africa between 1950 and 2015. Source: United Nations, Department of Economic and Social Affairs, Population Division (2015).

Answer given to 2 significant figures, because that is the precision of the data from the graph.

$$\text{rate of change of population} = \frac{\text{change in population}}{\text{time taken for change}}$$

$$\text{rate of change of population} = \frac{830 \text{ million}}{50 \text{ years}}$$

$$= 16.6 \text{ million/year}$$

Answer: **rate of population growth = 17 million/year**

Second rule of reading graphs: describe each phase of the graph, including ideas about the meaning of the **gradient**, and other **data** including **units**.

Is there a correlation?

Sometimes we are interested in whether one thing changes when another does. If a change in one factor goes together with a change in something else, we say that the two things are correlated.

The two graphs on the right show how global temperatures have changed over time and how levels of carbon dioxide in the atmosphere have changed over time.

Is there a **correlation** between the two sets of data?

Look at the graphs – why is it difficult to decide if there is a correlation?

The two sets of data are over different periods of time, so although both graphs show a rise with time, it is difficult to see if there is a correlation.

It would be easier to identify a correlation if both sets of data were plotted for the same time period and placed one above the other, or on the same axes, like this:

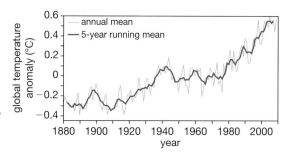

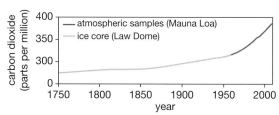

Graphs to show increasing global temperatures and carbon dioxide levels. Source: NASA.

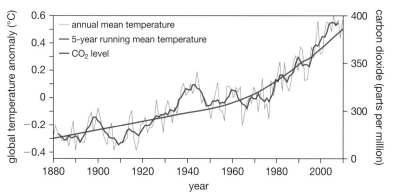

Graph to show the same data as the above two graphs, plotted on one set of axes.

When there are two sets of data on the same axes, take care to look at which axis relates to which line.

Another way to check for a correlation is to plot the two variables on a scatter graph.

Look at the scatter graph in the margin. Is there evidence that the two variables:

- are correlated?
- show a causal relationship?

Explaining graphs

Explaining the patterns or trends shown by a graph is different to describing them. It requires us to use scientific ideas to suggest what could be causing the observed patterns.

When a graph suggests that there is a correlation between two sets of data, scientists try to find out if a change in one factor *causes* a change in the other. They look for a mechanism that explains how one factor affects the other.

> **Third rule for reading graphs:** When looking for a correlation between two sets of data, read the axes carefully.

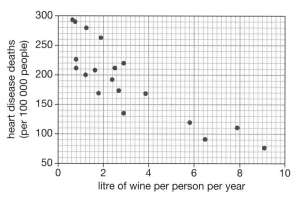

Graph showing that heart disease is less common in people who drink a moderate amount of wine, from a study in over 19 countries.

Displaying frequency data

Frequency data shows the number of times a value occurs. For example, if four students have a pulse rate of 86 beats per minute, then the data value 86 has a frequency of four.

Frequency data is presented using a bar chart or a histogram. It's important to know the difference between these two types of chart and when to use each one.

Bar chart: discontinuous data

Country	Number of nuclear power plants
USA	99
France	58
Japan	43
Russia	34
China	27
UK	16

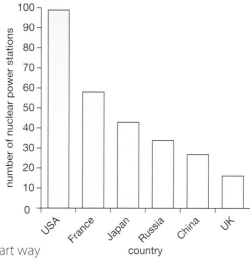

The data in the table has been plotted as a bar chart, showing the number of working nuclear power stations in different countries in June 2015.

Look at the bar chart displaying the number of nuclear power stations per country. Each country is separate, and it's not possible to measure a value part way between any two countries. The data are said to be discontinuous. A bar chart is used to display discontinuous frequency data.

A bar chart would also be used to summarise the number of trees of each species in a wood (species names on the *x*-axis), and the number of students studying chemistry in different schools (school names on the *x*-axis).

In a bar chart all of the bars should be drawn with equal width, and there should be a gap between each bar.

Histogram: continuous data

You may work with frequency data for a continuous variable, for example, height. Continuous data can be divided into groups known as class intervals. Collecting data in class intervals can be done by tallying. As a rule of thumb, try to divide the data into at least five class intervals.

Look at the data recording the heights of 31 people:

Height (m)	Tally	Frequency
1.60–1.65	I	1
1.65–1.70	IIII	4
1.70–1.75	IIII IIII II	12
1.75–1.80	IIII III	8
1.80–1.85	IIII	5
1.85–1.90	I	1

Note that the class interval 1.60–1.65 includes all the people with a height that is:

- greater than or equal to 1.60 m
- less than 1.65 m.

This means that a person who is 1.64 m tall is included in the class interval 1.60–1.65, but a person who is 1.65 m tall is included in the next class interval (1.65–1.70).

A histogram is used to display continuous frequency data.

In a histogram the bars are drawn touching, and are labelled at their edges on the *x*-axis.

Rearranging equations

Equations show the relationships between physical variables. They are used to calculate the value of one variable from the values of other known variables. Often you need to rearrange the standard equation to put the quantity you are trying to find on the left-hand side, before the equals sign (this makes it the subject of the equation).

There is a simple rule to follow when rearranging equations:

> Whatever you do to the left hand side of the equation you must always do the same thing to the right hand side – so the two sides remain equal.

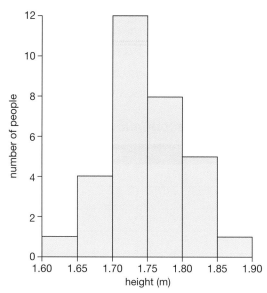

A histogram displaying the frequency of height in a group of 31 people.

Worked example: Changing the subject of the equation 🖩

Rearrange the equation for the area of a circle to make the radius the subject of the equation.

Step 1: Write down what you know.

A = area of a circle

r = radius

$A = \pi r^2$

> Tip: it is much easier to rearrange the equation using algebra symbols than using words.

Step 2: Decide what you need to do to get r^2 on its own. Divide both sides by π.

$$\frac{A}{\pi} = \frac{\pi r^2}{\pi}$$

Step 3: Cancel the π on the right hand side

$$\frac{A}{\pi} = \frac{\cancel{\pi} r^2}{\cancel{\pi}}$$

Step 4: Swap the two sides of the equation so that r^2 is on the left hand side.

$$\frac{A}{\pi} = r^2$$

$$r^2 = \frac{A}{\pi}$$

Step 5: take the square root of both sides, to give r.

$$\sqrt{r^2} = \sqrt{\frac{A}{\pi}}$$

Answer:

$$r = \sqrt{\frac{A}{\pi}}$$

Often you will be asked to find the value of a variable from other given variables. The worked example below shows the steps to take.

Worked example: Finding the value of a variable from the formula

What is the radius of a circle which has a perimeter of 30 cm?

Step 1: Write down what you know.

perimeter = 30 cm

Step 2: Write down the equation for the perimeter of a circle.

perimeter = $2\pi r$

Step 3: Decide what you need to do to get r on its own.

$$\frac{\text{perimeter}}{2\pi} = \frac{2\pi r}{2\pi}$$

Divide both sides by 2π.

$$\frac{\text{perimeter}}{2\pi} = r$$

Step 4: Swap the two sides of the equation so that r is on the left hand side.

$$r = \frac{\text{perimeter}}{2\pi}$$

Step 5: Substitute what you know into the equation.

$$r = \frac{30 \text{ cm}}{2\pi}$$

Step 6: Work out the value for r.

$r = 4.77$ cm

Answer:

$r = 4.8$ cm (to 2 significant figures)

You may find it easier to substitute in the values before rearranging, but the more often you practise rearranging the algebraic equations, the more familiar you will become with the different ways of writing the relationships.

Models in science

Find out about

- what a model is
- how models are used to investigate, explain, and predict
- the benefits and limitations of models
- representational, descriptive, and mathematical models

Key words

➤ model
➤ system
➤ representational model

Most children like to play with toys. A popular toy is a model car. It's called a **model** because it represents something in the real world. It has some of the main features of a real car, such as wheels, doors, a windscreen, and a roof. But some features, such as the engine, are not included. The model shows that the car can move when the wheels turn.

A model car is a simple way to represent the main features of a car, but much of the detail of a real car is not included in the model.

Models are everywhere

People use models all the time, even if they don't realise it. A model isn't always an object, such as a toy car. Models can be words, pictures, and numbers. For example, a map is a model.

Millions of people visit London every year, and they use maps to help them travel around. The usual map of the London Underground is a useful guide for getting from one Tube station to another. It's a good model of the city's underground train network because it shows how the stations and lines are connected. It is quick and easy to understand. It can answer questions such as: 'What is the most direct way to get from Bond Street to Westminster?'

This map is a simple model of the London Underground train network. It helps people to work out how to get from one Tube station to another.

This map is another model of London, but it includes features such as streets and local landmarks.

We can also use the model to make predictions. For example, we could predict that it would take longer to travel by Tube to Westminster from Camden Road than it would from Bond Street.

However, the London Underground map can't solve all of a traveller's problems. It doesn't show how the Tube stations relate to streets and landmarks on the surface. These features are not included in the model. To answer the question 'What is there to see around Westminster Tube station?' we can use a different, more detailed model – for example, a street map.

What is a model?

From the everyday examples of model cars and maps, we know that a model:

- is a simpler way of representing something in the real world
- includes some, but not necessarily all, of the features of the thing it represents
- can show how these features are connected or interact
- can be used to explain things, answer questions, and make predictions.

We also know that the usefulness of a model is limited by how closely it represents the real world and that different models are useful in different situations.

Usually, a model represents a collection of interacting parts. Scientists often refer to a collection of interacting parts as a **system**.

Using models in science

Models are useful in science. They help us to explain how things work and interact. They also help us to make predictions and investigate possible outcomes. Scientific models can be words, pictures, objects, numbers, graphs, or equations.

Many different models are used in science, but they can be grouped into three main types. These are described below. You've already used models in your science lessons. An example of a model that you should be familiar with is given for each type.

A number of scientific models are highlighted throughout this book – look out for the red boxes like the ones shown here.

Representational models

A **representational model** uses simple shapes or analogies to represent the interacting parts of a system. One example of a representational model is the particle model – it helps us to visualise the tiny particles (atoms and molecules) that make up substances.

Different models of the same thing can contain different amounts of detail. A model car made of blocks will roll on its wheels from the top of a slope to the bottom. A remote-controlled car contains a motor, so can be driven from the bottom of a slope to the top. The models can be used to demonstrate and investigate different behaviours.

The particle model of matter

All matter is made of very tiny particles with attractive forces between them. The particle model represents the particles as spheres. It helps us explain the arrangement and movement of the particles in different states of matter.

However, this model makes some simplifications. For example, particles of matter are not all identical spheres – they have different shapes, sizes, and masses. This means there are limitations to the model and what we can do with it.

solid
particles touching and unable to move away from their neighbours

liquid
particles touching but able to slide over each other

gas
particles far apart and can move freely

You should already know about some simple models of photosynthesis (the process plant cells use to make food).

A speed camera takes photographs of a car as it travels over markings on the road. The time between the photographs and the distance between the markings are used to calculate the car's speed.

Descriptive models

A **descriptive model** uses words to identify features of a system and describe how they interact. One example of a descriptive model is a simple account of the inputs and outputs of photosynthesis. It helps us to explain how plant cells can make their own food in the form of glucose (a type of sugar).

A simple model of photosynthesis

Photosynthesis is a complicated biological process, involving a number of chemical reactions inside cells. However, a simple description of the inputs and outputs can help us to understand what is going on.

Inputs	Outputs
light	glucose
water	oxygen
carbon dioxide	

This is a very simple way of summing up the process of photosynthesis. We could use this simple model to make a prediction, for example, that increasing the supply of inputs would increase the amount of glucose made.

However, this model misses out much of the detail. It does not tell us anything about the chemical reactions or where they take place.

Mathematical models

A **mathematical model** uses patterns in data of past events, along with known scientific relationships, to predict what will happen to one variable when another is changed. This involves doing calculations. If the calculations are very complicated, they can be done by a computer - this is a **computational model**. But a very simple example of a mathematical model is the relationship between speed, distance, and time.

Modelling the speed of a moving object

There is a simple, scientific relationship between the speed of a moving object, the distance it moves, and the time taken to move that distance. The relationship is:

$$\text{speed} = \frac{\text{distance}}{\text{time}}$$

This is a mathematical model. We can use it to calculate the speed of a moving object if we have values for the other two variables (distance and time). We can also use the model to make a prediction, for example if the car travels for a longer time at the same speed, it will travel further.

But this simple model is limited. It can only be used to calculate an average speed from the total distance and time – it does not include information about changes in speed such as acceleration or deceleration. Also, it does not include any information about the direction the car is travelling.

One type of mathematical model is a **spatial model**. A computer is used to make a model of one or more objects in a three-dimensional space. The model can be used to predict the outcome of changing a variable (e.g., temperature) in a given space (e.g., a landscape and the atmosphere above it). The space can be divided into sections and outcomes predicted for each section. Spatial models are often used to make predictions about weather and climate.

Why use models?

If we tried to describe and explain every unique situation in the world, we would never get finished! This is one reason why models are useful. A model is a general explanation that applies to a large number of situations – perhaps to all possible ones. For example, every cell in your body is different, but we can use a model of an animal cell to describe the main features that animal cells have in common.

A benefit of models is that they enable us to investigate situations that we cannot investigate using practical experiments – perhaps because it is not ethical, is too expensive, or is not possible to do so. For example, mathematical models enable us to investigate the future effects of human activities on the Earth's climate and biodiversity. This helps us to make predictions about the likely outcomes of different courses of action, which can affect the decisions we make.

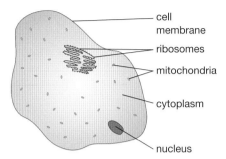

A simple model of an animal cell. Every animal cell is different, but the model includes the main features they have in common.

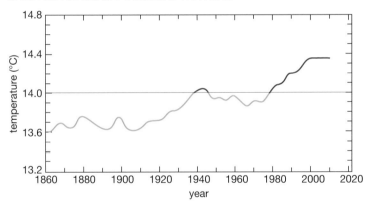

Measurements taken over the past 150 years show that the Earth's temperature is rising. We can use a mathematical model to predict how it may change in the future.

Models are very useful but we must always remember that they are limited. Even a very good model cannot represent the real world exactly, so outcomes in the real world could be different from a model's outcomes. Models help weather forecasters make predictions about the weather, but they don't always get it exactly right. Always think carefully about how much confidence you can have in claims based on a model – be realistic, and don't be too surprised if things turn out a little differently in the real world.

Key words

> descriptive model
> mathematical model
> computational model
> spatial model

Appendices

Electrical symbols

junction of conductors	
switch	
electric cell	
battery of cells	
power supply	
diode	
light-emitting diode (LED)	
ammeter	
voltmeter	
fixed resistor	
variable resistor	
light-dependent resistor (LDR)	
thermistor	
lamp	

Relationships

You will need to be able to carry out calculations using the equations listed here using the appropriate SI units. (See the Maths section for the units used for each of these physical quantities.)

We give the relationships both in words and symbols.

You need to recall and use these relationships using SI units.

Symbols and abbreviations used throughout this book:

Physical quantity	Symbol or abbreviation
force	F
mass	m
acceleration	a
kinetic energy	KE
speed, velocity, final speed	v
initial speed	u
work done, energy	W
distance, displacement	s
power	P
time	t
weight	$F_{gravity}$
gravitational field strength	g
height	h
spring constant	k
extension of spring or other stretchy material	x
frequency	f
wavelength	λ
charge	Q
current	I
voltage, potential difference	V
electrical resistance	R
density	ρ
volume	V
pressure	p
area	A
specific heat capacity	c
specific latent heat	L
length	l
magnetic field strength	B

Word equation	Symbol equation
force = mass × acceleration	$F = ma$
kinetic energy = ½ × mass × (speed)^2	$\text{KE} = \frac{1}{2}mv^2$
momentum = mass × velocity	momentum = mv
energy transferred (work done) = force × distance (along the line of action of the force)	$W = Fs$
energy transferred = power x time	$W = Pt$
efficiency $= \dfrac{\text{useful energy transferred}}{\text{total energy transferred}}$	
weight = mass × gravitational field strength	$F_{\text{gravity}} = mg$
gravitational potential energy = mass × height × gravitational field strength	$\text{PE}_{\text{gravity}} = mgh$
force exerted by a spring = extension × spring constant	$F = kx$
moment of a force = force × distance (normal to direction of the force)	moment = Fs
speed $= \dfrac{\text{distance}}{\text{time}}$	$v = \dfrac{s}{t}$
acceleration $= \dfrac{\text{change in speed}}{\text{time taken}}$	$a = \dfrac{v - u}{t}$
wave speed = frequency × wavelength	$v = f\lambda$
charge = current × time	$Q = It$
potential difference = current × resistance	$V = IR$
power = potential difference × current = (current)^2 × resistance	$P = VI = I^2R$
energy transferred electrically = charge flow × potential difference	$W = QV$
density $= \dfrac{\text{mass}}{\text{volume}}$	$\rho = \dfrac{m}{V}$

In addition, you should be able correctly to select and apply the following relationships:

(final velocity)^2 – (initial velocity)^2 = 2 × acceleration × distance	$v^2 - u^2 = 2as$
change in internal energy = mass × specific heat capacity × change in temperature	$W = mc\theta$
energy to cause a change of state = mass × specific latent heat	$W = mL$
energy stored in a stretched spring = ½ × spring constant × (extension)^2	$W = \frac{1}{2}kx^2$
force on a conductor (at right angles to a magnetic field) carrying a current = magnetic field strength × current × length of conductor	$F = BIl$
For transformers: potential difference across primary coil × current in primary coil = potential difference across secondary coil × current in secondary coil	$V_P I_P = V_S I_S$

Glossary

absorb (radiation) The radiation that falls on an object and is not reflected, or transmitted through it, is absorbed (e.g., black paper absorbs light). Its energy makes the object get a little hotter.

acceleration The rate of change of an object's velocity, that is, its change of velocity per second. In situations where the direction of motion is not important, the change of speed per second tells you the acceleration. Acceleration is measured in m/s^2.

accuracy How close a quantitative result is to the true or 'actual' value.

action-at-a-distance forces Forces that act all the time even when objects are apart. These forces get weaker when objects are further apart. Examples include gravitational, magnetic, and electrostatic forces.

activity The number of radioactive decays per second. Activity is measured in becquerels (Bq).

actual risk Risk calculated from reliable data.

air resistance A force on objects moving through the air. Always acts in the direction to slow the object down.

alpha particle The least penetrating type of ionising radiation, produced by the nucleus of an atom in radioactive decay. A high-speed helium nucleus.

alternating current (a.c.) An electric current that reverses direction many times a second.

ammeter A meter that measures the size of an electric current in a circuit.

amplitude For a mechanical wave, the amplitude is the maximum distance that each point on the medium moves from its normal position as the wave passes. For an electromagnetic wave, it is the maximum value of the varying electric field (or magnetic field).

area The area of a shape is a measure of the space that it covers. Area is measured in cm^2 or m^2.

atmosphere A layer of gas around a planet. The Earth's atmosphere is a mixure of gases (air), containing roughly 78% nitrogen and 21% oxygen, with trace amounts of other gases. Three-quarters of the mass of the atmosphere is within the first 11 km of height. The atmosphere protects life on Earth by absorbing ultraviolet solar radiation and reducing temperature extremes between day and night.

atom The smallest particle of an element. The atoms of each element are the same as each other and are different from the atoms of other elements.

attract Pull towards.

average speed The distance moved by an object divided by the time taken for this to happen. Speed is measured in metres per second (m/s).

background radiation The low-level radiation, mostly from natural sources, that everyone is exposed to all the time, everywhere.

balanced forces If forces are balanced, there is zero resultant force.

beta particle One of several types of ionising radiation, produced by the nucleus of an atom in radioactive decay. More penetrating than alpha radiation but less penetrating than gamma radiation. A high-speed electron.

biodiversity The biodiversity of the Earth, or of a particular area, is the combination of the diversity of living organisms, the diversity of genetic material the organisms have, and the diversity of ecosystems in which the organisms live.

biofuel A fuel produced from plants (such as bioethanol from sugar cane, or wood) or other recently living material (such as agricultural waste).

bond Attractive force holding atoms or ions together.

braking distance The distance travelled while braking to a stop.

cause When a change in a factor produces a particular outcome, and there is a mechanism to explain this link, then the factor is said to cause the outcome.

centripetal force The force needed to keep something moving in a circle: this force must be towards the centre of the circle.

CFL (compact fluorescent light bulb) A light bulb designed to be more efficient than a normal (incandescent) lamp.

change of state Changing from one state of matter to another, for example, melting, evaporating, condensing.

charged Carrying an electric charge. Some objects (such as electrons and protons) are permanently charged. A plastic object can be charged by rubbing it. This transfers electrons to or from it.

climate Long-term weather patterns in a region.

climate change A long-term change in the climate of the Earth, or a region of the Earth.

closed system A system in which the amount of mass doesn't change, and there is no energy transfer in or out.

compression (forces) The balanced inward forces on an object that reduce its size along the line of the forces.

computational model A type of mathematical model in which the calculations are done by a computer.

condensation The change of state from a gas to a liquid, for example, water vapour in the air condenses to form rain.

conservation of energy The principle that the total amount of energy at the end of any process is always equal to the total amount of energy at the beginning – though it may now be stored in different ways and in different places.

conservation of momentum The principle that the sum of the momentum of all the objects before a collision is the same as the sum of the momentum of all the objects after the collision, providing no external forces act on the objects.

contact forces Forces exerted by objects that are touching. These forces arise because the objects are touching.

contamination The presence of an unwanted (and possibly harmful) substance or organism in the body, in a substance, or on a surface.

correlation If an outcome happens when a specific factor is present but does not happen when it is absent, or if a measured outcome increases (or decreases) as the value of a factor increases, there is a correlation between the two. For example, there is a correlation between pollen count and the number of hay fever cases.

counter force A force in the opposite direction to something's motion.

crumple zone Part of a car designed to crumple in a collision.

deceleration Describes the motion when an object is slowing down. A negative acceleration.

decommissioning Taking a power station out of service at the end of its lifetime, dismantling it, and disposing of the waste safely.

density The mass per unit volume of a material.

descriptive model A type of scientific model that uses words to identify features of a system, and to describe how they interact. One example is a simple account of the inputs and outputs of photosynthesis. It helps us to explain how plant cells can make their own food in the form of glucose (a type of sugar).

diode A circuit component that has a very high resistance when connected one way in the circuit, but a low resistance in the other direction. It allows current to flow in one direction but not the other.

direct current (d.c.) An electric current that is always in the same direction.

displacement The length and direction of the straight line from the initial position of an object to its position at a later time. A vector.

displacement–time graph A graph showing the distance of an object from its starting point at each moment during its journey. Displacement on the y-axis and time on the x-axis. Displacement can decrease and it can be negative.

dissipated Energy is dissipated when it is spread out, and cannot be recovered. For example, when all molecules increase their kinetic energy a very small amount, causing a very small increase in temperature.

distance–time graph A graph showing the distance an object has moved at each moment during its journey. Distance on the y-axis and time on the x-axis.

domestic electricity supply A supply at 230 V, that produces alternating current at a frequency of 50 Hz in domestic appliances.

driving force The force pushing something forward.

duration The length of time, or time span, for which something continues to happen.

earth wire A wire that is connected to the ground that carries a high current if there is a fault.

Earth's magnetic field A magnetic field surrounding the Earth. It is thought the field is due to convection currents in the molten outer core interacting with the solid iron inner core. The magnetic North Pole is close to the geographic North Pole.

echo A sound, heard after it has been reflected from a distant surface.

efficiency The percentage of energy supplied to a device that is usefully transferred by it.

elastic An elastic material is one that returns to its original dimensions after any distorting forces are removed.

elastic limit In stretching, this is the greatest extension that can be obtained while the material extends elastically. It is often expressed as a percentage of the original length.

electric charge A fundamental property of matter. Electrons and protons are charged particles. Objects become charged when electrons are transferred to or from them, for example, by rubbing.

electric circuit A closed loop of conductors connected between the positive and negative terminals of a battery or power supply.

electric current An electric current is a flow of charges around an electric circuit. The rate of flow is measured in amperes (amps, A).

electromagnet A device that uses an electric current to create a magnetic field that can be controlled. Usually a coil of wire wrapped around an iron core. The core becomes magnetic when a current passes through the coil, but is not magnetic when there is no current. The strength of the magnet depends on the current in the coil and the number of turns.

electromagnetic radiation A kind of radiation consisting of vibrating electric and magnetic fields, which can travel in a vacuum. Visible light is one example.

electromagnetic spectrum The 'family' of electromagnetic radiation of different frequencies and wavelengths.

electron A tiny, negatively charged particle that is part of an atom. Electrons are found outside the nucleus. Electrons have negligible mass and one unit of charge.

element A substance made up of one type of atom.

emit To give out, for example, the Sun emits light.

energy Energy is the ability to do work. Energy transferred is equal to work done. Energy is measured in joules (J) and kilowatt-hours (kWh).

energy resources Materials or mechanisms for heating or generating electricity.

energy store An energy store is something (such as a food or hot object) that enables you to account for the energy at the start and end of a transfer by doing a calculation.

equilibrium An object is in equilibrium when there is zero resultant force on it – all the forces are balanced.

equivalent resistance The value of resistance of a single resistor that could replace a combination two or more resistors.

evaporation The change of state from a liquid to a gas. For example, when a puddle dries out the water has evaporated.

exposure How much of a hazard that a person will come in contact with and in what way. Risk is made up of hazard and exposure.

extension The difference between the original length of a stretched material and its stretched length.

extrapolation The process of extending the line of a graph to estimate values beyond the original data.

factor A variable that changes and may affect something else (the outcome).

fixed resistor An electrical component with a resistance that does not change over a wide range of conditions.

Fleming's left-hand rule A rule to predict the direction of the motor effect. Holding thumb, first finger, and second finger at right-angles to each other, align the first finger with the field and the second finger in the direction of the current. The wire will move in the direction indicated by the thumb.

force A push or a pull experienced by one object when it interacts with another. A force is needed to change the motion of an object. Force is measured in newtons (N).

fossil fuel Coal, gas, and oil are fossil fuels. They were formed from the remains of trees and sea creatures over millions of years and are finite, which means they cannot be replaced but will run out.

free-body force diagram A sketch showing the forces acting on an object.

free fall An object falling in the Earth's gravitational field with no other forces acting on it.

frequency (of a wave) The number of waves produced each second. Frequency is measured in hertz (Hz).

friction The force exerted on an object due to the interaction between it and another object that it is sliding over. It is caused by the roughness of both surfaces at a microscopic level.

gamma radiation (gamma rays) The most penetrating type of ionising radiation, produced by the nucleus of an atom in radioactive decay. The most energetic part of the electromagnetic spectrum.

global warming An increase in the average temperature of the whole Earth. The average global surface temperature increased by about 0.89 °C from 1901 to 2012.

gradient (of a graph) The gradient, or slope, of a graph is a measure of its steepness. It is calculated by choosing two points on the graph and calculating: the change in the value of the *y*-axis variable/the change in the value of the *x*-axis variable. If the graph is a straight line, you can use any two points on it. If it is curved, you should estimate the gradient of the tangent at the required point.

graduation A line on a container, ruler, or meter that marks a measurement.

gravitational field strength The size of the gravitational attraction per unit mass. Symbol *g*. Gravitational field strength is measured in newtons per kilogram (N/kg).

gravitational potential energy Energy stored in a gravitational field when two objects that are interacting (e.g., a lifted object and the Earth) are moved apart.

gravity A universal force of attraction between any two objects. This force depends on the mass of each object, and gets weaker if the objects are separated by greater distance.

greenhouse effect The atmosphere absorbs infrared radiation from the Earth's surface and radiates some of it back to the surface, making it warmer than it would otherwise be.

greenhouse gas Gases in the atmosphere that absorb radiation emitted by the Earth and thereby contribute to the greenhouse effect (warming). The most potent greenhouse gases are carbon dioxide, methane, and water vapour.

half-life The time taken for the amount of a radioactive element in a sample to fall to half its original value. It is also the time it takes for the rate of decay to decrease by a half.

hazard A source of potential harm to health or the environment.

heating A process of transferring energy when there is a temperature difference.

hydroelectric power Electricity generated using water falling downhill.

hypothesis A tentative explanation for an observation. A hypothesis is used to make a prediction that can be tested.

incident ray Ray of light falling on a surface.

induce Cause an effect to happen.

induced magnetism Some materials become magnetic in the presence of a magnetic field, but lose their magnetism when the field is removed. This effect is induced magnetism.

induced potential difference A potential difference produced when a conductor is in a changing magnetic field.

inertia The property of an object that causes it to resist changes to its motion (change of speed or direction).

inertial mass The mass of an object measured by how much it accelerates or its momentum changes when acted on by a force.

infrared (IR) Electromagnetic radiation with a frequency lower than that of visible light, beyond the red end of the visible spectrum.

instantaneous speed The speed of an object at a particular instant. In practice, its average speed over a very short time interval.

insulation (thermal) Material through which energy transfers slowly, a material with a low thermal conductivity.

intensity (of radiation) The amount of energy transferred by radiation to a receiver every second, per unit area.

interaction What happens when two objects collide, or influence each other at a distance. When two objects interact, each experiences a force.

interaction pair Two forces that arise from the same interaction. They are equal in size and opposite in direction, and each acts on a different object.

interface (computer) A device that allows sensors or other devices to communicate with a computer.

internal energy Energy stored in a material, often associated with temperature rise. It is a combination of kinetic energy of the particles in the system and energy stored in bonds between particles.

interpolation The process of taking a pair of values from a graph that are in between the data points that were plotted.

ion An electrically charged atom or group of atoms. A positively charged ion has a greater number of protons than electrons. A negatively charged ion has a greater number of electrons than protons.

ionisation The process of removing an electron from (or adding an electron to) an atom or group of atoms.

ionising radiation Radiation with sufficient energy to remove electrons from atoms in its path. Ionising radiation, such as ultraviolet, X-rays, and gamma rays, can damage living cells.

ionosphere A region high up in the atmosphere that reflects radio waves.

irradiation Being exposed to radiation from an external source.

isotope Two or more forms of the same element that have different numbers of neutrons in their nuclei, and hence different mass numbers.

joule The unit of energy/work. One joule is the energy transferred when a force of 1 newton moves an object a distance of 1 metre in the direction of its motion.

kinetic energy Energy stored in an object by virtue of its movement.

lattice A regular three-dimensional arrangement of particles in a crystalline solid (e.g., metals, salt, and diamond).

LED (light-emitting diode) An energy-efficient component that gives out light. It conducts a current only in one direction.

light-dependent resistor (LDR) An electric circuit component whose resistance varies depending on the brightness of light falling on it.

live wire A wire in a plug that connects the appliance to the mains so the potential difference between live and neutral is 230 V.

longitudinal wave A wave in which the particles of the medium vibrate in the same direction as the wave is travelling. Sound is an example.

lubrication Putting a material (such as oil) between surfaces to reduce energy transfer due to friction.

magnetic field The region around a magnet, or a wire carrying an electric current, in which magnetic effects can be detected. For example, another small magnet in this region will experience a force and tend to move.

magnitude The size of a vector quantity.

mains electricity Electricity generated in power stations and available through power sockets in buildings.

mass The amount of matter. Mass is measured in kilograms (kg).

mathematical model A type of scientific model that uses patterns in data of past events, along with known scientific relationships, to predict what will happen to one variable when another is changed. A simple example of a mathematical model is the relationship between speed, distance, and time.

mean value A type of average, found by adding up a set of measurements and then dividing by the number of measurements. You can have more confidence in the mean of a set of measurements than in a single measurement. The mean can be used as the best estimate of the true value.

medium (radiation) The material through which radiation is transmitted.

mechanical equivalent of heat A historic quantity that showed that the same amount of mechanical (or electrical) work always produced the same temperature rise.

mechanism A process that explains why some factor brings about a particular outcome.

meniscus The water surface in a narrow tube curves to form a meniscus.

microwave Radio waves of the highest frequency (shortest wavelength), used for mobile phones and satellite TV.

model A scientific model is a way of representing something from the real world, such as a system of interacting parts. It includes some, but not necessarily all, of the features of the system it represents. It can show how these features are connected or interact, and can be used to explain scientific ideas, answer questions, and make predictions.

momentum A property of any moving object, momentum is a vector quantity given by mass × velocity. Momentum is measured in kilogram metres per second (kg m/s).

motor A device that uses an electric current to produce continuous motion.

motor effect A current-carrying wire at right-angles to a magnetic field experiences a force perpendicular to both the wire and the field.

National Grid UK electrical distribution system that connects houses and factories to power station generators and other systems that generate electricity, such as wind and solar.

negative A label used to name one type of charge or one terminal of a battery. It is the opposite of positive.

neutral wire A wire in a plug that connects the appliance to the mains so the potential difference between live and neutral is 230 V.

neutron A subatomic particle found in the nucleus with about the same mass as a proton but no electrical charge.

neutron radiation High-energy neutrons emitted from the nucleus of an unstable radioisotope.

non-ionising radiation Radiation with photons that do not have enough energy to ionise atoms or molecules.

non-renewable Type of energy resource that will run out eventually (e.g., fossil fuels).

normal contact force The force exerted by a solid surface on an object that presses on it. The force is at a right-angle to the surface.

nuclear equation A summary of the changes that take place during radioactive decay. The equation shows the atomic number and mass number of the original nucleus and all the products of the decay.

nuclear model (of the atom) The atom contains protons, neutrons, and electrons. Protons and neutrons make up the nucleus, which is much smaller than the whole atom. Electrons are outside the nucleus. Most of the mass of an atom is concentrated in its nucleus.

nuclear power station A power station that uses nuclear fuel to generate electricity (and does not produce CO_2).

nucleon number The total number of protons and neutrons in the nucleus of an atom.

nucleus (atom) The tiny central part of an atom (made up of protons and neutrons). Most of the mass of an atom is concentrated in it nucleus.

order of magnitude If two numbers differ by an order of magnitude, then one number is about ten times bigger than the other. A value given to the 'nearest order of magnitude' will be given to the nearest power of ten.

oscillate Vary (in position or value) regularly, for example, a string on a guitar oscillates to make a sound.

outcome A variable that changes as a result of something else changing.

outlier A measured result that seems very different from other repeat measurements, or from the value you would expect. The measurement should be treated as data, unless there is a reason to reject it (e.g., measurement or recording error).

ozone layer A thin layer in the atmosphere, about 30 km up, where oxygen is in the form of ozone molecules. The ozone layer absorbs ultraviolet radiation from sunlight.

parallel circuit A circuit in which the components are each connected to the power supply, and all have the same potential diference across them.

particle In the particle model of matter a particle can be an atom of a metal, a molecule of a gas, or an ion of an ionic substance such as sodium chloride.

particle model of matter The particle model explains the differing properties of solids, liquids, and gases, and changes of state.

peer review The process whereby scientists who are experts in their field critically evaluate another scientist's scientific paper or idea before and after publication.

perceived risk People often judge a risk to be higher (or lower) than it actually is; this is perceived risk.

period (of a wave) The time to make a complete wave. It is the same as the time for one complete wave to pass any point. Period is measured in seconds.

permanent magnet A material that remains magnetic, unlike a material that can be induced to be magnetic, but loses its magnetism easily.

photon Tiny 'packet' of energy carried by electromagnetic radiation. The energy of a photon is proportional to the frequency of the radiation.

plastic (behaviour of a material) A material behaves plastically when it does not return to its original dimensions after any distorting forces are removed.

plum-pudding model of the atom A model of the atom suggested by J. J. Thomson. He said that an atom consists of tiny, negatively charged electrons moving about in a postively charged sphere.

positive A label used to name one type of charge, or one terminal of a battery. It is the opposite of negative.

potential difference (p.d.) The work done when one unit of charge passes between two points in an electric circuit. Also called voltage. Potential difference is measured in volts (V).

potential divider An electric circuit that uses two resistors to provide an output voltage as a fraction of the supply voltage.

power The rate of transfer of energy; the rate at which work is done. Power is measured in watts (W).

power rating (of an appliance) The number of watts or kilowatts that tells you the rate at which an appliance transfers energy.

precision A measure of the spread of quantitative results. If the measurements are precise, all the results are very close in value.

prediction A hypothesis is used to make a prediciton about how, in a particular experimental context, a change in a factor will affect the outcome.

pressure The force per unit area acting on a surface. Pressure is measured in pascals (Pa) or newtons per square metre (N/m^2). $1\ Pa = 1\ N/m^2$.

principal frequency The frequency of the radiation with the highest intensity emitted by a warm object.

principal wavelength The wavelength of the radiation with the highest intensity emitted by a warm object.

proportional Two variables are proportional if there is a constant ratio between them.

proton A subatomic particle found in the nucleus of atoms with a positive electric charge equal in magnitude to that of an electron.

proton number The number of protons in the nucleus of an atom (also called the atomic number). In an uncharged atom this is also the number of electrons.

radiation A flow of energy from a source. Light and infrared are examples. Radiation spreads out from its source, and may be absorbed or reflected by objects in its path. It may also go (be transmitted) through them.

radiation dose A measure, in millisieverts, of the possible harm done to your body, which takes into account both the amount and type of radiation you are exposed to.

radio waves Electromagnetic radiation of a much lower frequency than visible light. They can be made to carry signals and are widely used for communications.

radioactive Used to describe a material, atom, or element that produces ionising radiation from the nucleus of atoms.

radioactive decay The spontaneous change in the nucleus of an unstable element, giving out alpha, beta, or gamma radiation. Alpha and beta emission result in a new element.

radiotherapy Using ionising radiation to treat a patient.

random A random process is unpredictable – there is no pattern to help predict what will happen next. Radioactive decay is random – you cannot predict when a particular nucleus will decay.

random error A measurement error due to results varying in an unpredictable way, for example, due to the scientist having to make a judgement about timing or colour.

range Describes the spread between the highest and the lowest of a set of measurements.

rate A measure of how quickly something changes. In physics it is usually describes how a quantity changes with time.

reaction time The time it takes for the human body to respond to a stimulus.

reflect What happens when a wave hits a barrier and bounces back off it. If you draw a line at right-angles to the barrier, the reflected wave has the same angle to this line as the incoming wave. For example, light is reflected by a mirror.

refraction The wavelength of a wave changes as it travels from one medium to another in which its speed is different. For example, when travelling into shallower water, waves have a smaller wavelength as they slow down. If the waves pass from one medium to another at an angle to the boundary, they will change direction.

renewable Resources that can be used to generate electricity without being used up, such as the wind, tides, and sunlight.

repeatable Data are said to be repeatable when the same investigator finds the same or similar results under the same conditions. We can have more confidence in data that are repeatable.

repel Push apart.

representational model A type of scientific model that uses simple shapes or analogies to represent the interacting parts of a system. One example is the particle model – it helps us to visualise the tiny particles (atoms and molecules) that make up substances.

representative sample The characteristics of a representative sample are very similar to the characteristics of the whole population.

reproducible Data are said to be reproducible when other investigators have found the same or similar results under similar conditions. We can have more confidence in data that are reproducible.

resistance The resistance of a component in an electric circuit indicates how easy or difficult it is to move charges through it. Resistance is measured in ohms (Ω).

resistor An electric circuit component designed to control the current in the circuit.

resultant force The sum, taking their directions into account, of all the forces acting on an object.

risk An estimate of the probability that an unwanted outcome will happen. The size of the risk can be estimated from the chance of it occurring in a large sample over a given period of time.

sample It is usually not possible to collect data about a whole population of organisms or other specimens. For this reason a study usually collects data about a proportion of them. This is a sample. Conclusions about a sample can only be applied to the whole population if it is a representative sample.

Sankey diagram A diagram that shows all the energy transfers taking place in a process and the amount of energy in each transfer.

scalar A quantity with size but no direction, for example, speed and distance.

scale diagram A drawing with accurate directions and sizes. The sizes are all reduced or increased by a scale factor (the scale).

secondary data Data collected by somebody else, which can be compared with the primary data collected in the laboratory or field by the person doing the investigation.

sensor An electric circuit component that changes an electrical property in response to changes in its surroundings, for example, a light-dependent resistor or a thermistor.

series circuit A circuit in which all the electric components are in a single loop. The charges pass through them all in turn.

slope See 'gradient'.

solar cell (photovoltaic) Device that uses light to produce a potential difference.

solar power Using energy transferred from the Sun for heating or to generate electricity.

solar thermal panels Panels that contain pipes through which water flows. The water is heated by the Sun.

solenoid A coil of wire that conducts a current to produce a magnetic field for use in an electromagnet.

source (of radiation) An object that produces radiation.

spatial model A type of mathematical model in which a computer is used to make a model of one or more objects in a three-dimensional space. The model can be used to predict the outcome of changing a variable (e.g., temperature) in this space (e.g., a landscape and the atmosphere above it).

specific heat capacity The increase in internal energy required to raise the temperature of 1 kg of a substance by 1 °C (or 1 K). Specific heat capacity is measured in J/kg °C.

specific latent heat The increase in internal energy required to change the state of 1 kg of a solid to liquid (**specific latent heat of fusion or melting**) or of 1 kg of liquid to gas (**specific latent heat of vaporisation**). Specific latent heat is measured in J/kg.

speed–time graph A graph showing the speed of an object at every instant during its journey. Speed on the y-axis and time on the x-axis. Speed is always positive.

spring constant For an elastic material obeying Hooke's Law, spring constant $k = \dfrac{\text{stretching force}}{\text{extension}}$. Spring constant is measured in newtons per metre (N/m).

state of matter Solid, liquid, or gas are the three states in which most matter exists on Earth.

stopping distance The distance travelled between the driver seeing a hazard and the car being stationary.

sublimation The change of state directly from a solid to gas (and the reverse).

sustainability Using resources and the environment to meet the needs of people today without damaging the Earth for people of the future. One example is to use resources at the same rate as they can be replaced.

system A collection of interacting parts.

systematic error A measurement error that differs from the true value by the same amount each time a measurement is made. A systematic error may be due to the environment, methods of observation, or the instrument used.

tangent A straight line touching a curve or the circumference of a circle at a single point. It has the same gradient as the curve at that point.

tension The force in a cable or string when it is stretched tight. The direction is to reduce the stretching. If a cable has a tension of 100 N, there is a 100 N force pulling at each end of the cable.

theory A scientific theory is a general explanation that applies to a large number of situations or examples (perhaps to all possible ones). It has been tested and used successfully, and is widely accepted by scientists. An example is Newton's theory of gravity.

thermal conductivity The energy per second transferred through 1 m² of a material of 1 m thickness when the temperature difference across it is 1 °C.

thermal power station A power station that uses fossil fuels to generate electricity (and produces CO_2).

thermistor An electric circuit component whose resistance changes markedly with its temperature. It can therefore be used to measure temperature.

thinking distance The distance travelled between the driver seeing a hazard and applying the brakes.

tidal power Generating electricity from generators driven by the movement of water as the tide comes in and out each day.

tracer (radioactive) Used in medical diagnosis. The position of a radioactive substance in the body can be traced from outside the body by detecting the radiation emitted.

transfomer An electrical device used to 'step' voltage up or down to the level required, for example, in the National Grid. The device has two coils of wire wound on an iron core. An alternating current in one coil causes an ever-changing magnetic field that induces an alternating current in the other.

transmit When radiation hits an object, it may pass through it. It is said to be transmitted through it. We also say that a radio aerial transmits a signal. In this case, transmits means 'emits' or 'sends out'.

transmutation The changing of one element into another because the number of protons in the nucleus changes. This happens during radioactive decay.

transverse wave A wave in which the particles of the medium vibrate at right-angles to the direction in which the wave is travelling. Water waves are an example.

true value The actual value.

turbine The component of a power station that is normally driven by steam, water, or wind. It drives the rotating generator.

ultrasound Sound with frequencies too high to be heard by humans, above about 20 kHz.

ultraviolet (UV) Electromagnetic radiation with frequencies higher than those of visible light, beyond the violet end of the visible spectrum.

uncertainty An indication of the confidence a scientist has in the accuracy of a measurement. It can be expressed as a range of values within which the true value must lie.

unintended consequence A consequence of an action that was not expected or planned for.

unstable (atom) The nucleus in radioactive isotopes is unstable. It is liable to decay, emitting one of several types of radiation. If it emits alpha or beta radiation, a new element is formed.

valid The conclusions from an experiment are valid if the procedures ensure that the effects observed are due to the cause claimed, and if the analysis has taken account of other possible factors.

variable resistor An electric circuit component whose resistance can be changed.

variation Differences within repeated measurements of a quantity.

vector (physics) A quantity that has a magnitude and a direction, for example, a force.

vector diagram A diagram that shows the direction and magnitudes of vectors (e.g., for forces).

velocity The speed of an object in a given direction. Unlike speed, which only has a size, velocity also has a direction. It is a vector.

velocity–time graph A graph showing the velocity of an object at every instant during its journey. Velocity on the y-axis and time on the x-axis. Velocity can be positive or negative.

vibrate Move rapidly and repeatedly back and forth, like a string on a guitar or a particle in a lattice connected by bonds to its neighbours.

visible light The only electromagnetic radiation visible to the eye.

voltage The voltage marked on a battery or power supply is a measure of the 'push' it exerts on charges in an electric circuit. The voltage between two points in a circuit means the potential difference between these points.

voltmeter An instrument for measuring the potential difference (which is often called the voltage) between two points in an electric circuit.

wave equation The wave equation 'wave speed = frequency × wavelength' applies to all types of wave.

wave model (of radiation) In the wave model of radiation, sources emit energy by making something oscillate (vary regularly), which produces waves; the waves travel outwards from the source like ripples on a pond.

wave power Generating electricity from generators driven by the movement of water as waves hit the shore.

wave speed The speed at which waves move through a medium.

wavelength The distance between one wave crest (or wave trough) and the next.

weight The force of gravitational attraction on a mass. It is measured in newtons (N).

wind power Generating electricity from generators driven by the movement of air.

work (electrical) Energy transferred by an electric current as it passes through a device.

work (force) Work is done whenever a force makes something move. The amount of work is force multiplied by distance moved in the direction of the force. This is equal to the amount of energy transferred.

X-ray Electromagnetic radiation with high frequency, well above that of visible light.

Index

COVER: © The Trustees of the Natural History Museum, London

p2: Geospace/Science Photo Library; **p7(T)**: Alberto Masnovo/Shutterstock; **p7(C)**: Amriphoto/iStockphoto; **p7(B)**: Sutasinee Anukul/Shutterstock; **p8(R)**: Simon Fraser/NCCT, Freeman Trust, Newcastle-Upon-Tyne/Science Photo Library; **p8(L)**: Boryana Manzurova/Shutterstock; **p12**: Mauro Fermariello/Science Photo Library; **p14(T)**: NASA/Science Photo Library; **p14(B)**: Jerry Mason/Science Photo Library; **p15(TR)**: Phanie/Alamy Stock Photo; **p15(L)**: Mark Sykes/Science Photo Library; **p15(BR)**: Martin Dohrn/Science Photo Library; **p19**: Dabarti CGI/Shutterstock; **p16**: Medact/Wellcome Library, London; **p18**: Syda Productions/Shutterstock; **p20(L)**: Ted Kinsman/Science Photo Library; **p20(R)**: Ivan Smuk/Shutterstock; **p21**: NASA, JPL-Caltech, UCLA; **p22**: S.m.u.d.g.e/Shutterstock; **p24**: British Antarctic Survey/Science Photo Library; **p25**: Kodda/Shutterstock; **p30**: Berenice Abbott/Science Photo Library; **p36**: Geospace/Science Photo Library; **p37**: Phanie/Alamy Stock Photo; **p40**: Geoeye/Science Photo Library; **p42(T)**: Andrey_Popov/Shutterstock; **p42(B)**: Photobac/Shutterstock; **p43(T)**: Chris Curtis/Shutterstock; **p43(B)**: Grigvovan/Shutterstock; **p44(T)**: Onur Döngel/iStockphoto; **p44(B)**: RonFromYork/Shutterstock; **p45(L)**: Warin Keawchookul/Shutterstock; **p45(R)**: Nikkytok/iStockphoto; **p46**: Evgeny Tomeev/Shutterstock; **p48(R)**: Joe Belanger/Shutterstock; **p48(L)**: Ensuper/Shutterstock; **p49(T)**: Irin-k/Shutterstock; **p49(C)**: Adrian Reynolds/Shutterstock; **p49(B)**: Ivan Smuk/Shutterstock; **p50**: Lesley O'Farrell/123RF; **p51(T)**: Elgol/iStockphoto; **p51(BL)**: Chones/Shutterstock; **p51(BC)**: Paket/Shutterstock; **p51(BR)**: Mylisa/Shutterstock; **p54(T)**: Jeremy Reddington/Shutterstock; **p54(B)**: Michelangelus/Shutterstock; **p55**: Eyeidea/Shutterstock; **p56**: Fotorutkowscy/Shutterstock; **p57**: Maica/iStockphoto; **p58(T)**: Peter Bowater/Science Photo Library; **p58(B)**: Jarous/Shutterstock; **p59**: Ivan Smuk/Shutterstock; **p62(T)**: Ralf Gosch/Shutterstock; **p62(B)**: Alex Mit/Shutterstock; **p64**: Innershadows Photography/Shutterstock; **p65**: Lopolo/Shutterstock; **p66(T)**: Lisa S./Shutterstock; **p66(B)**: Robert Brook/Science Photo Library; **p67(T)**: Grace21/iStockphoto; **p67(B)**: Pedrosala/Shutterstock; **p68**: Claudio Divizia/Shutterstock; **p71**: Rui Saraiva/Shutterstock; **p72**: RonFromYork/Shutterstock; **p73**: Rui Saraiva/Shutterstock; **p76**: Olegbush/Shutterstock; **p86(T)**: JSAbbott/iStockphoto; **p86(B)**: Kazakov/iStockphoto; **p92**: Antb/Shutterstock; **p95**: EQRoy/Shutterstock; **p97**: SteveStone/iStockphoto; **p99(T)**: Sergei Drozd/Shutterstock; **p98(TR)**: G-stockstudio/Shutterstock; **p98(BL)**: Cordelia Molloy/Science Photo Library; **p98(BR)**: Cordelia Molloy/Science Photo Library; **p99(B)**: Anyaivanova/Shutterstock; **p100**: MilanB/Shutterstock; **p101(T)**: BanksPhotos/iStockphoto; **p101(B)**: Science Museum/Science & Society Picture Library; **p102**: ABB Asea Brown Boveri Ltd; **p107**: ABB Asea Brown Boveri Ltd; **p98(TL)**: Robert Kneschke/Shutterstock; **p98(C)**: Kondor83/Shutterstock; **p110**: ESA–S. Corvaja, 2015; **p112**: Arie v.d. Wolde/Shutterstock; **p113**: Ted Kinsman/Science Photo Library; **p114**: NASA/Science Photo Library; **p115**: Cinoby/iStockphoto; **p118**: Aphelleon/Shutterstock; **p121(T)**: Artens/Shutterstock; **p121(B)**: Bob Daemmrich/Alamy Stock Photo; **p122**: Jamesbowyer/iStockphoto; **p124(L)**: Maros Bauer/Shutterstock; **p124(R)**: ChameleonsEye/Shutterstock; **p126**: Images-USA/Alamy Stock Photo; **p129**: Izf/Shutterstock; **p131(T)**: Kenneth Eward/Biografx/Science Photo Library; **p131(B)**: Joggie Botma/Shutterstock; **p133**: coburn77/123RF; **p135**: Ruth Peterkin/Shutterstock; **p136**: Maxisport/Shutterstock; **p137**: Lakeview Images/Shutterstock; **p140**: MeeRok/Shutterstock; **p142**: Johan Swanepoel/Shutterstock; **p144**: Brian Kinney/Shutterstock; **p147**: TRL Ltd. /Science Photo Library; **p152**: Kzenon/Shutterstock; **p153**: Nic Vilceanu/Shutterstock; **p154(T)**: Natursports/Shutterstock; **p154(B)**: Sjo/iStockphoto; **p155**: Zhao jian kang/Shutterstock; **p160**: Julian Baum/Science Photo Library; **p162(TR)**: JPL-Caltech/Malin Space Science Systems/NASA; **p162(BR)**: Public Health England/Science Photo Library; **p162(TL)**: Kletr/Shutterstock; **p162(BL)**: Public Health England/Science Photo Library; **p163(T)**: Karen Hoar/123RF; **p163(BL)**: Ppart/Shutterstock; **p163(BR)**: Oleksiy Mark/Shutterstock; **p164(L)**: Science Photo Library; **p164(R)**: Science & Society Picture Library/Getty Images; **p165**: Magnetix/Shutterstock; **p167**: Natursports/Shutterstock; **p171**: © South Tyrol Museum of Archaeology - www.iceman.it; **p173(T)**: Geoff Tompkinson/Science Photo Library; **p173(B)**: Krzysztof Slusarczyk/Shutterstock; **p176**: Medact/Wellcome Library, London; **p175(T)**: Josh Sher/Science Photo Library; **p175(B)**: Public Health England/Science Photo Library; **p177**: Prof. J. Leveille/Science Photo Library /Science Photo Library; **p179**: Monkey Business Images/Shutterstock; **p181**: Prof. J. Leveille/Science Photo Library /Science Photo Library; **p184**: ORNL/Science Photo Library; **p187**: Andrew Leech, University of York; **p189(T)**: Vereshchagin Dmitry/Shutterstock; **p189(B)**: CreativeNature R.Zwerver/Shutterstock; **p190**: Tiago M Nunes/Shutterstock; **p192**: Adam Hart-Davis/Science Photo Library; **p194(T)**: R.Classen/Shutterstock; **p194(B)**: Eder/Shutterstock; **p188(L)**: Science Photo Library; **p196(T)**: Marzolino/Shutterstock; **p196(BL)**: Andrew Lambert Photography/Science Photo Library; **p196(BC)**: MilsiArt/Shutterstock; **p196(BR)**: Martin Damen/123RF; **p199**: Charles D. Winters/Science Photo Library; **p202(L)**: Andrey_Popov/Shutterstock; **p202(C)**: Africa Studio/Shutterstock; **p202(R)**: Auremar/Shutterstock; **p203(R)**: Giphotostock/Science Photo Library; **p203(L)**: Giphotostock/Science Photo Library; **p206**: Martyn F. Chillmaid/Science Photo Library; **p207**: Kozlenko/Shutterstock; **p209**: Adam Hart-Davis/Science Photo Library; **p212**: Steve Woodward/SolarAid; **p214(T)**: Corrie Wingate Photography/SolarAid; **p214(B)**: Steve Woodward/SolarAid; **p215(T)**: Hill120/Shutterstock; **p215(B)**: HyKoe/iStockphoto; **p216**: Grant Heilman Photography/Alamy Stock Photo; **p217**: Fouad A. Saad/Shutterstock; **p220(BR)**: Andrew Leech, University of York; **p220(BL)**: Patrick Landmann/Science Photo Library; **p220(CR)**: Joggie Botma/Shutterstock; **p220(CL)**: Jerbarber/iStockphoto; **p220(TR)**: Jarous/Shutterstock; **p220(TL)**: Simon Fraser/NCCT, Freeman Trust, Newcastle-Upon-Tyne/Science Photo Library; **p226**: Olegbush/Shutterstock; **p228**: Science Photo/Shutterstock; **p242**: Four Oaks/Shutterstock; **p260-p262**: Author Photo;

All artwork by Q2A Media

Project Team acknowledgements

These resources have been developed to support teachers and students undertaking the OCR suite of specifications GCSE Twenty First Century Science. They have been developed from the first and second editions of the resources.

We would like to thank Michelle Spiller, Sarah Old, Naomi Rowe, and Ann Wolstenholme at OCR for their work on the specifications for the Twenty First Century Science course.

We would also like to thank the following contributors to case studies in these resources: Tessa Kipping and Grace Power (SolarAid); Marc Charlton (Solarcentury).

Authors and editors from the first and second editions

We thank the authors and editors of the first and second editions: David Brodie, Peter Campbell, Simon Carson, John Lazonby, Robin Millar, Stephen Pople, David Sang, Elizabeth Swinbank, and Carol Tear.

Many people from schools, colleges, universities, industry, and the professions contributed to the production of the first edition of these resources. We also acknowledge the invaluable contribution of the teachers and students in the pilot centres.

A full list of contributors can be found on the website: https://global.oup.com/education/content/secondary/online-products/acknowledgements/?region=uk

The first edition of Twenty First Century Science was developed with support from the Nuffield Foundation, The Salters' Institute, and the Wellcome Trust.

The continued development of Twenty First Century Science is made possible by generous support from The Salters' Institute.

OXFORD
UNIVERSITY PRESS

Great Clarendon Street, Oxford, OX2 6DP, United Kingdom

Oxford University Press is a department of the University of Oxford. It furthers the University's objective of excellence in research, scholarship, and education by publishing worldwide. Oxford is a registered trade mark of Oxford University Press in the UK and in certain other countries

© Salters' Educational Resources Ltd and the Nuffield Foundation

Resources developed by the University of York Science Education Group on behalf of Salters' Educational Resources Ltd

The moral rights of the authors have been asserted

First published in 2016

All rights reserved. No part of this publication may be reproduced, stored in a retrieval system, or transmitted, in any form or by any means, without the prior permission in writing of Oxford University Press, or as expressly permitted by law, by licence or under terms agreed with the appropriate reprographics rights organization. Enquiries concerning reproduction outside the scope of the above should be sent to the Rights Department, Oxford University Press, at the address above.

You must not circulate this work in any other form and you must impose this same condition on any acquirer

British Library Cataloguing in Publication Data
Data available

978 0 19 835954 8

10 9 8 7 6 5 4 3 2 1

Paper used in the production of this book is a natural, recyclable product made from wood grown in sustainable forests. The manufacturing process conforms to the environmental regulations of the country of origin.

Printed in Great Britain by Bell and Bain Ltd. Glasgow

This resource is endorsed by OCR for use with specification J260 OCR GCSE (9–1) in Combined Science B (Twenty First Century Science). In order to gain OCR endorsement, this resource has undergone an independent quality check. Any references to assessment and/ or assessment preparation are the publisher's interpretation of the specification requirements and are not endorsed by OCR. OCR recommends that a range of teaching and learning resources are used in preparing learners for assessment. OCR has not paid for the production of this resource, nor does OCR receive any royalties from its sale. For more information about the endorsement process, please visit the OCR website, www.ocr.org.uk.

MIX
Paper from
responsible sources
FSC® C007785
www.fsc.org